THE
Nonfiction
NOW
LESSON BANK

GRADES 4–8

To my husband, Mehran, who is always by my side
and who tells me to never, ever give up.

THE Nonfiction NOW LESSON BANK

GRADES 4–8

Strategies & Routines for Higher-Level
Comprehension in the Content Areas

NANCY AKHAVAN

Foreword by Jennifer Serravallo

FOR INFORMATION:

Corwin
A SAGE Company
2455 Teller Road
Thousand Oaks, California 91320
(800) 233-9936
www.corwin.com

SAGE Publications Ltd.
1 Oliver's Yard
55 City Road
London EC1Y 1SP
United Kingdom

SAGE Publications India Pvt. Ltd.
B 1/I 1 Mohan Cooperative Industrial Area
Mathura Road, New Delhi 110 044
India

SAGE Publications Asia-Pacific Pte. Ltd.
3 Church Street
#10-04 Samsung Hub
Singapore 049483

Publisher: Lisa Luedeke
Development Editor: Wendy Murray
Editorial Development Manager: Julie Nemer
Editorial Assistant: Francesca Dutra Africano
Production Editor: Melanie Birdsall
Copy Editor: Melinda Masson
Typesetter: C&M Digitals (P) Ltd.
Proofreader: Jeff Bryant
Indexer: Sheila Bodell
Cover Designer: Shawn Girsberger
Interior Designer: Gail Buschman

Printed in the United States of America.

Library of Congress Cataloging-in-Publication Data

Akhavan, Nancy L., author.

The nonfiction now lesson bank, grades 4-8 : Strategies and routines for higher-level comprehension in the content areas / Nancy Akhavan.

p. cm.
Includes bibliographical references and index.

ISBN 978-1-4522-8650-1 (pbk. : alk. paper)

1. Language arts—Correlation with content subjects. 2. Content area reading. 3. Reading comprehension—Study and teaching (Elementary) 4. Reading comprehension—Study and teaching (Middle school) I. Title.

LB1576.A3985 2014
372.6—dc23   2013045107

This book is printed on acid-free paper.

22 10 9 8 7 6 5 4 3 2

Contents

Note: For titles of texts to use with lessons, see the Appendix.

REPRODUCIBLE FORMS

Visit the companion website at
www.corwin.com/nonfictionnow
for downloadable resources.

Foreword

You can tell Nancy is a classroom teacher first. Sure, she's also been a professor and principal and staff developer and authored many professional books. But when you read this resource you now hold in your hands, what shines through is this: *Nancy is a teacher.*

Only a teacher would know that this is just the right book for teachers, right now.

Right now, teachers need support with teaching kids to read nonfiction. The Common Core's call for a 50/50 balance of literature and informational texts by fourth grade means that now, more than ever before, teachers need to know how to teach children to read a wider range of nonfiction texts over more time. More than the handful of minutes it takes for a class to shared read a *TIME for Kids* article, more than using nonfiction solely for research purposes or to dip in and dip out based on a scan of the index. *Real* nonfiction reading. Helping kids understand main ideas and key details, wrestle with challenging vocabulary even when English might not be their first language, make sense of text structures and text features. This is big work, and this book helps.

Right now, with the pressures to help kids read more and more complex texts, Nancy Akhavan has a solution that is sensible: Make sure that kids are doing the work, not the teacher. Make sure to leave lots of time for independent practice. Nancy's practical suggestions for routines that she calls the Daily Duo are rooted in the work of educational heroes like Pearson and Gallagher, Wiggins and McTighe, Afflerbach, Calkins, and Allington. She helps teachers to hold tight to what works in a time when some might suggest we look the other way.

And now, with the ever-mounting pressures and, at times, minimal staff development, what might many teachers want most? A book filled with clearly laid-out, practical, and ready-to-use lessons based on research they can trust. Unlike many lesson books, however, in this book Nancy puts faith in the teacher's judgment and in her close and careful assessment of her students. The lessons are organized so they can be easily navigated, but are not meant to be used one after another like a script.

As I travel the country these days, working with teachers from New York to Seattle, I find I'm met with a lot of panic. Much of it I find to be rooted in misinterpretations that are based on instructional shifts described in the publisher's criteria, not the actual Standards themselves. Nancy gives it to us straight—telling us what the Common Core says about nonfiction reading and what it doesn't, and how the comprehension research of the last few decades intersects with new recommendations.

Now, just as it's always been, it's about *comprehension.*

—*Jennifer Serravallo*

Acknowledgments

I have had the privilege and honor of visiting and working in hundreds of teachers' classrooms during the last five years. This immersion into all types of settings, including primary, middle school, and high school, has brought me side by side with so many dedicated, talented, and incredibly hardworking teachers. I am grateful for their openness, and for their willingness to work with me as we all deepened our practices as teachers. Thank you to all of you, and, in particular, thank you to the teachers in the Fresno Unified School District.

This book has had the benefit of some very talented thinking partners whom I am honored to know. Lois Bridges has been a beacon of inspiration for many years about teaching and learning. The beginning of this book reflects her handprint. My talented editor, Lisa Luedeke, inspires me. She not only sees the potential in others, but also believes in others and their abilities to teach, to learn, and to enhance the literacy lives of our young people. This book exists because of her vision and inspiration. Writing a book takes many arduous hours beyond initial inspiration, to make sure that the words on the page live up to the heady goal of supporting teachers to teach. One person made this process possible: Wendy Murray. She has been a creative partner who improved my ability as a writer, and above all, she made it fun.

This book is now launched, and I encourage teachers to shape and re-form its lessons and ideas to their liking as they strive to help students read well. I wish all teachers "best teaching" as they craft their lessons, watch their students grow as readers and writers, and lay the foundation in our young people for becoming literate, critical thinkers. May we all continue to engage in the incredibly delightful and energizing world of learning.

PART I

The "Now" Factor of Nonfiction Reading

As we bring an abundance of nonfiction into our classrooms, we create not just a library of texts but a leg up in the world; think about it: Nonfiction *is* the world and all of its realities, from hardships to heroism and feats of discovery and creativity. So when we help students read these texts about real events, cultures, ideas, inventions, history, and science, we help them become citizens of the world, not just students in school.

However, I want to set our sights even higher than helping our readers develop content-area knowledge. The real goal and opportunity is to help our readers engage with the information enough that they are motivated to think with it and apply it—not just spout dates or read bar graphs. So as you read Part I, which gives you the lay of the land for reading nonfiction, remember that the ideas here and throughout the book are stepping-stones for students to become, to do—to know how to think like historians, scientists, sociologists, and journalists. For when our students read texts written by experts in history, science, and other disciplines with sufficient understanding, they in a sense have the mental space to also take in the discipline-specific processes behind the knowledge and information on the page.

Enjoy—and help your students enjoy nonfiction. *Learning by doing* is the name of the game.

Yes, We *Are* Asking More of Our Nonfiction Readers

This is a book about teaching strategic readers, readers who know how to read a non-fiction text and walk away with not only some good information, but also a good feeling about having read. It's designed to help you know how to channel the ease students have with toggling between all types of texts into slower, deeper, and more purposeful reading and understanding. Our students have been using technology since they were babies, and can run rings around most teachers in "speed of motion"—finding, gathering, reading, sharing, and manipulating text and visual information—but what education researchers are discovering is that their comprehension of these texts can be shallow, their attention spans short.

When students are out and about in the world, they will be expected to do more sophisticated thinking and application with texts. This book is about providing them with the tools for strategically reading and responding to any type of text they may encounter. This isn't an easy task! There are, however, some specific techniques we can use in our classrooms to create the magic and ensure our students are literate readers and consumers and creators of information.

What Is a Collaborative, Problem-Solving Reader?

At the risk of sounding flippant, it's not enough to be a good reader anymore. Readers have to be strategic (Duke & Pearson, 2002; Ganske, 2010; King, 2007; Pressley & Wharton-McDonald, 1997). Strategic readers do the following:

- Establish goals for reading
- Select reading strategies appropriate for the text they are reading

- Make connections between texts
- Infer
- Synthesize
- Visualize
- Monitor their reading to determine if they are comprehending or not
- Use fix-up strategies when understanding falters
- Question
- Have stamina and a can-do perseverance even with lengthy, complex texts
- Maintain a positive attitude toward reading

If we consider the above skills and behaviors in light of nonfiction reading, it's no wonder that so many of our students struggle with both comprehension and engagement. As professionals, we haven't done a good enough job of awakening them to all of the well-written, engaging informational texts available. And perhaps more to the point, we haven't modeled for them *how* to read nonfiction. Sure, we have talked about teaching students to *navigate* or *tackle* nonfiction, but we need to back up a few steps more: We have to model for students how to go into a nonfiction reading with a purpose in mind. I know this was true for my students—they often had no defined, driving purpose for reading or rereading a text, and that undermined comprehension and motivation.

I have worked with hundreds of teachers over the last 10 years, and they have reported to me that they find the same phenomenon happening with their students. Even their "good" readers can read most books and do well enough on assessments of comprehension, but they seldom go beyond the text in their thinking, or engage with it enough that it spurns other questions, or a quest for a complementary book.

"It's as though they plow into all texts as if the texts were the same," one teacher commented to me. This insight intrigued me, and led me to develop the ideas in this book, which show teachers and students just *how* nonfiction texts are different, and thus require some different moves and mind-sets on the part of the reader.

This book also provides teaching strategies for students who not only lack purpose, but are not proficient readers. These students do not employ comprehension strategies well, and comprehension often breaks down for them; over time, these students avoid reading.

I've organized this book into three parts to make it easier for you to rediscover strategies and lessons you want to use in the classroom.

Part I, *The "Now" Factor of Nonfiction Reading,* explores the kinds of informational texts available today, and the latest thinking on the comprehension processes involved in reading them well. To keep the focus on active student learning, I share practical strategies for two major emphases of reading nonfiction in school, one a genre and the other a process: textbook reading and close reading.

Part II, *The Daily Duo,* lays out routines for reading and writing that expand students' reading comprehension, of the information they are reading about and confidence with nonfiction. I call the routines the daily duo because when you plan your instruction with a tool that allows you to intentionally build understandings throughout the week, you will ensure you're giving students the time to read, write, and think with texts.

Part III, *The Lessons and Texts,* gives you exemplary lessons and authentic short non-fiction texts to use with students—right away. The lessons can be used in any sequence that suits your needs, yet are arranged in an order that involves students in a variety of interactions with a text, from skimming it before reading to analyzing it and connecting it to other texts.

Let's look at a few more key realities about today's readers, today's nonfiction texts, and today's academic expectations, because establishing these points helps set a context for the teaching ideas in subsequent chapters.

Our Students Now: Grazing Without Synthesis?

The students in our classroom now are different learners, thinkers, and consumers of print than we were at that age—or are now. Our students are also different learners, thinkers, and consumers of print than the students who filled our classrooms a mere decade ago. Although I have never bought into hard-and-fast definitions of the baby boomers, Generation X, Generation Y, or the more recent millennials, who are now in the job market, I find *iGeneration* an apt term for the students in our classrooms now.

Who are the iGeneration students? They are students who were born after 1997. Students from the iGeneration interact with texts within multiple literacies. Students today are used to a constant flow of information and often multitask better than any of our previous students. Brain researchers suggest that the connections within the brain look different based on exposure to a constant flow of information and stimulation from very young ages (Whitman & Goldberg, 2008). These students understand their world as a place where they not only access information through technology, but create information and participate in a virtual world through multiple avenues. Yet even though they are plugged in—texting, reading information on the Internet, creating text and uploading it for the world to read—they often have difficulty reading the texts we use in schools; these texts are more technical and information rich. They struggle with content-area reading for a host of reasons: the challenges of vocabulary, density of information, concepts, unfamiliar text structures—you name it. This book recognizes that these "school texts" won't, and shouldn't, go away, and provides instructional ideas for helping our students learn from them, and even learn to like them!

Reading Today: A Multigenre Mash-Up

The answer isn't to compel students to buck up and read textbooks and longer works in the spirit of simply having more "rigor" in reading. In a very real way, we have to take our students' lead and teach strategic reading strategies for all texts students encounter and use on a daily basis—including textbooks.

Readers of the Internet are exposed to electronic texts that provide new supports as well as new challenges. These supports and challenges can have an impact on the reader's comprehension of material (Coiro, 2003). Web-based reading is very different from print-based reading because readers have the option of creating their own path through the text via hyperlinks and multiple windows. Sometimes web readers develop a "snatch and grab" philosophy to reading, which is not an approach apparent in print-based reading (Sutherland-Smith, 2002). Our job as teachers is to help students sustain attention and comprehension while reading web-based and print-based texts.

Earlier I listed the qualities of a strategic reader, and there are specific reading strategies we can teach to help our students become strategic readers (Duke & Pearson, 2002; Ogle & Blachowicz, 2002; Trabasso & Bouchard, 2002). The lessons that appear later in this book focus on teaching these strategies. The following reading strategies are the ones you will find in this book, and probably also appear in your current reading program:

- Activate prior knowledge
- Monitor comprehension
- Repair comprehension through fix-up strategies
- Determine important ideas
- Visualize
- Determine key details
- Synthesize
- Draw inferences
- Ask questions
- Navigate text

These strategies provide teachers with a needed frame for their reading instruction and they apply seamlessly to narrative and informational texts (Serravallo, 2013). There are similarities and differences between using these reading strategies with print-based text and using them with web-based text. See *Online Text Characteristics and Reading Strategies* for a description of the characteristics and the reactions of the reader. Print literacy is converging with technology, and the possibilities for reading for our students are exciting and also a bit daunting. This book helps you teach students to read with high levels of thinking and understanding, no matter what and where they are reading.

Online Text Characteristics and Reading Strategies

Online Text Characteristics	Online Reading Strategies
Larger reading and navigating space	Skimming
Reading choices with hyperlinks	Scanning
Greater sense of control over what and how one reads	Searching
Larger amount and variety of information	Navigating

Online Reading Comprehension Strategies	Additional Reader Actions With Internet Texts
Prior Knowledge	• Draw on prior knowledge of informational website structures and web-based search engines
Inferential Reading Strategies	• Use inferential reasoning including matching, structural, and context clues (online reading requires you to infer what you need before you click a link) • Use multilayered reading processes across three-dimensional Internet spaces
Self-Regulated Reading Processes	• Use cognitive reading strategies connected with physical reading actions • Engage in rapid information-seeking cycles in very short text passages

Source: Adapted from Coiro & Dobler (2007); Schmar-Dobler (2003).

Eight Essential Informational Text Comprehension Strategies

Strategy	Description
Activate Prior Knowledge	Drawing on knowledge of a topic and knowledge of text structure to organize and remember information
Monitor and Repair Comprehension	Being aware of whether the text makes sense and taking action with "fix-up" strategies (reading, skipping ahead, applying word work strategies, etc.) if needed
Determine Important Ideas	Analyzing text to see what information is important for understanding
Determine Key Details	Analyzing text to determine what information and ideas are important for understanding
Synthesize	Merging new information with prior knowledge to develop an understanding
Draw Inferences	Reading between the lines to determine understanding and identify important information
Ask Questions	Asking questions of the text to increase understanding and develop motivation
Navigate Text	Using text features to identify information

Source: Pearson, Roehler, Dole, & Duffy (1992); Pressley (2002); Weaver & Kintsch (1991).

Why Nonfiction Has Favored Status in the CCSS

Today, I have spent several hours interacting with text in different ways. All of the texts I accessed were electronic, except for the local paper (still delivered to my doorstep). I spent 10 minutes looking through and the *Time* magazine I read while waiting for my daughter at a doctor's appointment. Online, I accessed and read texts on teachers' blogs, nonprofit organization sites, and a web platform for teaching courses electronically. I read e-mail, people's personal thoughts and opinions, and technical journals. My experience isn't unusual; actually, it is probably common. However, it is a bit different from my experience in the classroom, teaching. When I was teaching, I spent all day in front of, and beside, 30 learners who needed me to engage them with reading and writing, all in the same format: print. If it didn't appear in a book in the classroom, we didn't read or write about it. When I was teaching, I didn't have a lot of time to read, and on vacations, I relished the ability to sit down and read a novel. Today, I find I am reading not novels, but nonfiction, and lots of it.

Because we are all reading more nonfiction, and because the world now revolves around an insane amount of information accessible with the click of a mouse, we have to teach more nonfiction reading. Nonfiction reading, and specifically informational reading, is a driving force in the Common Core State Standards (CCSS). The CCSS require six instructional shifts as we move the teaching of language arts from our past repertoire to 21st century skills (Achieve the Core, 2013). One of these shifts is the balance of informational text and literary text. Informational text is a type of nonfiction text focused specifically on informing the reader. By the end of the elementary grades, at least 50% of what students read should be informational text; by the end of middle school, 55%; and by the end of high school, 70%. This includes an increase in exposure of literary nonfiction across the disciplines. We will need to be able to teach through and with informational texts.

Another instructional shift called for in the CCSS is building knowledge in the disciplines. This shift applies to the standards in Grades 6 and above, and applies to teachers teaching English language arts, social studies, science, and technical subjects. Teachers in the content areas will need to use their technical expertise to help students understand the challenges of reading and writing in their field. This means that teachers of content areas will need to teach content-area literacy.

Read and Do: A Greater Emphasis on Application

If our students are reading more nonfiction, they must be able to think about what they read in deep ways. It isn't enough for students to plow through a text and grasp the main idea; they need to wrestle with the words, the meaning, and the problems or paradoxes that the text might present. To do this, students need to think at higher levels. Higher-order thinking skills include critical, metacognitive, logical, reflective, and creative thinking. To think at higher levels, students involve themselves in the situations and outcomes presented to them, and then they apply thinking skills to dive deep into text (King, 2007).

Situations are the context of reading. These are the real-life situations that ground a text and help students apply what they are reading to previous knowledge about a new issue or new information. Think of situations, or the context of a reading, as dilemmas, challenges, obstacles, doubt, problems, and questions presented by a text. The outcomes of wrestling with text—for example, creating arguments, hypotheses, insights, judgments, conclusions, predictions, plans, recommendations, and compositions—come from the thinking process and are not generated from regurgitation of facts or answering low-level comprehension questions. These real-world applications with real-world texts are motivating for readers (Gutherie et al., 2007).

What thinking processes are involved in helping students move from understanding the context of content read to coming up with an outcome based on the reading? These processes include analysis, creative thinking, evaluation, inquiry, synthesis, and reflection.

Graze, Dive, Engage: How Readers Approach Texts

With the new literacies and participatory expectations of our students (they are not only consumers but creators of web-based text), it is important to understand how readers approach text. The students in our classrooms approach information gathering in very different ways than previous students did (Jacobs, 2011). As teachers, we need to understand this new way of filtering and accessing information. Our students are exposed to a constant flow of information and have to choose where to place their attention to make sense of, and not overload on, all of the information. Palfrey and Gasser (2008) describe the way students access information as a three-step process: (1) grazing, (2) deep diving, and (3) engagement.

When students graze, they are checking posts, blogs, feeds, and texts frequently. The information accessed when grazing is sorted, so the focus can be easy to identify and process. The sources students graze are superficial, and little mental effort is required to make sense of the information. Students take a deep dive into information when something captures their attention while grazing. The readers may access Internet sites and texts that provide in-depth information on a topic. Deep diving requires different skills than grazing. Students need to be able to access information, connect it with prior knowledge, and apply thinking skills to use the information for real purposes. Engagement refers to the students' participation with the information. Students don't always engage with this step, but if they are deeply affected by information presented, they might write about it, blog about it, pass the information along on social networking sites, or make comments on Internet sites. In the classroom, their connection with engagement could include print-based or web-based writing. During this step, students are creating and sharing their thinking with classmates and even the world.

The Distinctions Between Types of Nonfiction Texts

If there were only one type of text, the world would be a boring place. Writers write to share their experiences, persuade us to think, argue with us about ideas and information, inform our lives and thinking, and also describe experiences, information, and life. Nonfiction is not fiction, although in some forms, like narrative nonfiction, text features are shared. Before we can think about how each form of nonfiction differs from the others, we need to understand the individual forms.

How Types of Nonfiction Invite
Different Purposes for Reading

I've suggested, thus far, that students need to read more nonfiction text, but this doesn't mean just handing students nonfiction books and assuming we've done all we need to help them read this genre. Students don't encounter one type of nonfiction text in their lives; there are many different types of nonfiction text. Some types used in our day-to-day lives include letters, journals, advertisements, descriptions, instructions, notices, signs, catalogs, and forms. These types of nonfiction texts do require thinking, including understanding conventions of writing, noting differences in language features, distinguishing fact from hype, seeing bias, understanding logical sequences, understanding nonfiction conventions, handling complex layouts of information, and understanding and evaluating the effectiveness of messages. Other types of nonfiction text relate specifically to written bodies of information. These include biographies, autobiographies, memoirs, journals, essays, historical documents and speeches, periodicals, interviews, articles, reports, and media accounts, and they require such thinking skills as analysis, synthesis, logical reflection, metacognition, and creative thinking.

Each type of nonfiction text has a specific purpose. Students need to know how to access, how to use, and how to think while reading each type of text (Williams, 2007). *Types of Nonfiction Text* shows different types of nonfiction text and their features, as well as what students should be learning when interacting with each type.

Types of Nonfiction Text

Type	Definition	Forms
Recount	Text that retells experience from the past	Newspaper articles, diaries, letters, biographies, autobiographies
Procedural	Text that tells how to do something	Recipes, directions, instructions
Informative/ Explanatory	Text that describes a phenomenon or event, similar to procedural text, and that does not include personal opinions	Lab reports, scientific material
Informational/ Expository	Text that gives information, shares ideas, and provides explanations and evidence	Advertisements, descriptions, tables, essays, speeches, surveys, catalogs, references, arguments

When we teach writing, we tend to follow standards to guide and inform our writing units. We often find ourselves teaching specific forms of nonfiction. Knowing and understanding these forms will not only help our students be good creators of nonfiction text; it will help them be great consumers of nonfiction text. There are basically four forms of nonfiction text that students need to be familiar with: (1) expository, (2) descriptive, (3) persuasive, and (4) narrative.

Each form has its own characteristics. Expository nonfiction is used to explain or inform. Descriptive nonfiction describes information clearly, often using sensory images; a picture can be an example of descriptive nonfiction. Opinion and argument are the cornerstones of persuasive nonfiction, and narrative nonfiction employs the text features of narrative fiction writing; however, the characters and setting are real. The lessons in this book provide support in teaching these four forms of nonfiction so that students can delve into a text and use their understanding of its form to comprehend what they are reading and analyze its meaning. In the next chapter, we look at what it means to read nonfiction in our classrooms and how to help our students get the most out of reading in multiple literacies.

Model It

*Four Lessons for
Introducing Close Reading*

"Frontloading text is dead!" a teacher bemoaned to colleagues as she left a session on the Common Core State Standards (CCSS) at a conference I attended recently. "What am I supposed to do now to help my students read really hard text? They can't all read well enough to read on their own without support!"

"Students using background knowledge is a no-no; preteaching vocabulary is prohibited; students need to do a cold read of a hard text without instruction . . ." We teachers are all reading and hearing these statements. But are they true? The "Key Design Considerations" of the Introduction to the CCSS says this:

> By emphasizing required achievements, the Standards leave room for teachers, curriculum developers, and states to determine how those goals should be reached and what additional topics should be addressed. Thus, the Standards do not mandate such things as a particular writing process or the full range of metacognitive strategies that students may need to monitor and direct their thinking and learning. *Teachers are thus free to provide students with whatever tools and knowledge their professional judgment and experience identify as most helpful for meeting the goals set out in the Standards.* (National Governors Association Center for Best Practices & Council of Chief State School Officers, 2010, emphasis added)

So, while it's natural to be alarmed at the thought of the above assertions being mandated, they actually are not; they are widely held misconceptions. So, let's take a deep breath and remind ourselves that as teachers, we always have the power to adjust instruction so it works for our students—and the CCSS support this. It would *not* make sense as teachers to throw away everything we know about literacy, the teaching of reading, and what our students need to engage with reading.

In that can-do spirit, let's look at close reading, an instructional practice that is central to achieving the CCSS, and see how to harness its power for reading nonfiction texts.

The truth is that frontloading text is not dead because of the CCSS. Also true is that students are expected to engage deeply with texts, some of which may be difficult for them to read when they don't have any background knowledge on the topic. First, let's look at exactly what the CCSS say about close reading. The anchor standards for college and career readiness, which are the same for all grade levels, state, "Read closely to determine what the text says explicitly and to make logical inferences from it; cite specific textual evidence when writing or speaking to support conclusions drawn from the text" (www.corestandards.org/ELA-Literacy/CCRA/R). Although this is an end goal—what students need to know and be able to do at the end of their K–12 school career, with complex text at the 12th-grade level—we have to teach our students to meet this goal along the way, with close reading at their grade level; this begins in kindergarten. Richard Paul and Linda Elder, two researchers who have focused their work on critical thinking, have defined four purposes for reading in our lives: for sheer pleasure, to figure out a simple idea, to gain specific technical information, and to understand and appreciate a new worldview (Paul & Elder, 2008). This last purpose, *to understand and appreciate a new worldview*, requires close reading through texts that stretch our minds, and our students are never too young to approach a text to stretch their minds and be filled with the wonder of the world.

Close and Critical Reading

It is difficult to envision teaching close reading at a specific grade level if we don't have a working definition of *close reading*. Close reading is not a new skill that evolved from the CCSS; students in college-level literacy classes have been expected to use this skill for a very long time. Although it has been embedded in past individual state standards, it may not have been called out as *close reading*. A close reading is a mindful, careful, meticulous look at a text, picture, or scene (Brummett, 2010). When we do a close reading, we take ownership of a text's ideas, using our intellectual skills to analyze and bring meaning from our own knowledge to the text.

We read for meaning. We see something and read it. It might be a real-life scenario; it might be a movie, a picture, or a text. We do a close reading when we want to make critical analysis of what we read. In fact, close reading leads to critical reading. When we lead students to critically analyze a text, we ask them to do several specific tasks *as they read*. In a close reading, they don't take on these tasks before or after reading; they focus on the tasks *as they read*. For example, students intellectually interact with the author as they read. They actively ask questions and seek deeper understanding of the text as they read. Asking questions and seeking meaning occur not after reading, but *while* reading. Students involved in a close reading also make connections to themselves, other texts, and the world. They evaluate as they read and bring important ideas to their own thinking. In a close reading, this occurs during the reading, not before or after the reading (Beers & Probst, 2013; Brummett, 2010; Fisher, Frey, & Lapp, 2012).

One of the best ways to meet the CCSS is to recognize how much of these standards we already address with our students. To some extent, to become "Common Core" in our teaching is to intentionally label what we teach using the language of these standards.

When Is Close Reading an Appropriate Kind of Reading?

As teachers, we know that we have to *know* when to engage our students with different types of reading, and all types of reading are *not* appropriate at all times, or with all texts. Close reading is not a way to approach text all the time. Think about how we read newspapers, magazines, and e-mails. We graze over some pieces and do deep dives into others, depending upon our interests, our purposes, and the demands of the text. So this gets mirrored in our teaching: We engage our students with different types of reading, and all types of reading are not appropriate at all times, or with all texts (Beers & Probst, 2013).

We should utilize close reading when we want students to do the following:

- Determine deep meaning of text
- Analyze author meaning and purpose in relation to text structure
- Tackle texts above their current reading level, but gain insight into a subject area, an author's thinking, or a historical, political context connected to a text

Close reading is *not* the teaching tool of choice when

- Students need to get the gist of the text
- Students are reading to glean information
- The goal is for students to read for pleasure
- The text is above the students' heads both in complexity and in content
- The groups of students working with the text are struggling readers, or mostly English learners

How to Do a Close Reading

To read any text well, it isn't a matter of grasping the one and only interpretation possible, or thinking that you can ever fully know the author's intended meaning, or trying to match your thinking about the theme of the text with the instructor's. The key is to think critically about the text, make statements about your thinking, and support your thinking with evidence from the text. It is a shift from "What does the teacher want me to think about the text?" to "What do I take from and think about the text?"

Students Involved in a Close Reading Lesson

The Three Levels to Delve Into

When teaching students to think about a text, it helps to consider the text at different levels. Dan Kurland (2000) breaks this down into what the text *does*, what it *says*, and what it *means*. I think of the three levels in this way:

- The surface level
- Digging for meaning
- Exploring, analyzing, and evaluating the logic of the author's meaning

When students read at the surface level, they need to grasp the text meaning and message. It helps for students to state the meaning of individual sentences in their own words. When digging for the thesis or the author's message, the second level to consider, the focus is on understanding what the author is trying to say—the deep meaning of the text. At this level, the students don't interpret what the text means through personal text connections; rather, they focus on discovering the actual intent of the author. It does help students, however, to relate the meaning of the text to concrete examples from the real world, so they should focus on text-to-world connections. Then, at the third level, students take their thinking about the text a bit deeper and consider the factors that might have influenced the author while writing. The students analyze and evaluate what they are reading. One factor to think about is the author's reasoning and its implications; students can also think about the assumptions the author is making and his or her point of view. An important thing to consider when thinking about the author's point of view is the historical context, or the social and political events that characterize the period in which a text was written. Finally, the student needs to consider the bias of the author in writing the text, and what that bias may mean for the reader.

Some general steps are followed in every close reading. First, you read the text—you give it a go on your own. After doing a first reading of a text, you read it a second time to discern the meaning. A third reading is often necessary so that you can analyze the text and surmise its meaning, determine the author's purpose, support conclusions and implications of the text, and identify significant information. Sometimes students may need to read the text a fourth time and think about what it means to them as readers. Let's take a look at each of these steps individually.

The First Reading: What Does the Text Say?

In the first reading of the text, you are asking an essential question, "What does the text say?" As a reader, you may be paraphrasing and capturing the essential meaning of the text. You may focus on visualizing the meaning of the text and use context clues to gain a more precise understanding. Reading strategies involved in the first reading include summarizing and restating.

The Second Reading: How Does the Text Say It?

In the second reading of the text, you are asking a different essential question, "How does the text say it?" This reading is focused on the meaning of the text and how the author portrays it. During this reading, you may analyze inferences based on the text. Analyzing inferences requires you to deeply interpret the text by applying background knowledge and supporting conclusions. Reading strategies involved in the second reading include determining the craft and the structure of the text.

The Third Reading: What Does the Text Mean?

In the third reading of the text, you are asking a question focused on getting to the thesis, or the author's message of the text, "What does the text mean?" This reading is focused on the analysis of the text, including identifying the author's purpose and making conclusions about the concepts and implications of the text. To grasp the deeper meaning of the text, students need to make connections to the text, with a focus on text-to-world connections. Too often, students try too hard to relate to a text, and sometimes they make things up just to "have a connection." At this stage of reading, they should connect ideas in the text to their knowledge of the real world. Strategies involved in the third reading include determining the theme of the text, identifying the author's purpose, and making text connections.

The Fourth Reading: What Does the Text Mean to Me?

A fourth reading of the text may be necessary for students to relate the text back to themselves and their knowledge of the world. During this reading, you are asking another essential question, "What does the text mean to me?" This stage of reading requires you to relate the text's meaning back to your own knowledge, your connections to the text, and your reflection on the text and its meaning. During this stage, students may evaluate the text, think about whether it is significant, and consider its depth, logic, and fairness. Reading strategies involved in the fourth reading include making text connections, visualizing the meaning of the text, and reflecting on reading.

Four Lessons for Introducing the Fundamental Steps of Close Reading

Here are four lessons that gradually introduce students to close reading. Consider these tips before you jump into the lessons:

- **First, model, model, model.** Our students need lots of experiences with texts, and they need lots of experiences watching us work with texts. When we show students how to interact with texts, our teaching will stick.
- **Second, take it slow.** Students don't usually have well-developed "thinking muscles." We need to help them exercise their thinking brains a little bit at a time. If we just throw students into the reading without breaking the learning sequence into chunks, our students might just "drown" and give up!
- **Third, take the teaching suggestions with a grain of salt.** I created these teaching moves after working with students and teachers in many different contexts, but that doesn't mean that the teaching will work for you as written. Feel free to make the lessons your own!

SAMPLE LESSON: Close Reading a Picture

This is the simplest introduction to teaching close reading.

LESSON OBJECTIVE: Reading a picture or an image

Reading a picture is something we do every day, especially when we look at advertisements in magazines, newspapers, or another venue, like a webpage. In fact, companies *depend* on us to read advertisements and bring meaning to the picture. Reading a picture is a great way to help students begin to look closely at an image and think about the embedded meaning.

Classroom
CLIP

MATERIALS NEEDED: Projector for sharing the image with the class; projectable image ready (see *Boy and His Dog*).

GROUPING: Large or small group

TIME: 10 minutes

Step 1. Have Students Examine the Picture

Tell your students to look at the picture of the boy and his dog for a moment. Then say:

"As you look at the picture, what goes through your mind?"

Step 2. Model Your Thinking Aloud for the "First Read"

After the students have looked at the picture for a minute or two, model a think-aloud about the picture. You might say:

"At first glance, after the quick reading, I am thinking, 'Oh, it's a boy and a dog.' But then, I take a longer look, and I notice some details in the picture. I notice that the boy

Boy and His Dog

is talking to the dog, that he is leaning in and holding the dog's leg firmly. It appears that the dog is in the boy's lap. I also notice that the dog looks relaxed and somewhat content with the position he is in in relation to the boy. It also appears that they are in a park and that the dog has some sort of scarf around its neck."

Step 3. Encourage Students to Share Their Thinking

Give students a few more seconds to look at the picture after you finish your short think-aloud. Invite students to share their thinking. You might want to write down their thoughts and ideas as they share.

Step 4. Encourage Students to Probe Deeper With Their Thinking

After several students have shared, ask the class to probe deeper and read the picture more closely. A close reading should take them deeper into the context of the picture than what might be perceived at first glance. To get the conversation started, you could say:

"We could wonder about the relationship between the boy and the dog. I wonder if the artist was portraying a utopia vision of what childhood should look like, where every child has a pet. You might find absolutely no connection to the picture as it might not show what you think of as an owner–pet relationship. Maybe we could also look at the picture and see if it is saying anything about our world. I think a bit of a stereotype is portrayed in the picture about how every child should have a pet and be in love with his best friend."

Classroom CLIP

SAMPLE LESSON: Close Reading a Cartoon

Another simple way to begin to teach close reading is to read a cartoon.

Cartoon for Close Reading Exercise

LESSON OBJECTIVE: Reading a picture or an image

Reading a cartoon provides different opportunities for discussion than the previous lesson provided. Students need to spend more time with the third and fourth readings to determine the meaning of the picture and accompanying text, as well as to examine their feelings and thoughts about the cartoon, to understand what it means to them.

MATERIALS NEEDED: Projector for sharing the image with the class; projectable image ready (see *Cartoon for Close Reading Exercise*).

GROUPING: Large or small group

TIME: 10 minutes

Step 1. Have Students Examine the Cartoon

Begin with the first reading. Remember, you are asking students to consider the essential question, "What does the text say?" You might say:

"Think about what this this cartoon says. *[Pause, giving students a minute to examine the picture.]* This is our 'first read' of the picture. I am noticing that the cat, obviously injured, is describing the suspect to the police artist and the police artist is drawing the suspect as the cat talks."

Step 2. Encourage Students to "Read" the Picture Again

Give students a few more seconds to look at the cartoon after you share your thoughts. Invite students to share their thinking. You might want to write down their thoughts and ideas as they share. You can say:

"In the second reading, we need to think about how the artist shows us what the text says. Remember, we focus on 'How does the text say it?' This author says it through the illustration's details. Notice the cat's hand waving in the air as he describes the suspect. Notice the injuries of the cat and the suspect he is describing, the dog. Look at the context of the room the two characters are in. It is sparse. Notice the look on the face of the police artist, and the ability of the police artist to capture what the cat is describing."

Step 3. Encourage Students to Examine the Picture and Evaluate Meaning

Rally the class and get the students talking about the cartoon. Focus on students thinking about whether the cartoon is funny or not, and encourage them to explain why using details from the cartoon. You can say:

"In the third reading, we ask the question, 'What does the text mean?' *[Pause for a minute.]* I want you to think about what the text means. In this simple cartoon, the artist is trying to get us to smile and to laugh. A process that is used in police work is made funny because it is a cat that is injured and describing the suspect, which is a dog. When considering the context of this cartoon, we know that it was written in the United States where the relationship between dogs and cats is considered adversarial. That is what makes us smile when looking at the cartoon!"

Step 4. You're Done!

Your students just did a close reading with three "readings" of the cartoon. First they thought about literal meaning of the cartoon; after the third reading, they asked answered questions about text meaning; and they also evaluated the picture and accompanying text to determine the deeper meaning of the cartoon.

SAMPLE LESSON: Close Reading a Short Article

When moving from a picture or cartoon to text in terms of teaching close reading, use short, easy-to-understand text that discusses new ideas or provides information.

LESSON OBJECTIVE: Close reading of a short article

Reading a short article may be something you do in your classroom already. In this lesson, you walk your students through the text with three readings. In teaching close reading, don't preteach vocabulary or provide background knowledge; instead, let the students delve into the text on their own, noting their ideas and thoughts in the margins. This lesson assumes that you have taught students to annotate a text; see *Prereading and Think-Aloud Lessons for Main Idea and Details* in Part III.

MATERIALS NEEDED: Copy of article "A Day at School in Kyrgyzstan" for each student (see pages 18 and 248); chart or projector to record notes and ideas

GROUPING: Large or small group

TIME: 40 minutes or two 20-minute sessions. You can teach the first and second reading in 20 minutes and the third reading in another 20-minute session. It helps to break it up if your students' "thinking muscles" are getting tired!

Step 1. Have Students Read the Text Through for the First Time

Have students read the article "A Day at School in Kyrgyzstan," by Kathryn Hulick. Say:

> "We have learned to closely read a picture and a cartoon as a warm-up for learning to closely read a text. Today we are going to closely read 'A Day at School in Kyrgyzstan.' Because we are focused on a close read right now, I am going to teach you the steps of close reading while you are practicing with this article. When we do a close reading, we start by jumping in and reading the text. We don't talk about the text first; we talk about it *after* we give it a go. You can mark up the page with your ideas about the text. Remember, just like when we examined the picture and the cartoon, we are thinking about the question, 'What does the text say?'"

Circulate the room while students read, reminding them to annotate the text. If you created a text annotation chart from previous teaching (see *Annotating Text* in Part III), you can point to it to remind students how to take notes in the margins while reading.

Step 2. Go Through the Text as a Group and Paraphrase Sentences

Once students learn to closely read a text on their own, they will paraphrase the text and take notes as they read. Because this is the students' first lesson in close reading, you will complete the paraphrasing process as a group, to teach the process of paraphrasing and capturing what the text says. Say:

> "Now that we have read the text, we are going to examine the text closely as a group. We are going to look at the text line-by-line and paragraph-by-paragraph and say the text in our own words."

See an example of paraphrasing "A Day at School in Kyrgyzstan" in *Paraphrasing Example* on page 19. This is the time to discuss difficult vocabulary with your students; however, your focus needs to be on words that the students identify as hard, not on words that you have chosen to teach! In a close reading, you don't teach vocabulary. Save that for a different lesson—for example, *Understanding Key Vocabulary* in Part III.

Step 3. Read the Text for a Second Time and Focus on How the Text Says What It Says

In the second reading of the text, you are focused on asking a different question, "How does the text say it?" This reading is concentrated on what the text says *and* how the author says it. Say:

> "Now I want you to read the text a second time. This time, while you are reading, think about what the text says—you can look at our paraphrasing chart to help you remember—and then think, 'How does the text say that?' For example . . . Once you are done with the second reading, we are going to talk about how the text says what it says all together as a group." *[Circulate and monitor students as they read the text the second time, and encourage them to think about what the text says (remember, the information is recorded on the chart you created with them) and how it says it.]*

Step 4. Go Through the Text as a Group and Discuss How the Text Says What It Says

During the second reading, students may begin making inferences about the text. Making and analyzing inferences requires students to deeply interpret the text by applying background knowledge and supporting conclusions, for which you will support them in this step. Encourage students to look at the craft and structure of the text as well as to begin thinking about how the ideas in the text connect to each other, or to other things. Say:

> "Let's talk about what you noticed in the article about how it says what it says. I know that it's funny to think about that. You may be thinking, 'Well, it just says it!' but authors use craft and structure to write their ideas down. Authors also use things they know about the subject of the article to write. Let's use our paraphrasing chart to help us. The first thing on our paraphrasing chart is . . . *[Refer to an example on the chart you created with the class (see* Paraphrasing Example *for guidance).]* Now, let's think, 'How does the author say this?' I am noticing that, in the article, the author . . ."

Walk the students through the article, examining what the text says and how the text says it. Encourage your students to think about the directness or indirectness of sentences (do the sentences present the main idea simply?), metaphors in the text, and the text structure. Help them make inferences about what the author might know and how the author shows what he or she knows in the writing. It helps to have students talk about and tie ideas in the text to concrete examples in the real world. Encourage students to compare their life to the life of a student in Kyrgyzstan.

Step 5. Read the Text for a Third Time and Focus on Text Meaning

This reading is focused on the analysis of the text. The essential question asked in this pass through the text is "What does the text mean?" This analysis includes identifying the author's purpose and making conclusions about the concepts and the implications of the text. Encourage students to consider some essential ideas about the author's thinking:

- The question the author is trying to answer
- The basic concept the author is portraying
- The author's purpose in writing the article
- The author's point of view
- Assumptions the author is making
- The implications of the author's reasoning
- The information the author chooses to use, or to leave out

Say:

> "Now we are going to read the text a third time. This time, I want you to think carefully about the author's meaning. Ask yourself, 'What does the text mean?' as you read. I want you to start by thinking about the author's purpose. Why did the author write this article? What does the author want us to think about? What does the central or 'big' idea in this article mean in our world? That last question is a big question, so I'll repeat it: 'What does the big idea in this article mean in our world?' We are going to discuss this question and what we think the author's purpose was in writing this article once you are done reading it again.
>
> "Don't get tired! I know that you have looked at this article two times already—but I think we can learn some things by looking at it again. Now, give it a go and write your ideas down in the margins just like we've done before."

A Day at School in Kyrgyzstan

by Kathryn Hulick

It's 7:30 a.m. and I'm on my way to school. I'm wrapped in a gigantic coat, hat, and scarf to keep out the winter chills as I walk. It's still dark out, but I pass vendors setting up shops, families driving donkey carts, and men standing outside their cars. I also pass groups of students, who wave to me and say, "Hello, Miss Kathryn!"

I am their teacher, a Peace Corps volunteer in Kyrgyzstan, a small country in the mountains of Central Asia. When I arrive at school, I climb the stairs to the third floor and unlock my classroom. It's a large room, with a row of windows and posters and maps all over the walls. The white board I bought leans against an ancient, unusable blackboard across the room from the windows. I flick the lights. Nothing happens. "Svet Jok," I think to myself, the Kyrgyz words for "No electricity." Although the sun is rising, it's still dark in the building. My first class, 11th grade, piles into the room, speaking among themselves in a mix of Russian and Kyrgyz. My job is to teach them English. It's going to be hard to follow my lesson plans when the students can't even see the white board, and it's so cold in the room that we're all still wearing our bulky coats and hats! Luckily, the lights blink on near the end of my first lesson. I ask my students to finish writing letters to their pen pals in America for homework.

A Kyrgyz high school goes up to the 11th grade. After graduation, many students will get married. The brightest students will go to university for five years, however most of them will end up back in this village, raising families, taking care of livestock and farming beans and potatoes. A select few will work their way to a job in the capital city of Bishkek. The common dream, however, is to travel to America or Europe, which is only possible if they first learn English.

For now, they are still students and teenagers. They giggle and whisper to each other in my class. They write to their pen pals about Britney Spears and 50 Cent, who they like as much as popular Russian, Turkish, and Kyrgyz pop stars. They watch American action movies, dubbed in Russian, on TV. A few kids have cell phones and collect clips of music to play for their friends. They do homework, take tests, play sports, and organize talent shows. But being students is just one aspect of their lives. When they go home after school, the girls make soup and bread from scratch, haul water in buckets and basins, and take care of younger siblings. The boys tend cows and sheep, learn to repair cars, and work in the fields.

Even in school, students are responsible for more than their homework. Students stay together in the same group of about 20 kids from first grade until graduation, meaning that classmates are like brothers and sisters. Each class has its own homeroom, and the students are responsible for the upkeep of this room. That's right, the students spend at least one afternoon every week with buckets, mops and dusting cloths cleaning their own classroom! When the weather is warm in the spring and fall, the director of the school may call a subotnik, which means that instead of classes, the whole school works outside cleaning up trash, gardening, and raking.

But today it's the middle of December. I wait ten minutes for my next class and finally one girl peeks in, "Sorry, Miss Kathryn! We have no lesson today. We are in the Actovnly Zal." That's Russian for "auditorium." I follow her downstairs and discover my students lined up on the stage, singing a song about winter to a group of teachers. If there's a performance going on, there probably won't be any lessons for the rest of the day. As I settle in to watch the show, I am full of hope for the futures of these students of mine, who juggle being teenagers, housekeepers, farmers, custodians, and entertainers all at once.

Paraphrasing Example

For the first four paragraphs of the text of
"A Day at School in Kyrgyzstan" by Kathryn Hulick

What the Text Says	Saying This in Our Own Words
It's 7:30 a.m. and I'm on my way to school. I'm wrapped in a gigantic coat, hat, and scarf to keep out the winter chills as I walk. It's still dark out, but I pass vendors setting up shops, families driving donkey carts, and men standing outside their cars. I also pass groups of students, who wave to me and say, "Hello, Miss Kathryn!"	A person is going to school in the morning. It is cold and dark because it is winter.
I am their teacher, a Peace Corps volunteer in Kyrgyzstan, a small country in the mountains of Central Asia.	The person going to school is a teacher in Kyrgyzstan.
When I arrive at school, I climb the stairs to the third floor and unlock my classroom. It's a large room, with a row of windows and posters and maps all over the walls. The white board I bought leans against an ancient, unusable blackboard across the room from the windows. I flick the lights. Nothing happens. *"Svet Jok,"* I think to myself, the Kyrgyz words for "No electricity."	The classroom seems sparse and doesn't have electricity.
Although the sun is rising, it's still dark in the building. My first class, 11th grade, piles into the room, speaking among themselves in a mix of Russian and Kyrgyz. My job is to teach them English. It's going to be hard to follow my lesson plans when the students can't even see the white board, and it's so cold in the room that we're all still wearing our bulky coats and hats! Luckily, the lights blink on near the end of my first lesson. I ask my students to finish writing letters to their pen pals in America for homework.	The teacher is teaching English. Because there is no electricity it will be hard for her to teach in the dark and in the cold. The lights do come on and the students write letters.
A Kyrgyz high school goes up to the 11th grade. After graduation, many students will get married. The brightest students will go to university for five years, however most of them will end up back in this village, raising families, taking care of livestock and farming beans and potatoes. A select few will work their way to a job in the capital city of Bishkek. The common dream, however, is to travel to America or Europe, which is only possible if they first learn English.	High school in Kyrgyzstan is much different than it is in the United States. Some students, but not many, get to go to college. Most students get married and work. They dream of going to America.
For now, they are still students and teenagers. They giggle and whisper to each other in my class. They write to their pen pals about Britney Spears and 50 Cent, who they like as much as popular Russian, Turkish, and Kyrgyz pop stars. They watch American action movies, dubbed in Russian, on TV.	The teenagers admire American, Russian, Turkish, and Kyrgyz rock stars. They do things American teens do, like watch TV.
A few kids have cell phones and collect clips of music to play for their friends. They do homework, take tests, play sports, and organize talent shows.	Teenagers in Kyrgyzstan like things that other teens like.
But being students is just one aspect of their lives. When they go home after school, the girls make soup and bread from scratch, haul water in buckets and basins, and take care of younger siblings. The boys tend cows and sheep, learn to repair cars, and work in the fields.	Teens in Kyrgyzstan are expected to do a lot. They work hard around the house and the farm.

Step 6. Have Students Work in Pairs to Discuss the Article

Remember, this third reading is focused on the analysis of the text. The essential question asked in this pass through the text is "What does the text mean?" Before discussing a reading in a group, have students talk in pairs so that they can "practice" their thinking with a partner. This helps to engage more students in the big conversation you will lead because they can prepare their ideas with a partner before sharing with the whole group. Say:

> "Now I want you to get with a partner and have a quick discussion about what you thought about the meaning of the text. Compare what you have noted with what your partner has noted. Make sure to, and help each other, have at least two ideas about the meaning of the text."

Step 7. Go Through the Text as a Group and Discuss What the Text Means

During the third reading, students are digging to make meaning. The thinking in this round is focused on the analysis of the text, including identifying the author's purpose and making conclusions about the concepts and implications of the text. You have already provided a structure for some meaning making: First the students read the text on their own, then they talked about it with a partner, and now it is time to discuss it as a group. To support them through the meaning making required for this step, make a chart with the information listed in *Author's Purpose Thinking Points*, or project the text box in *Author's Purpose Thinking Points* and discuss each bullet point. Say:

> "Now, let's talk about what we think the article means. We are going to think about what the article means by thinking about the author's reasoning in writing this article. Look at the points in this chart. [*Show* Author's Purpose Thinking Points.] Let's start our discussion with the author's purpose. What do you think the author's purpose was, and why?" [*Go through a few of the bullet points in* Author's Purpose Thinking Points, *having students share their thinking. Record the class's thinking on a chart or projected image.*]

Step 8. You're Done!

Your students just did a close reading with three passes through an article. First they thought about the literal meaning of the article; after the third reading, they asked and answered questions about text meaning; and they also evaluated the author's reasoning.

Author's Purpose Thinking Points

- The question the author is trying to answer
- The basic concept the author is portraying
- The author's purpose in writing the article
- The author's point of view
- Assumptions the author is making
- The implications of the author's reasoning
- The information the author choses to use, or to leave out

SAMPLE LESSON: Close Reading a Challenging Text

Teaching close reading with a challenging text takes practice. You taught close reading of a nonfiction text with "A Day at School in Kyrgyzstan," but students will read more difficult texts than this article. It is important to practice a close reading with a difficult text to understand how to apply the steps of a close reading to a text that isn't so easy to understand on the first read. This lesson uses a difficult text that appears on the pedestal of the Statue of Liberty. The poem, "The New Colossus," was written by Emma Lazarus. You can read about Emma Lazarus on the National Park Service website (www.nps.gov/stli/historyculture/emma-lazarus.htm).

LESSON OBJECTIVE: Close reading of a challenging text

In this lesson, you walk your students through a challenging article with four readings. Remember, in teaching close reading, not to preteach vocabulary or provide background knowledge, but to let the students delve into the text on their own, noting their ideas and thoughts in the margins.

MATERIALS NEEDED: Copy of article for each student; chart or projector to record notes and ideas; projectable copy of *Thinking About the Text: Author Questions*

GROUPING: Large or small group

TIME: 50 minutes or two sessions, one 20 and the other 30 minutes. You can teach the first and second reading in 20 minutes and the third and fourth readings in the 30-minute session. It helps to break it up if your students' "thinking muscles" are getting tired!

This lesson follows the same steps as in the previous lesson, *Close Reading a Short Article*. Follow Steps 1–7 of that lesson, and then continue the close reading of a complex text with a fourth reading. The directions for a fourth reading appear below.

Step 8: Fourth Reading of the Text

During the fourth reading, students work to understand what the text means to them. Their thinking in this round is focused on the analysis of the text and how it relates to their experiences with information and the world. This step includes some evaluation of the text and identification of relevant information, including evaluating the text for accuracy and significance. You have already provided a structure for some meaning making: First they read the text on their own, then they talked about it with a partner, and finally they discussed the meaning of the text as a group. Now you are ready to lead students to discuss the text and what it means to them. Say:

> "We are going to read the poem one more time, and while you are reading, I want you to think about what the poem means to you. We have already decided what the poem says and what the poem means, so now let's think about the question, 'What does the text mean to me?' To think about this, it might help to write down the thoughts you have about the poem. What did you notice about your feelings while we read and discussed the text? Were you irritated, angry, or excited? Think about why you might have been feeling these things while reading. Make sure to have your notebooks handy for jotting down your thoughts and ideas."

Now model your thinking for the class. To prepare for the modeling, make a chart with the information listed in *Thinking About the Text: Author Questions*, or project the text box in *Thinking About the Text: Author Questions* and discuss each bullet point. Say:

> "Let me give you an example. I am going to talk about what some of the lines mean to me. I am struck by the lines 'Here at our sea-washed, sunset gates shall stand a mighty woman with a torch.' These lines have meaning for me. I picture the Statue of Liberty standing at the edge of the water. I had never thought about New York City as a sun-washed gate for people, but that is what it is for many—a gate to a good life, a new life—and 'sun-washed' means to me that it is a bright new beginning. I think about what the author's intent was—we already discussed that during our third reading of the poem—and then I think about how the author

The New Colossus

by Emma Lazarus

Not like the brazen giant of Greek fame,

With conquering limbs astride from land to land;

Here at our sea-washed, sunset gates shall stand

A mighty woman with a torch, whose flame

Is the imprisoned lightning, and her name

Mother of Exiles. From her beacon-hand

Glows world-wide welcome; her mild eyes command

The air-bridged harbor that twin cities frame.

"Keep, ancient lands, your storied pomp!" cries she

With silent lips. "Give me your tired, your poor,

Your huddled masses yearning to breathe free,

The wretched refuse of your teeming shore.

Send these, the homeless, tempest-tost to me,

I lift my lamp beside the golden door!"

Source: Lazarus, Emma, "The New Colossus," *A Century of Immigration, 1820–1924* (handwritten) (sonnet), Library of Congress.

Note: See more at http://www.poets.org/viewmedia.php/prmMID/16111#sthash.G6Epj5ce.dpuf

Example of "The New Colossus" and Gloss Notations

Gloss	Text
The first two lines of the sonnet tell about conquering. What is being conquered? (Students write their ideas in the margin.)	Not like the brazen giant of Greek fame, With conquering limbs astride from land to land;
The next two lines describe the Statue of Liberty and where she is located. How would you describe who she is and where she is? (Students write their ideas in the margin.)	Here at our sea-washed, sunset gates shall stand A mighty woman with a torch,
Skipping forward a couple of lines, the sonnet describes a *beacon-hand* and *world-wide welcome*. What do you think these terms mean? (Students write their ideas in the margin.)	From her beacon-hand Glows world-wide welcome;
Later in the sonnet, a line describes a type of people. What do you think about the description? What is the sonnet saying? (Students write their ideas in the margin.)	"Give me your tired, your poor, Your huddled masses yearning to breathe free,
In the next line, *refuse* is used to describe the people leaving one country and coming to America. *Refuse* means "garbage." Why do you think the author described the people as *wretched refuse*? (Students write their ideas in the margin.)	The wretched refuse of your teeming shore.
The last two lines of the sonnet describe what the woman might be saying as a welcome. She describes the people as homeless, and America as the golden door. What do you think about her words? (Students write their ideas in the margin.)	Send these, the homeless, tempest-tost to me, I lift my lamp beside the golden door!"

takes the idea of welcoming new people to the United States and how relevant it is that she described Liberty standing at a gate of new beginnings."

Go on with your description as needed to make sure your students are following along with your thinking. Then, *don't describe more of the text and your thoughts,* but let your students read the poem again and give a go to their thinking about the poem's meaning to them. Remember, in a close reading, we don't frontload the thinking; we model how, and then let the students try, to read and think. We support them by talking through the text *after* the reading.

Step 9. You're Done!

Your students just did a close reading with four passes through a poem. This reading exercise not only got them talking and thinking about what the poem says and means, but they related the poem to their own thinking and explored what the poem means to them.

Thinking About the Text: Author Questions

- Is the author clear, or vague and confusing?
- Is the author accurate, and how does the author's message reflect the world at the time it was written?
- Is the author precise in description?
- Does the author display fairness or bias in the writing?
- Is the writing rich in important complexities, or is it superficial?
- What does the text make you think of, and what does the author's message make you think of?
- How did you react to the author's message?

What to Do if Students Are Not Ready for Close Reading

As you might notice, close reading of text assumes that students can read with some comprehension. Specifically, students should be able to decode a text and have some idea of what it means. True, not all of our students have this capability, at least not with grade-level, complex text, but we can differentiate a close reading to teach students this type of critical thinking and have them give it a go with text they can read and understand.

One approach you can take to support students not ready for close reading is to gloss the text (Richgels & Hansen, 1984). Glossing makes the reader–text interaction easier (Otto, White, Richgels, Hansen, & Morrison, 1981). Glossing focuses on a specific strategy and helps the student apply that strategy. When students gloss a text, they write in the margins to help them note important information, ask questions where they don't understand something, and note important vocabulary, following instruction and directions from the teacher. Gloss notation prompts can be prepared by the teacher, and then used by the student while reading to mark up a text (see *Example of "The New Colossus" and Gloss Notations*). When using glossing as a strategy, be sure to provide students with a copy of the text that they can write on.

Another approach is teaching students to get the gist of the text. When students work on skimming, scanning, and understanding the main idea of a text, they are focused on getting the gist of the text. In this type of reading, students read the text and work to glean its important ideas.

A final approach is teaching students to read nonfiction text written at a less complex level and then to write down the important parts, or main idea of each section, in a notebook. This approach focuses on summarizing and allows students to practice writing short summaries of text. *Student Outline of a Text From His Notebook* shows a student's notebook; the student created an outline of a text by listing the main ideas of each section.

How the Four Close Reading Questions Tap Different Purposes for Reading and Distinct Levels of Understanding

Two purposes exist for guiding students through texts. One is to learn content information, and the other is to analyze the text. Both purposes lead to student learning; however, one purpose focuses more on a literal level of understanding of factual information, and the other focuses on an inferential and evaluative level (Alvermann & Eakle, 2003; Fisher et al., 2012; Ganske, 2010). An inferential level of understanding and thinking involves learning information from text, whether the information is clearly provided or embedded in the meaning, while an evaluative level of understanding requires students to reflect on their emotional response to a text and connections they make to it (Barone, 2010; Keene, 2010).

These two purposes, a literal level of understanding and an inferential and evaluative level of understanding, align with the four questions of close reading discussed above. Remember, the first question focuses on learning content information, and the second, third, and fourth questions focus on making inferences and judgments about a text:

- What does the text say?
- How does the text say it?
- What does the text mean?
- What does the text mean to me?

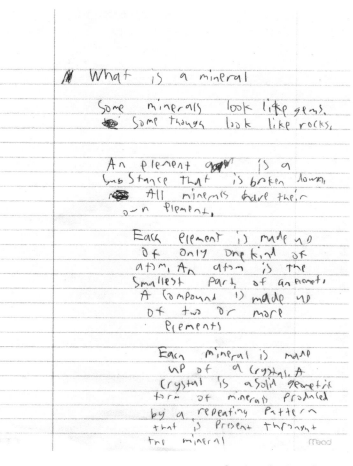

Student Outline of a Text
From His Notebook

Writing About Texts

As we've seen, close reading is a series of during-reading analytical moves, but of course the importance of reading a text radiates well beyond the time we sit down to read. Especially when texts have really engaged us, we think about the reading for days and weeks; we might talk about it with others, share it with others, find other texts related to it, and so on. In the classroom, we should provide students with experiences that do all of this, but one of the most potent ways of ensuring students deeply understand a text in a more lasting way is to have them write about it (Dreher, 2002; Herrington, 1981). Thinking about text goes beyond talking about text; it requires writing about texts. Teaching students to write about the texts they read is sometimes as simple as having them write down their thinking about the four questions they ask while close reading. Your lesson needs to go beyond that, too, but writing down their thoughts about the four questions is a start.

Writing *is* thinking. When students write about their reading, it can help them in two specific ways: to remember information they have read and to navigate the process of text analysis and evaluation. Singer and Donlan (1980) created a five-step process called the Learning From Text Guide to help students remember and retain information.

The Learning From Text Guide

The Learning From Text Guide focuses on three levels of student thinking: literal, inferential, and generalizable/evaluative. At the literal level, students read and recall literal elements from the text. At the inferential level, students make inferences, ask questions, and think about things that they can search for in the text. At the generalizable/evaluative level, students think beyond the text, ask questions of the author, wonder about the author's purpose, and think about the text's impact on their own thinking. The steps of the Learning From Text Guide focus on students asking questions and writing statements about the text:

Step 1: Read the text to determine important content. Write the important ideas down. Make statements or ask questions.

Step 2: Categorize the information learned from the text at three levels: in the text (literal), things to think about and search for in the text (inferential), and thoughts "in my head" (generalizable/evaluative).

Step 3: Write a short paragraph about learning from the text based on the categorized statements and questions.

Selecting Texts for Close Reading

Determining how easy or difficult a text is for students to read is not easy. The dimensions of text complexity can make the process difficult to understand, much less apply to the texts you use in your classroom. The Common Core State Standards look at text complexity as a three-part model. First, consider the qualitative dimensions of the text, or the aspects that measure levels of meaning, structure and clarity of language, and demand for knowledge. Second, consider the quantitative dimensions of the text, or items that can be measured, like word length, word frequency, and text cohesiveness. A computer often does this type of measurement. Third, consider the reader himself and the task of reading. This includes the reader's motivation and depth of knowledge of the subject, as well as the complexity of the reading assignment (Fisher et al., 2012).

Two questions are essential in preparing to teach a close reading: (1) How do you know your students can read the text, and (2) how difficult is the text? I often work with new teachers who are confused by these questions. They look at me, quizzically, thinking, "The text is appropriate for my students. It is in my textbook." A few weeks into teaching, the new teachers understand why I asked these questions. Not all texts are created equal.

I don't find determining text complexity easy. It is an exercise that takes thinking and practice.

Look out for some signals in the text to help determine its complexity. These factors work together to make a text either easier or harder to read. Recently, in choosing a book for a graduate course I was teaching, I considered the level of the students in the program, the density of content in the text, the voice of the text, and the length of chapters and size of the font. I decided on a hands-on text with a practical voice—appropriate for teachers busy in the classroom by day and taking graduate courses by night. The chapters were short, and the text was peppered with text boxes and bold print outlining important ideas and information. This text was less complex than other texts I could have chosen for my students to read.

Certain factors can help you determine complexity. Hess and Biggam (2004) created a list of factors that interact and influence text complexity:

- Word difficulty and language structure
- Text structure
- Discourse style
- Genre and characteristics of the text
- Student familiarity with the content, or background knowledge
- Level of reasoning required
- Organization of the text
- Length of the text

In the next chapter, we look at teaching students how to read textbooks, which brings in unique challenges.

CHAPTER 3

Taming the Textbook

Strategies for Helping Students Handle These Tomes

Our students are going to have to read more than trade books and high-interest articles during their school careers, and front and center in upper elementary and middle school is the textbook. While textbooks may not be your go-to texts for engaging your students in a content area, I've made my peace with them. They do manage to provide students with knowledge in many important curriculum areas, their content is well researched, and they represent a "text type" that students will be expected to access, use, and read in middle school, high school, and beyond. In many professional fields, articles and texts are sometimes dense with information and not written for the purpose of engaging the reader, and reading textbooks gets students used to accessing information in technical texts.

But, as the saying goes, it's how you play the game that determines whether students learn from these texts. For example, recently, I was in a ninth-grade social studies classroom and observed as the teacher taught a short lesson to start work for the day. After she finished, she said to the class, "Work with your partner to answer the questions on the board about pages 244 to 278 in the textbook." The students moved into pairs, and each pair retrieved a big, heavy textbook from the shelf in the back of the room. The students hunched up over the books, reading together and pointing to words and sentences, and then began writing in the notebooks they had out on their desks or in their laps. I meandered through the classroom, curious about the work the students were doing. A few pairs of students seemed to be able to read the textbook effortlessly; others were working through the text slowly; and a few seemed to be pretending to read, and trying to look busy. I decided to sit with one of the pairs; these students were reading the textbook slowly.

"So, what are you working on?" I asked.

"This reading, the teacher put on the board," one of the students answered.

"Oh, is it hard?"

"Yeah, kinda. It's about the war and stuff," the other student answered.

"OK, I see," I said. "Do you know why you are reading it?"

The two students looked at each other, and then at me. For a moment, no one said anything. "'Cause we have to," the first student said, while the second student nodded.

Then I sat down with a pair of students who weren't really reading, but were trying to make me think they were.

"So, what are you working on?" I asked.

"That—on the board over there," one student answered.

"Oh, I see. It looks like you are having trouble getting into the work," I said.

"Yeah, Justin, here—man, he keeps distracting me."

"Got it. How are you going to read that?" I asked as I pointed to one section on the textbook page. "I mean, it looks hard."

"Yeah," the other student answered, I guess we could look at some of the pictures here . . ." Then the student hit the other student in the shoulder, and they both started laughing.

"OK—I'll leave you two alone, but I think looking at the pictures and reading the headers (I pointed to the headings) might help you."

Both pairs of students needed help to understand what they were reading. The pair that was reading, but reading slowly, could access the words, but they were plowing through the book section as if all the words had the same level of importance. They didn't have a clear strategy for reading the text, and they didn't have a goal for the reading other than that the teacher expected them to read it. The pair that couldn't read the text (they told me it was too hard) weren't getting anything out of the text at all, in spite of the informational pictures and text boxes that were easier to read than the text. These students had no strategies for accessing the textbook section they were assigned.

This situation isn't very different from those in many other classes I have visited when students are working with a textbook: Some students just don't know how, and even the capable readers read all of the information in the same way. Students need to *use* textbooks, not just read them. We can do a few things to make this happen.

Protocols and Graphic Organizers to the Rescue

Textbooks are unwieldy books that often can be uninvolving and too difficult for developing readers of informational text (Birr Moje, 2010). These texts can also be boring for strategic readers of informational text. But as I said, they do expose students to the technical text genre, and as such they perform an important function. We can put in place some strategies to help students' skills grow with textbook use. In essence, we can help them tame the unwieldy textbook! We can

- provide background reading about the subject with engaging short texts, articles, and other media sources;
- use graphic organizers to help students tackle textbook sections;
- use graphic organizers and note-taking protocols to help students remember information from the texts; and
- have students keep notebooks to outline information in a specific way to aid learning (Andreassen & Bråten, 2011; Knoell, 2010; Meyer & Ray, 2011; Ogle & Blachowicz, 2002).

Reading protocols and graphic organizers can scaffold textbook reading for students. A reading protocol is a set process students go through when approaching a text and readying themselves for reading (Riley, 1992). Graphic organizers can lead student thinking and embed a set of action, or a protocol, and make it a habit. The graphic organizers presented in this chapter are designed to be more than a sheet of paper that students fill out to prove they have done some work; instead, they outline a set of actions for students to take when

- getting ready to read a textbook section;
- reading a textbook section for facts and details; or
- recounting what a textbook section is about.

Five Graphic Organizers That Help Readers Connect, Map, and Remember

First, I advise you to let your students in on a little secret: Without saying it's OK to hate the textbook, share your stance. For example, you might say you've always found textbooks difficult going, too. Reading them can feel like a giant beast of facts coming at you, and sometimes your attention wanders. But you've learned how to tame them, and you're going to help your students conquer their mightiness, too. You might say:

> "I don't read a textbook like I read a novel. I *use* it, like I use a cookbook or an encyclopedia, or even a dictionary. That is, it's a tool that I use for very specific purposes. It makes me feel more in control when I define for myself why I am reading it, consulting it. I'm the boss of it. One purpose may be to fill out a graphic organizer focused on recall of facts from the text reading. Another purpose could be to take notes to prepare for a test. Yet another reason could be to gather information about something I want or need to know (my favorite reason for using textbooks).
>
> "I am going to share a graphic organizer that works for all three purposes."

Get across to students that, yes, no matter how you slice it, they have to get good at understanding and recalling information and facts, but doing so is easier with the graphic organizers, which help them remember that, often, they can glean information from the book without reading the text straight through.

How the Organizers Scaffold the Cognition Behind High-Level Comprehension

Students need to use specific strategies along with the graphic organizers to tackle the textbook—that is, to be aware of the thinking skills involved in learning new information (Dreher, 2002). The five graphic organizers presented in this chapter are all designed to address a key strategy for comprehension: connect, map, and remember (Akhavan, 2008). You'll need to demonstrate and coach students toward independence with knowing how to do the following:

- Connect to information they are reading in textbooks
- Map the information by creating connections so they can learn the new information
- Remember information, facts, and details for their writing, discussion, and perhaps class projects
- Use metacognitive strategies to help guide their reading of textbooks (Baker, 2002; Meyer & Ray, 2011)

As you introduce the organizers, get across the idea that they help readers tap into different levels of thinking. (You may be familiar with levels of thinking as Bloom's taxonomy!)

Thinking Levels in Action

Benjamin Bloom's taxonomy of thinking levels was revised in 2001 to embody a truer representation of the active nature of knowing and thinking. The original taxonomy laid out six major categories in the cognitive domain, ordered from simple thinking to complex thinking and from concrete thinking to abstract thinking. Additionally, a hierarchy of mastery organized these categories of thinking, with simpler categories considered a prerequisite to more complex categories.

The revised taxonomy organizes thinking into a knowledge dimension and a cognitive process dimension. I think about the knowledge dimension as addressing the *outcomes* of subject matter learning: factual knowledge, conceptual knowledge, procedural knowledge, and metacognitive knowledge.

The cognitive process dimension is the verb of learning—it captures the active "doing" of thinking and has six categories: remember, understand, apply, analyze, evaluate, and create.

This revision gives us a deeper way of focusing on our teaching and student learning. When we teach content, students need to remember and retain factual knowledge. Knowing things, and being able to remember the information, is really important for all of us in developing expertise in an area. With the taxonomy revision, we don't have to consider these processes as *lower* levels of thinking. Instead, these forms of knowledge are different ways for students to act on information. The levels we consider higher levels of thinking—to analyze, evaluate, or create—are ways students interact with the information so that they can begin to own the information for themselves. The textbook tamer graphic organizers help students tap into both dimensions.

Source: Krathwohl (2002).

The Knowledge Dimension

There are four types of knowledge in the knowledge dimension. We learn and process information with these types of knowledge in different ways.

Factual Knowledge: Knowledge that is basic to a discipline.

Conceptual Knowledge: Knowledge about the interrelationships among the basic elements within a larger structure that enable them to function together. For example, classifications, principles, theories, models, and structures.

Procedural Knowledge: Knowledge about how to do something, specific to a discipline, including methods of inquiry and criteria for using skills, techniques, and methods.

Metacognitive Knowledge: Knowledge of cognition in general as well as awareness and knowledge of one's own cognition, including strategic and reflective knowledge.

Source: Anderson & Krathwohl (2001).

Structure of the Cognitive Processes of Revised Bloom's Taxonomy

There are six cognitive processes in the revised taxonomy. We learn and process information differently based on the type of cognitive process involved in the task at hand.

- ❏ Remember
  - ❏ Recognizing
  - ❏ Recalling
- ❏ Understand
  - ❏ Interpreting
  - ❏ Exemplifying
  - ❏ Classifying
  - ❏ Summarizing
  - ❏ Inferring

- ❏ Comparing
- ❏ Explaining
- ❏ Apply
  - ❏ Executing
  - ❏ Implementing
- ❏ Analyze
  - ❏ Differentiating
  - ❏ Organizing
  - ❏ Attributing

- ❏ Evaluate
  - ❏ Checking
  - ❏ Critiquing
- ❏ Create
  - ❏ Generating
  - ❏ Planning
  - ❏ Producing

Source: Anderson & Krathwohl (2001); Krathwohl (2002).

In this matrix, the knowledge dimensions are related to the six cognitive processes. You can use this matrix to develop tasks for students based on the type of knowledge and cognitive process you are emphasizing in your lesson.

The Knowledge Dimension	1. Remember	2. Understand	3. Apply	4. Analyze	5. Evaluate	6. Create
A. Factual Knowledge						
B. Conceptual Knowledge						
C. Procedural Knowledge						
D. Metacognitive Knowledge						

Source: Anderson & Krathwohl (2001).

The five textbook tamer graphic organizers in this chapter are organized by the levels of knowledge and the cognitive processes that they incorporate:

- Scanning text features
- Skimming tabs
- Summarizing from notes
- Analyzing sections
- Interpreting text

Using the Textbook Tamers Daily

These graphic organizers are not designed to be an end in themselves—a final product of student learning; rather, these tools help students learn throughout a unit, which may lead to a final product like a writing assignment, project, or text. Using the graphic organizers for 20 minutes or so each day helps students get their arms around the difficult lengthy reading in textbooks, largely by helping them *organize* the information while reading the text. The goal of using these organizers is to help students own the information in the reading, set up a successful plan for students to tackle the reading, and quell the overwhelming sense of resistance that can consume students when faced with a large text that doesn't motivate them to read.

Graphic Organizer: Scanning Text Features

Strong readers often familiarize themselves with the text features within nonfiction texts *before* they begin to read, scanning ahead to notice charts, the sheer length of the piece they are embarking on, subheads, and so on. This kind of previewing works very well with textbooks, and when we train our students to look at text features, it goes a long way; a neglected aspect of reading stamina is the reader's initial "courage" to face the scope of the piece. So many students just dive right in without checking the "depths of the water" around them first. The following tips can be modeled and shared with students in demonstration lessons:

- If students are reading a text *section*, they should orient themselves by asking themselves questions about what they are going to read. What chapter is the section in? What is the chapter title? What is the chapter about? Is the chapter in turn part of a larger unit or theme? What is the content of the prior section?
- If students are reading a textbook chapter, they will ask themselves similar questions, but be focused on the chapter overall. Where does the chapter appear in the book—the beginning, the middle, or the end? What information was shared in the book in the prior chapters? What will be shared in subsequent chapters? What is the chapter title? What is the textbook about? How does this textbook relate to the information learned in class?
- Before reading, students need to orient themselves to the features of the textbook and, in particular, the section or chapter they are going to read. The text features might include boxes, graphics, pictures, graphs, primary source texts, and glossaries. Students can glean important ideas about the text from these features.

The textbook tamer *Scanning Text Features* gives students a place to record things they notice or think about the textbook reading. Students who are unfamiliar, or who struggle, with textbook reading don't have a well-established path for tackling the text. They need a structure to rely on, and this graphic organizer provides one, in basically three steps.

1 Students start with the right-hand boxes of the graphic organizer. In the top box, titled "Important Ideas," students write down what they think are important ideas about a text they are going to read by looking at the text features.

2 Students move next to fill in the box titled "Important Vocabulary." As they scan the text, students should notice vocabulary that pops at them and record the words. They may or may not know the words; the important point is that they can spot words that seem key to understanding the chapter or text section.

Reviewing students' responses in this section will give you a chance to check their thinking and teach words that the class has identified as important to the text. It is important to teach words students are thinking about because this validates, or accepts and confirms, their thinking and thus connects them to the textbook reading. Of course, you may feel other words are important for them to know, so you'll teach those as well. Remember: Validate, validate, validate.

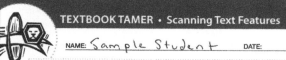

TEXTBOOK TAMER • Scanning Text Features

NAME: Sample Student   DATE:

Important Ideas
(Look at the text features)

- continents richest country is South Africa
- rich and poor cities
- people of many descents
  - also many languages
- World's largest producer of Gold.

Get the Gist
(Summarize key points)

South Africa is Africa's wealthiest country, and the world's largest producer of gold. South Africa is very diverse with about 43 million people. There are a couple wealthy cities, but mostly poor towns, and the average lifespan in South Africa is 56 years old.

Important Vocabulary
(Bold words, important terms)

- people live an average of 56 years in S. Africa
- Capitals - Cape Town, Pretoria
- About 43,426,386 population

Scanning Text Features Graphic Organizer Filled Out
Based on a Section of a Textbook

3 In the third step, students fill in the "Get the Gist" column with ideas on what they think the text is about. To do so, students may read several paragraphs. Overall, strategic readers scan text and text features before reading to get an idea of what they are going to read, and then they plan their reading based on what they glean from the scan. If the material is unfamiliar, strategic readers may slow down, read some sections more closely than others, or read paragraph by paragraph and then check themselves for understanding.

Key to having students use this graphic organizer is to quickly check in with them before they begin reading; by doing so, you can assess their readiness to read the text—and intervene if they are not ready with vocabulary work or other frontloading.

Graphic Organizer: Skimming for Information

Once students are oriented to what they are going to read, they need to decide *how* they are going to read. Most strategic readers make a reading "plan" without even realizing it; they sum up the task of the reading, consider their purposes for reading, and scan the text to decide how to read: slowly and deeply, or quickly to skim. As teachers, we often focus our students on deep understanding of the text they are reading, but sometimes deep reading isn't the goal. For example, skimming text to quickly gather information and

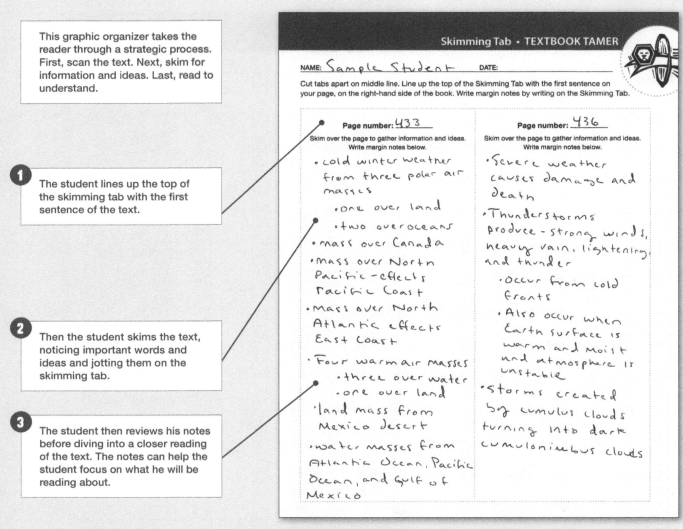

This graphic organizer takes the reader through a strategic process. First, scan the text. Next, skim for information and ideas. Last, read to understand.

1 The student lines up the top of the skimming tab with the first sentence of the text.

2 Then the student skims the text, noticing important words and ideas and jotting them on the skimming tab.

3 The student then reviews his notes before diving into a closer reading of the text. The notes can help the student focus on what he will be reading about.

Skimming Tab • TEXTBOOK TAMER

NAME: Sample Student   DATE:

Cut tabs apart on middle line. Line up the top of the Skimming Tab with the first sentence on your page, on the right-hand side of the book. Write margin notes by writing on the Skimming Tab.

Page number: 433

Skim over the page to gather information and ideas. Write margin notes below.

- cold winter weather from three polar air masses
  - one over land
  - two over oceans
- mass over Canada
- mass over North Pacific – effects Pacific Coast
- mass over North Atlantic effects East Coast
- Four warm air masses
  - three over water
  - one over land
- land mass from Mexico desert
- water masses from Atlantic Ocean, Pacific Ocean, and Gulf of Mexico

Page number: 436

Skim over the page to gather information and ideas. Write margin notes below.

- Severe weather causes damage and death
- Thunderstorms produce – strong winds, heavy rain, lightening, and thunder
  - Occur from cold fronts
  - Also occur when Earth surface is warm and moist and atmosphere is unstable
- Storms created by cumulus clouds turning into dark cumulonimbus clouds

Skimming Tab Graphic Organizer Filled Out Based on a Section of a Textbook

ideas can be helpful for a struggling reader to access the textbook. Sometimes the goal is a quick skim when we are returning to a text we have already read to try to locate content. In any case, students need a reading plan and a defined purpose for reading:

First: Scan the text.

Second: Skim for information and ideas presented in the text.

Third: Read to understand.

Students who are not strategic readers of nonfiction text don't automatically create a reading plan for themselves in their minds. We must teach them to do this. The skimming tab organizer (see *Skimming Tab*) is a like a bookmark. Students can take notes on it for a particular page they are preparing to read in any given textbook. The skimming tab organizer is a way for students to "write in the margins" without writing in the actual book.

For an example of this graphic organizer in use, see *Skimming Tab*.

Graphic Organizer: Summarizing With Notes

Often students have difficulty discussing what they have read after reading a textbook. This might be because the amount of information they've read is vast, and they are unsure of what is most important to discuss. Sometimes students don't know if they are supposed to discuss a main idea/theme or a series of events/facts. In any case, when students are given a tool that compels them to record important facts as they read, report them

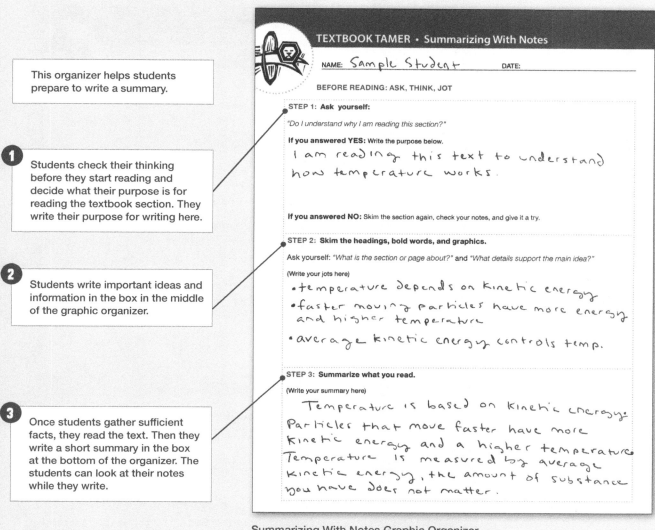

This organizer helps students prepare to write a summary.

TEXTBOOK TAMER · Summarizing With Notes

NAME: Sample Student   DATE:

BEFORE READING: ASK, THINK, JOT

STEP 1: Ask yourself:

"Do I understand why I am reading this section?"

If you answered YES: Write the purpose below.

I am reading this text to understand how temperature works.

If you answered NO: Skim the section again, check your notes, and give it a try.

STEP 2: Skim the headings, bold words, and graphics.

Ask yourself: "What is the section or page about?" and "What details support the main idea?"

(Write your jots here)

- temperature depends on kinetic energy
- faster moving particles have more energy and higher temperature
- average kinetic energy controls temp.

STEP 3: Summarize what you read.

(Write your summary here)

Temperature is based on kinetic energy. Particles that move faster have more kinetic energy and a higher temperature. Temperature is measured by average kinetic energy, the amount of substance you have does not matter.

1. Students check their thinking before they start reading and decide what their purpose is for reading the textbook section. They write their purpose for writing here.

2. Students write important ideas and information in the box in the middle of the graphic organizer.

3. Once students gather sufficient facts, they read the text. Then they write a short summary in the box at the bottom of the organizer. The students can look at their notes while they write.

Summarizing With Notes Graphic Organizer
Filled Out Based on a Section of a Textbook

in an organized fashion, and then use them to write a summary, students become more sure-footed about what is worthy of discussion. Rather, they become able to more deeply comprehend, and then find summarizing more possible.

Writing is a way of knowing, and when students write, it can help them remember and understand what they have read. Lengthy pieces of writing aren't always necessary! In fact, one way to approach this activity is to have students write important facts on sticky notes as they read and then organize their thinking in a notebook after reading. They can write each important fact on an individual sticky note and then pull the sticky notes from the textbook and place them in an order that helps them report the information in a written summary.

The *Summarizing With Notes* graphic organizer is another way to help students track important information from their reading.

This organizer is helpful because you can assess students' ability to glean important facts from the reading by checking what they write in the boxes. You can check the facts they chose before giving the students the go-ahead to write a summary.

Graphic Organizer: Analyzing Sections

After guiding students to make a reading plan and checking their thinking as they skim the text and identify important details, we can focus on helping students to retain information from the texts they are reading.

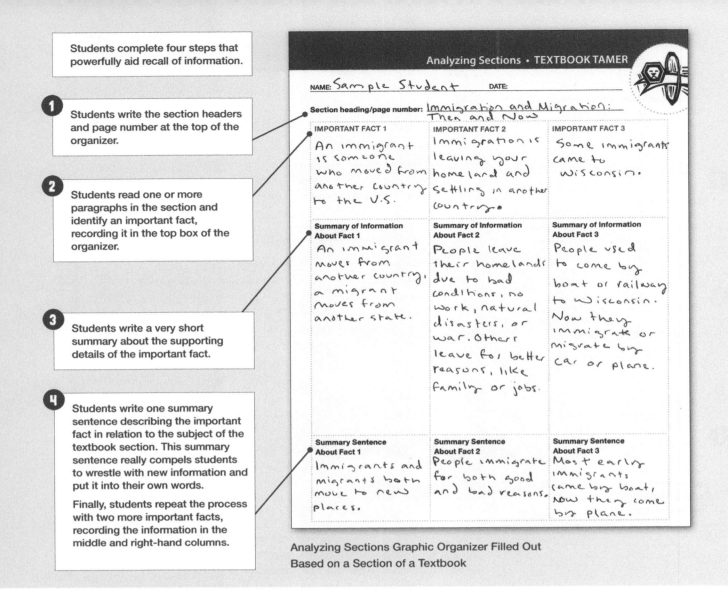

Students complete four steps that powerfully aid recall of information.

1 Students write the section headers and page number at the top of the organizer.

2 Students read one or more paragraphs in the section and identify an important fact, recording it in the top box of the organizer.

3 Students write a very short summary about the supporting details of the important fact.

4 Students write one summary sentence describing the important fact in relation to the subject of the textbook section. This summary sentence really compels students to wrestle with new information and put it into their own words.

Finally, students repeat the process with two more important facts, recording the information in the middle and right-hand columns.

Analyzing Sections • TEXTBOOK TAMER

NAME: Sample Student   DATE:

Section heading/page number: Immigration and Migration: Then and Now

IMPORTANT FACT 1
An immigrant is someone who moved from another country to the U.S.

IMPORTANT FACT 2
Immigration is leaving your homeland and settling in another country.

IMPORTANT FACT 3
Some immigrants came to Wisconsin.

Summary of Information About Fact 1
An immigrant moves from another country, a migrant moves from another state.

Summary of Information About Fact 2
People leave their homelands due to bad conditions, no work, natural disasters, or war. Others leave for better reasons, like family or jobs.

Summary of Information About Fact 3
People used to come by boat or railway to Wisconsin. Now they immigrate or migrate by car or plane.

Summary Sentence About Fact 1
Immigrants and migrants both move to new places.

Summary Sentence About Fact 2
People immigrate for both good and bad reasons.

Summary Sentence About Fact 3
Most early immigrants came by boat, now they come by plane.

Analyzing Sections Graphic Organizer Filled Out
Based on a Section of a Textbook

Most textbook chapters are made up of multiple sections that build information in a sequence of events, or in a knowledge-building sequence. Students often cannot retain all of the important information from one section to the next because the text is so dense with information, facts, and details. Another problem students can have when reading textbooks is that they cannot determine important facts within a section of text, or recognize the supporting details of those important facts. To help students learn information while reading textbooks, it helps to focus students on identifying important facts in specific textbook sections, and then identifying supporting details for those facts.

The *Analyzing Sections* graphic organizer is designed to help students identify important facts in their reading, section by section. Students should use one or two *Analyzing Sections* organizers per textbook section. After recording information on the graphic organizers, a student would have a set of notes that he or she could use to read or study in order to learn and retain information from the text.

Analyzing Sections is a simple three-step process that helps students to do the following:

- Discern important information
- Identify facts and details
- Synthesize information into a short sentence

Notice how this organizer encourages students to make a judgment about the information they read and express it in their words. This graphic organizer is a boon to developing students' interpretive skills.

1 Students read the text once to get the gist of the section.

2 Students reread the text to identify three important points in the text. These three points can be recorded in the left-hand column of the organizer.

3 Students carefully consider the three important points they outlined and use this information to write a summary of the text section. When summarizing, students are developing their understanding of what they have read. It is good practice for students to revisit the text as many times as needed to reread, refocus, and check their understanding while writing the short summary. Students can write this summary in the upper right-hand box of the organizer.

4 As a next step, students think about what the information means. The point is for students to relate this new information to previous things that they have learned about the subject. Students can jot a few notes about this in the box in the middle of the organizer.

5 Finally, in the box at the bottom of the organizer, students make a judgment about the information—perhaps why the information read is important, or not—and state why.

TEXTBOOK TAMER • Interpreting Text

NAME: Sample Student   DATE:

Three Important Ideas
(Outline your ideas)

1. Constitutional Convention is to improve the Articles of Confederation.

2. The Virginia plan proposed a three branch government with representation based on state population

3. The Great Compromise gave the States a House of R. based on state size and a Senate based on a fixed number of 2 per state.

Summarize the Text

leaders of the country met to improve the Articles of Confederation. The Virginia Plan proposed gov. representation based on state population, this upset small states. The Great Compromise appeased both the small and large states.

Interpret the Text
(Jot why the text's meaning is important or why it is not)

The text's meaning is important because the way that the country's Constitution was written is very important history.

Make a Judgment
(State your opinion about the text)

The text does a good job of explaining the details of the Constutional convention, it gives a full picture of the events.

Interpreting Text Graphic Organizer Filled Out Based on a Section of a Textbook

---

Graphic Organizer: Interpreting Text

When students interpret text, they show understanding by determining meaning. Interpretation is the focus of the *Interpreting Text* graphic organizer—for students, developing factual knowledge, developing their evaluative thinking regarding the factual knowledge, and developing their ability to understand what they read. Good to jump-start students' thinking, this organizer prompts students to put four kinds of thinking into play:

- Determining important information
- Summarizing sections of text
- Interpreting the meaning of information read
- Evaluating the importance of the information

Five steps make up the use of the *Interpreting Text* organizer. These five steps are focused on students remembering and retaining information read by determining facts, summarizing meaning, and evaluating importance.

Troubleshooting Tips That Maximize the Benefits of Graphic Organizers

When using the graphic organizers in class, be aware of common pitfalls:

- Students may fill out the sheet just to get the assignment over with.
- Students may not understand anything they have read in the textbook.
- Students working with a partner may just copy their partner's answers.
- Students may get their thinking mixed up.

You can avoid these pitfalls. First, if your students cannot use the graphic organizer independently, complete the thinking and fill out the organizer together in small or large groups. Another way of supporting student work with the graphic organizer is to stretch one out over several days. For example, you might spend 15 minutes one day and work on just part of the organizer with the class. Then, you can follow up the next day and finish the work.

Remember, the goal is to nurture student thinking, not to fill in the blanks, so pace the use of the organizers in ways that make sense for you and your students.

1. Know your students. Knowing your students is harder if you are a secondary teacher in a departmentalized setting rather than a self-contained setting, but it isn't impossible. The easiest way to get to know your students and their abilities to read and comprehend their reading is not to lecture. Rather than talking at students for long periods of time, structure your teaching with short lessons and lots of group work. You can walk around the classroom while students are working together and take notes. This is a time to notice who is doing what, how they are doing it, and what they are doing with the task at hand.

2. Design instruction to engage. While disengaged students come to class with a lot of baggage that teachers cannot necessarily change, we can do some things once we know our students. We can provide as much engaging instruction as possible. To do this, get students working together and thinking together. Have students read the text with one another, or have them work in groups using the graphic organizers to support their thinking and learning. Set up some accountability in this teaching structure so that students cannot just copy from the one student in the group who "gets it" and knows what to do. Use a random selection technique, like popsicle sticks with student names or numbers written on them, and use the random technique to call on students to report what their group has been doing, or report what the group wrote on the graphic organizer.

3. Let your students talk. A quiet classroom is a deadly classroom for student thinking. Our students need to talk to understand. It is important that they talk about what they are reading, thinking about, and learning, so I am suggesting not social talk but purposeful talk. Talk can help a student who has fuzzy thinking strengthen his understanding by going over points and details with another student. Talk can help an English learner understand important points in the text when a friend explains it to her. Talk can help all students consolidate and make sense of new information, facts, and details. This action of consolidating thinking is a way of understanding, storing, and retrieving information from our memories. Talk also builds a collaborative classroom community where students feel free to take risks and don't feel pressure to produce perfect oral and written work, or to be correct all of the time. Talk helps students learn.

Scaffolding Leads to Deep Comprehension

Remember, students who need instruction to support their comprehension don't always receive the help they need (C. Brown & Broemmel, 2011; Means & Knapp, 1991). These graphic organizers designed to help students tame textbooks and give them independent strategies for tackling a textbook, provide direct, explicit instruction as scaffolding to support their learning. Also remember that these graphic organizers and the explicit instruction they engender need not be bound to the basal; you can use these graphic organizers with informational materials of all types.

Should you use them a few times a week for months and months? Not necessarily. My general advice is that students need deep and sustained scaffolding until you see it can be pulled away. Deep scaffolding occurs when you provide more meaningful scaffolding that meets your students' needs prior to and during reading (C. Brown & Broemmel, 2011). Deep scaffolding develops in-depth schema building and critical understanding of text (Schoenbach & Greenleaf, 2009). You may do this in one lesson using a specific organizer or spread out the instruction over the week. You may teach the organizers explicitly at the beginning of the year and then just have them handy for reference later in the year once the students can use the organizers independently. If you are a middle school teacher, you may encourage the librarian to keep copies of the textbook tamers handy for students to use when reading textbooks from other classrooms.

Help your students read textbooks in an appropriate way—as information sources. Keep the focus of your instruction with textbooks on deep scaffolding as you prime students prior to reading, help them navigate a text while reading, and amplify their understanding after they read. The beauty of the organizers is that students use them temporarily as supports to lean on, but use the thinking skills they strengthen for a lifetime.

The Key Strategies for Deep Reading Nonfiction

Teaching nonfiction text can be arduous sometimes if my mind-set is to just "get it covered," but when I take a big breath and do a deep dive into it, teaching and learning can be downright fun, for both my students and me. The key is to use real-world texts, for real-world reasons (Kern, 2012). In this chapter, we look at the strategies at work when we plunge deeply into a nonfiction text, and consider how to help students turn the strategies into skills.

Proficient readers of nonfiction call upon seven key skills when reading text and grappling with new learning (Ogle & Blachowicz, 2002). These strategies bring the most power to readers and are most important for us to develop in our students. They are also aligned with the outcomes laid out in the Common Core State Standards; that is, they foster our students' ability to think about text, learn from text, and apply ideas from text to understanding the world in greater depth. When teachers help their students become strategic readers, they focus on teaching a repertoire of comprehension strategies and guide students' ability to use the strategies until they become skilled at their use (Duffy, 2002). With this focus, it becomes possible for students to do the kind of deep reading we're after. And here are the strategies we need to develop as skills in our students:

- To think about and learn from text, readers do the following:
    1. Understand text structure
    2. Identify main ideas
    3. Identify key details
    4. Recognize and explore key vocabulary
    5. Summarize text

- To apply the ideas they have learned from text to help them think more knowledgeably about the world, and to help them more deeply understand other disciplines, readers

  6. converse about the ideas of the text with others; and

  7. write about reading (McConachie & Petrosky, 2010; Ogle & Blachowicz, 2002; Trabasso & Bouchard, 2002).

The Strategies Defined

In this chapter, I define the "what"—the strategies that we want to become skills in our students. The "how" comes in later chapters, in the lessons and teaching sequences you can use to address these seven skills. Readers use skills and strategies to understand what they are reading. Through modeled instruction, interactive reading, and think-aloud mini-lessons, we can ensure that strategies become skills (Kern, 2012). This occurs once the strategies our students use become an automatic process (Stahl, 2006).

Skilled Versus Strategic

Skilled readers unconsciously apply strategies to comprehend a text (we discussed those strategies in Chapter 1). A skill is the talent to do something with a savvy and adroitness that we don't feel when first learning something new. Strategic readers employ a plan when reading unfamiliar text, somewhat like a blueprint in their brain. Strategic readers *consciously* use strategies in their repertoire to be successful when reading; they reason strategically when encountering barriers to understanding. Afflerbach, Pearson, and Paris (2008) point out that the terms *skills* and *strategies* distinguish between automatic processes (*skills*) and deliberately controlled processes (*strategies*).

Understanding Text Structure

Think back to a time when a text made you feel dumb. I recall reading the manual to my first computer (an Apple IIe), and I was certain I would *never* be able to use a computer! I imagine we all have these moments. Now think of a sixth grader starting a textbook chapter on classifying plants and animals, and within a page he is hit with *species, genus, organism, vascular,* and *nonvascular*—and that's just in the main text, aside from sidebars on plant classification and a formidable graph on cells. If he earnestly attempts to understand it all without any tools—reading it page by page as he would a novel—there is a darn good chance he's going to get overwhelmed trying to retain and recall so much *all at once*.

But if, instead, he anticipates the way the information has been organized for him, theoretically to aid his comprehension, then he will be less likely to get lost. And believe me, I have seen my students get lost in a text, and it isn't because they are enchanted by what they are reading; they are lost because they cannot see the structure of the text. If a reader doesn't know the structure, and how the writer has employed devices to put forth the content and combined features to tell a big-picture story, then he doesn't know that it's more than OK to tackle one part of a text at a time, and use other techniques for making meaning. Being familiar with the basic structures of nonfiction can help students prepare for reading this type of text, and they can check themselves for understanding while reading (Dymock, 2005; Meyer & Ray, 2011). Skilled readers with a good understanding of structure have fewer problems with comprehension than students who do not have this understanding (Armbruster, Anderson, & Ostertag, 1989; Duke & Pearson, 2002; Dymock & Nicholson, 1999).

We can guide our students to develop the skill of recognizing and using text structures by talking them through various nonfiction texts and showing them how the authors use different structures to relay information (Meyer & Ray, 2011). Project examples of each kind onto a screen, and be explicit! Students learn these structures quite easily when we provide concrete models and opportunities to spot them in whole-class, small-group, and individual settings.

The Main Nonfiction Text Structures

The main nonfiction text structures include descriptive, cause and effect, problem/ solution, question and answer, chronological or sequential, string, narrative informational, and compare and contrast (Dymock, 2005; Fountas & Pinnell, 2001; Meyer & Ray, 2011; Sanders & Moudy, 2008).

Descriptive: Has main topic with descriptive details, and information begins with general facts and moves to specific details.

- List: A descriptive structure including information in any order. For example, a book or article, or a section of it, might be entirely organized as a list.
- Web: A descriptive structure showing attributes with common links.
- Matrix: A descriptive structure focusing on comparing and contrasting two or more topics, like a list of features or attributes.

Cause and Effect: Shows causal relationships between events and often involves a chronological presentation of events with definite links between at least two events.

Problem/Solution: Conveys a problem and possible or actual solutions.

Question and Answer: Descriptive overall, but uses a question-and-answer format to organize sections, headings, and content. Newspapers and magazines often use this format to present interviews with prominent people and celebrities.

Chronological or Sequential: Events are explicitly organized by time. Writers use this structure when addressing a big span of time and when it's important to know "who did what when." For example, a textbook chapter of early explorers of North America would use a chronological or sequential structure. True-crime writers might employ this structure too because it's a good one for establishing facts.

String: Chronological order or steps in a process.

Narrative Informational: Has elements of fiction, including characters, setting, and plot, and reads like a story, built around facts and real events.

Compare and Contrast: Scaffolds information by connecting new ideas and information to something familiar, and may include whole-to-part and part-to-whole.

Identifying Main Ideas and Key Details

Knowing how to read for the main idea—and use key details to both identify and confirm a hunch about the main idea—is the epicenter of reading nonfiction well. But let's face it—it can be hard to teach, and I confess that sometimes a text is written in such a way that the main idea is subtle, or there seems to be more than one main idea, and I am uncertain. Most important is to emphasize for students that when we ask them to read for main ideas and details, we want them to understand the text's concepts, not just get caught up in a string of facts that lead to a superficial reading of text. Sometimes, students read to please—they check out the assignment's questions, skim the text to look for details that seem to match the question, copy down the relevant information, and then move on to the next question. When my students do this, they are just skimming for main ideas and details. That can be fine on a second reading when completing the assignment, but it can't preclude a full read.

I realized I needed to be more mindful of how I focused assignments. For example, when I assigned students questions about a reading, my true intent was to assess mere coverage of material and get proof that my students covered everything. While it is important to know that students are completing class assignments, I realized I needed to focus on teaching and assessing *understanding*, not *coverage*.

Reading for the main ideas and details is about understanding the concepts presented in the text—not grazing text to find the main idea in a superficial way. Teaching students to understand the concepts helps them understand the foundational ideas for the concepts and the points that back up the foundational ideas (King, 2007). One way to foster deep understanding of ideas and details in a text is to teach our students to ask themselves questions about their reading, *as they read*. For examples of how this looks in action, see "Lessons That Support Students While Reading for Main Idea and Details" in Part III.

Posing "Why" Questions

One way to begin teaching students to question in order to understand the concepts in a text is to begin with "why" questions. When students ask "why" questions, they learn and remember more information (Pressley et al., 1992; Pressley & Wharton-McDonald, 2002). "Why" questions can help our students orient themselves to the main ideas and details and understand them by asking "why" and then rereading or continuing to read to try to answer the questions. This helps students get in the habit of figuring out why the new ideas in the text make sense (Martin & Pressley, 1991; Pressley & Wharton-McDonald, 2002).

Asking other questions can also help students understand the concepts in a reading, and the key is for students to notice their thinking. Asking questions can also motivate students to read a "real-world" text, if they understand their purpose for reading (Kern, 2012). These questions help students go beyond skimming for the main idea of a text and finding supporting details with a "read-to-please" focus. Check out the types of questions students can ask themselves in *Questions Students Can Ask While Reading* and *Questions to Help Students Notice Their Thinking*.

Questions Students Can Ask While Reading

- Do I get what I just read?
- Is this clear?
- What parts of the text do I just not "get"?
- What's fuzzy in my head about the reading?
- Who is the focus in this article?
- What happened? or What seems to be really important?
- When did the main events take place?
- Where did the things occur?
- Why did the people in the text do what they did?
- How did the people make things happen?
- How do I think this issue is going to end?

Source: Adapted from Buehl (2007).

> ### Questions to Help Students Notice Their Thinking
>
> - Did I think about things I knew something about or had heard of before?
> - Did I wonder about some things (what, why, how)?
> - Did I picture something in my head as I read?
> - Did I look for clues in the text to figure it out?
> - Did I find things that seemed really important?
> - Can I sum up what I read in a few words?

Source: Adapted from Buehl (2007).

Recognizing Key Vocabulary

Next to main idea and key details, skill with vocabulary is critical to understanding nonfiction. In a way, it's a twofold skill for students—a matter of both possessing a wide vocabulary that makes reading easier, and knowing strategies to lean on while reading to tackle unfamiliar words and concepts.

As busy teachers, we cannot teach students all the words they need to know to be successful readers of nonfiction text. Fortunately, students who are skilled readers learn quite a bit of vocabulary through incidental reading (Nagy & Anderson, 1984; Sternberg, 1987). However, just because students can learn vocabulary through reading, it doesn't mean that we should assign our students reading of nonfiction texts and let them "have at it" and hope the meanings of the words sink in deeply. Rather, we need to focus students on recognizing and exploring key vocabulary in text.

Struggling readers read less than their more skilled peers, and because they are reading less, they are exposed to less information and encounter fewer words. Both issues limit their learning of vocabulary words (Stanovich, 1986). Struggling readers also have less developed metacognitive strategies to help them learn words, and they often have trouble using surrounding words and grammatical clues to figure out the meanings of unknown words (Lesaux, Kieffer, Faller, & Kelley, 2010). So, this means we need to help our students with vocabulary before, during, and after reading nonfiction texts.

Our vocabulary instruction, whether we are working with skilled or struggling readers, becomes more powerful when we are highly strategic. We need to focus on teaching fewer words deeply (Graves, 2006; Stahl & Nagy, 2006). It's helpful to think about it in terms of teaching concepts, not words. We must be truly careful here, because we might gravitate toward the low-frequency but intriguing words that appear in nonfiction text. Sometimes, the publishers themselves even choose these words for targeted instruction. But rather than focus deeply on these types of words, we need to focus on words that have utility and are general-purpose academic words (Beck, McKeown, & Kucan, 2002). Helping our students build strong skills in vocabulary while reading nonfiction texts means we need to teach them words that *have usefulness over a variety of texts*, and we need to hone students' ability to understand unknown words in the text. Thus, the two focus points for vocabulary instruction are (1) to teach words with utility and purpose across genres, and (2) to equip students with the thinking tools they need to learn words independently.

Teach Words

Instruction with repeated opportunities to practice with new words yields high results for students in learning vocabulary (Jenkins, Matlock, & Slocum, 1989). When we teach words, we teach carefully selected words (with utility and purpose across genres!) in fun and engaging ways with our students. We do not have them look up words in dictionaries and copy down the definitions. We focus on the power of combining thinking and discussion to learn new words (Akhavan, 2007). We also give students lots of opportunities to practice word and word definition use. Repeated opportunities to practice might include the following:

- Teaching word definitions
- Substituting word definitions in meaningful sentences
- Providing synonyms
- Discussing multiple meanings
- Learning word roots, suffixes, and prefixes
- Teaching word concepts
- Providing examples of concepts opposite to word meanings
- Drawing pictures representing the concepts of word meanings
- Creating semantic representations of words

Teach Word Learning Strategies

Contrary to teaching words when we teach word meanings, when we teach word learning strategies, we teach students skills to explore vocabulary words and what they mean. Of course, once students figure out word meanings in text, it doesn't mean that they have learned the words, but it does mean that they are thinking about words, word meanings, and the meaning of the text (Jenkins et al., 1989). This gives our students the power to tackle nonfiction text without giving up. When we teach students to derive word meanings, we are teaching students to do the following:

- Examine clues in the text
- Locate clues outside of the sentence that contain the target word (text boxes, for example)
- Substitute a word or expression for the unknown word
- Check for context clues that support the substitution
- Ask a peer or the teacher to confirm their prediction of the word meaning
- Explore possible word meanings
- Revise their ideas about what the word might mean to fit the context of the sentence (Jenkins et al., 1989; McKeown, 1985)

This includes teaching vocabulary word meaning skills by

- Modeling through think-alouds how to figure out word meaning from context
- Communicating important context to figure out and compile information about a word's meaning
- Modeling how to test alternative ideas for word meaning through substitution
- Presenting a text containing an unknown word and working through figuring out the meaning of the word, showing how information from text can confirm or eliminate a possible word meaning (McKeown, 1985)

Summarizing Text

Summaries are distinct from other texts that students write in and out of school. Naming how they are different helps us appreciate their function as a tool for understanding nonfiction. Here's how I think about it: In most writing activities, students generate ideas and details (even in writing based on their reading or research) and then plan the content and structure of the piece. Sure, one is making choices, for example to leave things out, but it's mostly a process of elaborating on one's ideas. The summary-writing process, on the other hand, is about winnowing down another's ideas. To write a summary, a student bases her writing on material already written, and decides what to include and exclude (Anderson & Hidi, 1989).

I'm often asked by teachers, "Is summarizing the same as retelling?" To me, one important difference is the teacher's purpose in assigning these activities. For example, teachers often use retelling as an assessment of text comprehension. With summary writing, my intent is to help students gain control over what they understand about their reading. I want my students to *own* their reading and the information they gather from a text. Being able to whittle dozens of pages and facts down to a succinct summary gives them this mastery.

Teaching students how to write summaries compels them to focus their attention as they read and reread. They know they must in a sense have their eyes open and ears pricked in order to sense the information, concepts, and ideas that are "summary worthy."

You can teach summary writing in a few ways, and which one you use will depend upon students' development as readers. Younger or struggling readers tend to make decisions about what goes in a summary on a piecemeal, sentence-by-sentence basis, whereas older and more proficient readers tend to consider the meaning of the whole text (Brown, Day, & Jones, 1983).

Summary writing involves these two thinking processes:

- **Making selections:** Judging what information should be included or excluded.
- **Making reductions:** Condensing ideas and information by substituting general ideas for specific ideas, and avoiding unnecessary detail (Anderson & Hidi, 1989; New York City Department of Education, n.d.).

You can help your students develop this type of thinking by teaching them to make generalizations about the text. When you teach them to make generalizations, you are encouraging them to think about the text and get the gist of what they read. When our students are "getting the gist" of what they read, their brains are involved in three processes: deletion, generalization, and construction. All three processes are truly helpful in teaching students to write summaries, so we want them to engage in these processes as much as possible. When students process through deletion, they leave out specific details *unless* the idea is necessary for understanding and interpreting main ideas. When they process through generalization, they substitute a sentence that pulls together specific ideas from a group of ideas or paragraphs. When they process through construction, they form a new idea based on the generalization they have made.

I recommend that you directly teach your students how to write summaries. One way to do this is through making generalizations (see *Guidelines to Generalizations*). Another way is to have your students apply a set of rules when they write. This way of teaching can be done by using a simple list of four rules:

- **Collapse lists.** Teach students to substitute a word or phrase for a list of things.
- **Use topic sentences.** Help students learn to identify topic sentences, and if there isn't a topic sentence (which often there is not!), teach them to write one.
- **Get rid of unnecessary detail.** Texts repeat information by saying the same thing in a number of different ways. Texts also include unimportant detail. Teach students to restate only the important information.
- **Collapse paragraphs.** In any text, some paragraphs are more important than others. Help students learn to decide which paragraphs to keep or get rid of, and how to join a couple of paragraphs together in writing their summaries (Hare & Borchardt, 1984).

A sample summary rule list appears in *Rules for Summary Writing*, and can be used for lessons or enlarged for a class poster.

Guidelines to Generalizations

A generalization is a conclusion, a broad statement about the text based on information, observations, and experiences.

Build your generalization by following these steps:

1. Read a selection and make a statement that relates to the purpose of the material.

2. State your generalization like a "big umbrella" to cover the facts and information from the text.

3. Check clue words to support your generalization: *all, none, most, many, few, never, sometimes, usually, generally.*

4. Check if your generalization includes, or implies, an idea or information from the text.

5. Check that your generalization matches information from the text, your past experience, or information that you already know.

6. Check that your generalization makes sense, with a focus on the logic and reasoning of the statement.

7. Check that examples back up your statement.

Source: Adapted from "Making Generalizations: Description of the Strategy," University of California at Santa Barbara (http://education.ucsb.edu/webdata/instruction/hss/Generalizations/Description_of_Strategy.pdf).

Rules for Summary Writing

1. **Collapse lists.** If you see a list of things, think of a word or phrase that can be a name for the whole list.

2. **Use topic sentences.** Look for a sentence that summarizes the whole paragraph. If you don't see one, make one up for yourself.

3. **Get rid of unnecessary detail.** Some information can be repeated, or the same thing can be said in different ways. Other information may be trivial.

4. **Collapse paragraphs.** Some paragraphs explain others, and some expand a beginning paragraph. Keep the necessary paragraphs and join together information from paragraphs that connect.

5. **Polish the summary.** Read your summary, and if anything sounds unnatural (this happens on a first draft), fix it up.

Source: Brown, Day, & Jones (1983); Hare & Borchardt (1984).

Cell Phone Use In Schools

Writing about Reading

When I read about teachers who may let students use phones for education, my first thoughts were about the efficiency and easy access. Since so many kids and teens have smart and cellular devices, what an opportunity for teachers to take advantage of the fact that they no more have to pay hundreds and thousands of dollars on books that the student will eventually rip up! Students would take much better care of their phones. There are also plenty of calculator, compass, and other apps that people could buy instead of heavy and costly products. Not to mention they wouldn't forget to bring supplies to school when everything is in their pocket. When I was smaller, I couldn't believe people didn't have the same teaching techniques as now so I would not be surprised if using phones and devices became one of the main ways to teach and learn.

Student Writing Sample of
Writing About Reading

Writing About Reading

The deepest dive we can take with our students—helping them flex their thinking muscles while reading nonfiction—is to apply ideas from text to their knowledge about the world. They do this by writing. Writing to learn is a catalyst for further learning and meaning making (Knipper & Duggan, 2006). Writing to learn is different from learning to write and often misunderstood in the content areas. Writing to learn is not process writing where students produce a polished work. Writing to learn is recalling information, grappling with it, and writing down a few thoughts to memorialize it. When students write to learn, they recall, clarify, question, wonder, discover, and communicate (Fisher & Frey, 2004; Knipper & Duggan, 2006).

Asking students to write about their reading, or write to learn about content they have seen or heard, takes a bit of instruction. Students don't show up in our content classes knowing how to write like mathematicians, historians, or scientists. We have to teach them what writing should look like in each discipline. However, this doesn't mean teaching process writing such as they might experience in an English class. Instead, modeling and providing examples of how writing should look gives the students time to make decisions about their writing, to make mistakes and practice writing about the content in ways that make sense to them (Bromley, 2003; Knipper & Duggan, 2006; Sinatra, 2000).

Writing about reading is not about writing answers to the questions that often appear at the end of texts. Writing about reading is about comprehension. It is extended writing and a way to help students learn the material, think about it, and go beyond recall by making inferences about its meaning. Notice the student's thinking about a reading in *Student Writing Sample of Writing About Reading*.

Going beyond recalling surface details by making inferences and identifying alternative perspectives is a skill even high school students struggle with in content reading (Myers & Savage, 2005). Students can participate in this type of writing by applying concepts from texts in new situations, perhaps prompted by the teacher. They can apply concepts from their reading to solve problems, or use developing evidence from texts to support a point of view. They may also express an individual interpretation of the information. A new focus in writing is to teach students to construct arguments—a skill students will need to be successful in high school and beyond. All types of writing about reading, from recall to extended writing, help students learn new ideas and concepts (Hebert, Gillespie, & Graham, 2012).

PART II

The Daily Duo

When planning my teaching, I think about how my instruction can expand and deepen students' learning. I look for ways to engage students sooner in meaningful work. When I use reading routines like the Daily Duo, my students spend more time actually reading and writing about a text. Using the routines frees me from the pressure of activities, and ensures a daily focus of instruction on comprehension, critical thinking, and creativity, with a good dose of student voice.

This section of the book lays out routines for making reading and writing the focus of student work during the day. When the duo of reading and writing take center stage (and more superficial "skillsy" practice gets thankfully elbowed out of the way), students have the opportunity to deeply engage with texts, information, and ideas, and in so doing build the skills and strategies to do ever more sophisticated reading and writing in specific disciplines or content areas.

The Daily Duo

A Sequence That Promotes Student Reading and Writing to Learn

Have you longed for a simple structure that engages students in deeply reading nonfiction—independently? In this chapter, I introduce the Daily Duo, a reading sequence that guides students to read, reflect, and then write about their reading in ways that meet standards, enhance comprehension, and build disciplinary understandings. As noted in previous chapters, students are often intimidated by complex, information-laden texts, and respond by taking a passive stance as they read. Even if they highlight and take notes, they do so without a "plan of attack." The Daily Duo guides students to inquire, question, and analyze their way through an interesting text, and then use brief bursts of writing as a way to moor their understanding of what they have read. Many of the instructional ideas presented in earlier chapters can be put into action during Daily Duo time.

The Daily Duo in Action

The Daily Duo is about independent reading and writing. It comes into play after a minilesson or short lesson introduction, providing a structure to reading practice. Students need lots of practice actually reading text and then writing about it—on their own. This is true for struggling readers as well as more capable readers; although you will need to provide differentiated text for struggling readers, they need as much, or more, practice reading and writing about texts as good readers. The Daily Duo focuses on the guided and independent phases of instruction, when students use short texts, articles, or even textbook sections to practice an idea, a skill, or a strategy introduced in a lesson or group of lessons.

Learning by Doing

There are attributes of effective teaching, known for years by great teachers, and also identified and reinforced by researchers. These attributes are reflected in teaching moves. Your teaching moves during the Daily Duo reinforce the gradual release of responsibility. The gradual release of responsibility is a framework that helps teachers model new learning, to guided practice, to independent practice (Fisher, 2008; Pearson & Gallagher, 1983). Specifically, the Daily Duo taps into the following attributes of dynamic teaching and learning:

- "Setting the stage" so students have context for new content and ideas

- Modeling how you use strategies to read, write, and think about new ideas and information

- Revealing the intricacies of your thinking as you read and write, so students can "see" your cognitive strategies

- Guiding and coaching learning, gradually moving responsibility of the new learning to your students as you help them own the new skill or strategy

- Focusing on the flow of student thinking to ensure students comprehend the texts they are reading, understand the content they are reading about, engage in thinking about the text and content through writing, and inquire into purpose and connections with texts and topics

- Evaluating and analyzing products of thinking, reading, and writing so you can apprentice students' thinking as they learn to grab a text, read it, write about it, and then share their thoughts with peers

See *Daily Duo Structure* to see how the Daily Duo matches these teaching moves.

Daily Duo Structure			
Daily Duo Steps		**Effective Teaching Ideas**	
Reading Steps	**Writing Steps**	**Teaching Moves**	**How It Looks in Practice**
Preparing to read	Note taking	Setting the stage	Giving students context for the reading and information in the text
		Modeling	Thinking aloud, showing, describing, and demonstrating
Reading	Short writing	Revealing	Helping students "see" your cognitive strategies
		Guiding and coaching	Moving the responsibility of learning to the students
Noticing	Extended writing	Focusing the flow	Guiding the timing and processes of students' thinking to help them become independent learners and inquirers
		Evaluating and analyzing	Apprenticing students' thinking, reading, and writing

The Reading Component

The reading component of the Daily Duo involves preparing to read, reading, and noticing what one reads. Key for students here is to be in control of the reading—and *actually read*; teachers do not read for students, have students listen to others read (as in round-robin reading in class, or a taped recording), or assume students are reading when they may just be lost and not reading at all. To implement the reading component successfully, we must look for students' engagement and active involvement in the reading process.

STEP 1: Preparing to Read

When we help students wrap their minds around reading a text, we help them set goals for reading. I'm not talking about activities that build background knowledge and tap prior knowledge (see sidebar). To launch the Daily Duo, I'm suggesting something quicker and simpler, something that involves a student taking a few moments just before reading a text to ask and answer the question, "So, why am I reading this?" This brief first step gives students a helpful time-out to focus their attention before digging in. The answer will differ for each individual student, but the key is for students to think about their *purpose* and decide, for themselves, why they are reading the text. Maybe they are curious about the topic, or perhaps they are reading to finish an assignment or participate in group work.

For more elaborate prereading lessons, see Part III. In particular, see *Survey the Text* (page 112), *List, Group, Label* (page 134), and *Get the Gist to Get Good at Section-by-Section Summarizing* (page 189).

STEP 2: Reading

In this step, students need to read. That may seem like a terribly obvious point, but many teachers, pressed for time, don't schedule in-classroom independent reading, or don't consider that some students may only be "fake" reading. During Step 2 of the Daily Duo, students only read. They do not take notes—that comes later. Depending on the length and complexity of the text, this step takes about 15 to 20 minutes.

How to Select Books for the Daily Duo

For students to engage in reading for the Daily Duo, the text needs to be within their reading zone, or the level at which they can read independently without frustration. Students should be stretched at this level, but be careful—the students are reading independently. They need to be challenged to read more complex texts, but not pushed so far that they give up. In the reading zone, students can read independently (but not too easily—they should be engaged with some mental effort) and maintain comprehension.

Teachers can measure students' reading level in many ways, including assessing students and matching their reading level to a book level, but before you focus on this more complex matching of text (for independent reading), think about providing a variety of opportunities for students to read a variety of nonfiction materials. There are times for supporting students through more complex texts than those they can read on their own (check out close reading in Chapter 2, and taming the textbook in Chapter 3), but during the Daily Duo, the texts need to challenge students enough that they practice fixing up their own comprehension when it falters, but not so hard they give up in frustration. Let students' motivation and engagement be your mantra when selecting books.

STEP 3: Noticing

Good readers notice things about what they read and connect a text's ideas to what matters to them; weaker readers tend to finish reading a text, and then drop it like a stone. They do nothing with it in terms of reflection or applying their understandings. Good readers do not necessarily routinely reflect during and after reading in a deep, complex way, but their brief, "casual" thinking makes a difference, leading to strong comprehension and, most importantly, an openness to the next reading experience.

To capture and precisely describe readerly reflection is difficult, but good readers ask themselves "So what?" questions. When reading, what do students wonder about, recognize, connect to other information or texts, or find curious? Good readers go through this brief thinking process many times before they finish a text. (The next time you read nonfiction, notice your questions and connections: "Why am I reading this?" "Will it get too technical for me to enjoy?" or—the "So what?" factor—"How does this relate to what I want to learn?").

As teachers, we want to cultivate this kind of complex comprehension activity in our students, and the second step of the Daily Duo is a great

Giving students lots of opportunities to try out their understandings of a text in writing compels them to check their comprehension and sharpen their thinking.

way to begin. (The lessons that appear in Part III of this book help you take comprehension further.) For now, the key is to simply give students time for reflective thinking after reading. With this step, we make a space in our really busy day for students to notice things immediately after they read a text. We give them a moment to think, "Aha! *That's* what this is about! *That's* the author's main point!" They can jot their ideas down, which leads us into the writing component of the Daily Duo. Give the "noticing" step about 5 to 10 minutes.

The Writing Component

While the reading component of the Daily Duo involves independent reading, this component involves independent writing about reading. Just like in reading, where practice makes better readers, students need writing practice to become better writers. The brief and extended writing tasks involved in the Daily Duo process range from note taking to writing about reading to give students writing practice. This practice leads to ways that show and deepen students' thinking. While writing longer pieces is critically important (see Step 6 of the Daily Duo and also the "Writing About Reading" section of Part III, beginning on page 224), the goal of this component is brief writing practice to encourage student engagement in thinking about their reading and sufficient practice to develop both fluency and confidence.

STEP 4: Taking Notes

Imagine your students have just finished reading a nonfiction text, and have taken a moment to think about what they noticed in and about the text: This is the perfect time for them to write about their thinking. The first move: Take notes. Note taking helps students remember what they have just read, and can be a great springboard for further writing or discussion. You can use any note-taking procedure that works well for you, but the key is to set a note-taking standard for your students to follow. Teach them how you want their notebooks to look—perhaps formatted as a reading log or a reading journal—and encourage them to jot down their noticings. This step takes about 10 minutes. See *Samples of Student Notebooks—Taking Notes After Reading* for samples of student notes.

T = Planets .

   I = The Sun

      • a star that "anchors" the solar system

      • without its heat/energy, we would die

      • 10,000°F (5,500°C

      • 74% (hydrogen) 25% (helium) 1% (heavy elements)

   I = Mercury

      • dead planet and most heavily cratered object

      • races around sun in 88 Earth days

      • A year is shorter than a day

      • One of the hottest and coldest planets

   I = Venus

      • Considered Earth's twin

      • hottest planet

      • harsh and strong planet

      • 2nd from the sun

C = Planets

pg	My thoughts
pg 1	I feel very sad for his disease. I though feel happy that he is happy because he feels special and unique. He is unique because he is only 2 feet tall.
pg 2	the doftors, cant explain why he only grew 40cm since birth. He left school and earns money from dancing at department stoBs. He also plays the role of a drug dealer in a film. I think that he is getting money and has apart in a film.

Samples of Student Notebooks—Taking Notes After Reading

Students can note other aspects of a text *after they read*. For example:

Some After-Reading Responses to Text

- ☐ Text structure
  - ☐ Confirming or disconfirming a judgment on text structure or a textbook section
  - ☐ Outlining details and support for text structure (see the lesson *Use Concept Maps for Problem-Solution Pieces* in Part III)
  - ☐ Conceptualizing examples of text structure to prepare to write (see the "Main Nonfiction Text Structures" section in Chapter 4, as well as the lesson *Recognize Many Text Structures* in Part III)
- ☐ Key ideas and details
  - ☐ Recording notes about reading (see the lesson *Inquiry Charts* in Part III)
  - ☐ Making predictions (see the lesson *Prediction Relay* in Part III)
  - ☐ Making inferences (see the lesson *Pause, Describe, and Infer* in Part III)
- ☐ Questioning
  - ☐ What do students wonder about the text?
  - ☐ What have students learned from reading the text?
  - ☐ What else do students want to know about the author's point of view or knowledge of the subject (see the lesson *Ask Great Questions* in Part III)?
- ☐ Summarizing
  - ☐ Writing short statements about key ideas (see the lesson *Using 3-2-1 Exit Cards to Assess Students' Understanding* in Part III)
  - ☐ Stating key ideas through recall (see the lesson *Say Something to Develop Understanding* in Part III)
  - ☐ Paraphrasing ideas from text (see the lesson *Creating Summaries* in Part III)

STEP 5: Brief Writing Tasks

The Daily Duo is a great comprehension check for students. When their pencil hovers above a blank page of paper, students must reconcile with, *Did I understand what I read and can I articulate that on the paper?* Remember, the goal is not to set up a "gotcha" dynamic wherein the students feel constantly tested; as a teacher, you want to convey that the purpose is *writing practice, not writing perfect*. Tell your class that you want to see just short snippets, or bursts of ideas and thinking. Don't correct or grade the students writing on grammar or content, do allow them to include relevant personal connections along with more text-based responses, and don't succumb to dull end-of-chapter–type questions. Help your students get over their writing reluctance by encouraging them to write freely, without fear of being wrong.

In the *Brief Writing Tasks That Engage* box, I provide ideas for writing tasks to offer. No matter which activity you choose, remind students to consult the notes they made in Step 4 of the Daily Duo for help. The time this step takes will vary with the writing task you choose. Much of the time students will write in class, but other times you may have them write as homework; either way, students should be writing for 10 to 15 minutes.

Brief Writing Tasks That Engage

- ☐ Free writing
  - ☐ Nonstructured response writing by which students write anything they want in relation to what they have read
- ☐ One-minute papers
  - ☐ Very short, timed writings, completed on an index card or small piece of paper (see the lesson *Microthemes* in Part III, for one example of a one-minute paper)
- ☐ Exit tickets
  - ☐ Writing based on a prompt and turned in at the end of a lesson or class period
- ☐ Brain "dumps"
  - ☐ Writing down everything one knows, essentially dumping *one's brain* in relation to a topic (Akhavan, 2004)
- ☐ Slogans
  - ☐ Creative, short, and striking phrases about a topic or text
- ☐ Response logs
  - ☐ Journal-type writing connected to prompts provided by the teacher

STEP 6: Writing About Reading

In the final step of the Daily Duo, students move from writing and thinking *practice* to writing extended summaries, exploration papers, reports, and opinion pieces. You should only occasionally engage your students in Step 6—full-blown writing about reading—perhaps at the end of a unit of study, or as a summative activity to an inquiry, or as a way for students to express learning from a book or text set study. Even then, you are inviting students to give you are inviting students to give-a-go to creating extended writing pieces but not always take their works through a full writing and revision process. Instead, this extended writing should flow from students' notes, but also fit the Daily Duo time frame. The time you devote for writing will depend on what extended writing task you chose. Plan to spend 20 to 30 minutes for this step, and perhaps adding additional writing time outside of class. For some extended writing tasks, see the ideas that follow.

Extended Writing Tasks That Engage

- ☐ Response to nonfiction text
  - ☐ Text-to-text, text-to-world, and text-to-self connections fully explained in a short piece of writing that refers to the text and other sources to justify and exemplify thinking. The focus for students is on relating knowledge and information from their memories or other sources to the reading—not on sharing connections that relate to their thoughts (unconnected to the content) or feelings
- ☐ Summary
  - ☐ Writing to summarize as described in the "Summarizing to Comprehend" section of Part III
- ☐ Short opinion pieces
  - ☐ Writing to state one's thoughts about a text, evaluating the concepts presented or the author's writing and writing approach
- ☐ Evaluation reports
  - ☐ Writing that evaluates, or makes a judgment about, a reading, providing references to the text to justify points made

The Premise Behind the Daily Duo

Reading and writing are powerful partners in helping students' thinking about and comprehending the world. As many educators have said before me, writing *is* thinking and deserves a much bigger role in teaching and learning. Writing is a tremendous tool in guiding students' ability to think, retain information, and comprehend texts (Applebee, 1985). When we teach students to write to learn, we also have the opportunity to teach them to think, and writing assignments can become opportunities to teach the particular patterns of thinking and inquiry in a content area. Discipline-specific thinking can range from the processes of observation to general problem-solving processes to applying a principle to a specific situation for analyses (Herrington, 1981).

As you have seen from Steps 4–6 of the Daily Duo, writing to learn means writing to promote the comprehension of reading. Writing to learn activities range in complexity and length from short, impromptu, and informal writing tasks to deeper and longer analyses and persuasive or response papers (Kiefer, 1990). Most writing to learn tasks can be completed in class in brief writing sessions. Longer papers require students to write in and outside of class (see the "Writing About Reading" section of Part III for how to teach both short and long writing tasks).

When students read to learn, they need to write to learn. We must teach our students how to read and write together—a skill that does not come naturally to most of our students. But by using the Daily Duo in your teaching, it can become a habit all students will tap into for the rest of their lives.

The Daily Layout of Teaching Nonfiction

In the previous chapter, we considered the six steps of the Daily Duo, each of which helps stoke students' independence with reading nonfiction texts. Now we are going to look in more detail at how the Daily Duo fits into your already busy curriculum (see *Cheat Sheet*). My main mission for you? To think about how to shift the layout of your daily routines to embed lots and lots of student practice. A three-phase lesson will help you accomplish this goal. Let's look at this and other sequences first, and then I'll show you with a particular nonfiction book just how practical these lesson structures are.

The Focus Lesson: What to Do

With the focus lesson, you claim the attention of your students and present what you want them to learn (Fisher & Frey, 2008; Lemov, 2010). As the name implies, you zero in on one succinct point or strategy (yes, one only!) so as not to overload students with too many concepts and learning goals at once.

The focus lesson has four parts that you move through in 10–15 minutes:

- Connect
- Teach
- Give It a Go
- Wrap Up

Cheat Sheet: Three Phases That Push Student Practice

Let's look at how the Daily Duo fits into your 45–50 minutes of reading time. One operating assumption on my part is that you organize your reading time into three phases (see *Three-Phase Lesson Design*).

Focus Lesson: During the first phase of instruction, you model, demonstrate, and detail for students what you want them to learn. Each focus lesson is relatively short, 10–15 minutes of a 30- to 40-minute writing session (but can also be only 5 minutes if you are reteaching), and can be structured as direct instruction (breaking the learning objective into parts and showing students the information one part at a time) or inquiry (framing the learning through a key question).

Practice: The next phase of reading time is devoted to practice—when the sequences of the Daily Duo come alive. The student practice is based on students being very active learners and thinkers. This phase takes between 25 and 30 minutes.

Share: In the last phase, a share, students discuss their work with the class, and you ramp up the learning objective by reviewing what was modeled, experimented with, and discussed throughout the student work time. This phase takes about 5 to 7 minutes.

These three phases of instruction focus on the students.

Three-Phase Lesson Design

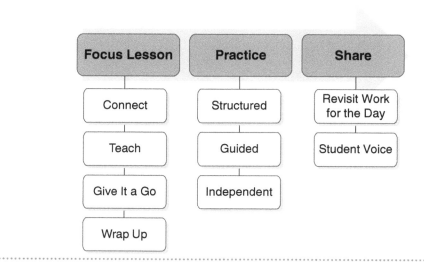

Connect: Start the lesson by connecting students to your teaching point in an engaging way, often finding a link between what they already know and the new information. With this "listen-up" message designed to immediately grab students' attention for the new learning you expect (Akhavan, 2008), essentially, you prepare your students' brains to receive new information. The Connect step is short, maybe a minute.

Teach: Now you are active in the "I Do It" phase of the Gradual Release of Responsibility Model, and your students are taking in new ideas and information as you demonstrate a nonfiction reading strategy or whatever you want them to soon practice (Lemov, 2010). You might think aloud as you read a text passage; you might model writing about reading—the point is to be explicit so there is nothing mysterious about your process. The Teach time is meaty, but remember the entire focus lesson is 10–15 minutes, so keep your teaching taut and brief, giving students time to dive into the reading and writing work.

Give It a Go: After you "Teach," invite students to immediately interact with the new learning just presented—to try it for themselves for a few moments—but don't exceed only a few minutes! The format is up to you: Students might talk with a partner about what they just observed you doing; they might practice the strategy you just outlined; or they might simply take the time to add to their notes about the concept you just modeled. This quick rehearsal helps ensure the new ideas stay in students' short-term memories long enough for the students to apply the lesson to their own reading and writing.

Wrap Up: Now it's time for a quick review of the new learning you shared, a chance for you to cheerlead—to restate and reiterate the process, the language, and all that's involved in what you want your students to embark on in the practice phase. Notice that in none of the four facets of the focus lesson are students ever in a passive stance. Their involvement is always expected, so energy remains high.

Practice: What Students Do

Now you have arrived at the second of three phases of reading time, and you can structure it in a few different ways (see *Three-Phase Lesson Design*). In **structured practice**, you model a step or strategy, and then students immediately practice it. In **guided practice**, students work independently, and you rove around the class, coaching them individually as you circulate. Or, if you discern students are ready to own what you have taught, plan an **independent practice**, in which most students work on their own; you might use this practice time to teach a small group of students who need extra help (Lemov, 2010).

The Share: Recapping the Learning Together

The share phase allows you to close the Daily Duo. Students have been reading and writing, using reading strategies to work independently or with your help, and now they spend a few minutes sharing their work with one another. A wonderful opportunity for students to talk aloud about the work, trading insights and written products with peers, the share time can be filled with student voice—an aspect of literacy development so often neglected, but so crucial to comprehension.

See *A Teacher's Daily Duo Lesson Plan in Progress* for a snapshot of a Daily Duo lesson plan with ideas jotted in. Use *Daily Duo Focus Lesson Plan* as a template for planning your own three-phase lessons.

A Teacher's Daily Duo Lesson Plan in Progress

Lesson: How to Collapse a List

Unit: Summary Writing

Objective: Substitute a word or phrase for a list of information appearing in text

This plan is written out as examples of what you would say for each step of the lesson.

Connect	We've been working on learning to write summaries, and today I want to show you how to take a list of information from a text and shorten it down to a couple of words. This is called collapsing, like when a balloon deflates. We are going to collapse a list to make it smaller.
Teach	When I read a text looking for lists of information, I go through and star parts of the text that I think might be a list. Look at how I did this with this excerpt from a short article on when ancient man started to walk upright. I starred this part right here on what the scientists thought. See, it's a list. (I point to the part in the text.) This list tells us about the thinking of the scientists. It's a list about the 3D statistical analysis of the ancient man's gait. This is a long paragraph, but I'm going to shorten it up and write in the margin, "Ancient Man walks twice as early as previously thought." See, I took this long list of information and turned it into a short sentence. This will help me remember the information—and it will help me when I skim my notes to write my summary.
Give It a Go	Now, I want you to work with a partner. Take out one of the texts you've been reading, or check out a section in the textbook—is there a part that looks like a list? Can you collapse that list into a few words? Work on that for a minute or two together.
Wrap Up	I'm going to have a few of you tell us what you worked on with your partner—what did the text say, and how did you collapse it? After we hear from a few of you, we are going to use this technique today while reading our texts to prep for writing a summary. Remember, collapse the lists like deflating a balloon. Make the list small and state it in a few words.

Daily Duo Focus Lesson Plan

Lesson:

Unit:

Objective:

Connect

Teach

Give It a Go

Wrap Up

Organize Instruction: Consider Sequences of Reading and Writing

So, time for a recap. The Daily Duo fits most easily into the practice time. And as we saw in Chapter 5, the Daily Duo involves the two processes of reading and writing, with a focus on writing to learn.

The reading component includes

- Preparing to read
- Reading
- Noticing

and the writing component includes

- Taking notes on reading
- Brief writing tasks
- Extended writing about reading

Now, let's think about how to weave reading and writing into sequences that help you target students' needs. The following suggested sequences do just that, and each involves five steps, thus providing consistency to students during reading. How do you know which sequence to choose? Base your decision on the text you want students to read and your objective for the lesson.

Sequence 1

In this sequence, students just read; they don't write—yet. Students prepare to read, read, notice, reread, and notice by circling. I often share this list with students on the chalkboard or on a sheet of paper:

- Prep
- Read
- Notice
- Reread
- Circle to note

Note: You can repeat or slow the steps based on the speed of learning; that is, you want to give students ample independent practice time. The speed of learning is the speed at which your students take up and own for themselves new ideas, information, and skills. Each student moves at an independent pace, but you can teach and scaffold to a degree and at a rate appropriate to your grade level and then differentiate as needed.

Sequence 2

This sequence delves deeper into students' reading and writing about reading, and includes preparing to read, reading, noticing, taking notes, and writing brief pieces about a text. Here's the list of five steps:

- Prep
- Read
- Notice
- Take notes
- Write short texts

Intentional teaching begins with effective instructional planning. Use the ideas in this chapter to make the planning process easier.

Sequence 3

To help students move farther along in their ability to write about reading, this sequence includes preparing to read, reading, noticing, taking notes, and writing extensive pieces about a topic, concept, or text. Here are the five steps:

- Prep
- Read
- Notice
- Take notes
- Write extended pieces

All three sequences really help me to plan out my teaching across days and adjust my plans as I assess how quickly or slowly students respond to my instruction.

The benefit for students is that the sequences provide a classroom routine that, over time, deepens to become a way of approaching texts in any setting. Now let's look at an example of the Daily Duo in action with a nonfiction text about diamonds.

Classroom CLIP

The Daily Duo in Action With a Nonfiction Text

Now that we have looked at the Daily Duo and how it fits into three phases of a class period, let's see it in action with a text, "The Wonder of Diamonds." Remember from Chapter 5 that the reading comes first, before the writing. In the reading part of the Daily Duo, you teach students to prepare to read, reread, and then notice points about the reading. In the writing part of the Daily Duo, you teach students to take notes about a reading, create brief writing based on the reading, and sometimes write more extensively

The Wonder of Diamonds

Have you ever noticed a flash of fire when a woman's diamond ring caught a ray of sunshine? Diamonds are the sparkly stones that adorn women's engagement rings. Even though diamond jewelry is a highly prized item, we don't often to think about why!

A diamond isn't just a pretty rock, it is a rare and beautiful mineral that formed deep in the earth in localized places around the world. Diamond is the hardest known substance in the world. Diamonds are used for industry, and diamond gems are used in jewelry and other art. Of the diamonds in the world, only 20% are of gem quality, the remaining diamonds have industrial uses (Fleet, Hart & Wall). Let's explore the types of diamonds, how they are formed, and the history of diamonds.

What is a Diamond?

Diamonds have a simple and elegant crystal structure. Diamonds are made of entirely of carbon. This was discovered by the English chemist Simon Tennant. Carbon has two polymorphs, graphite and diamond. In diamond, each carbon atom is bonded to four other atoms in a tetrahedral formation. The carbon atoms are densely packed in an array with strong bonds. This combination of the array and the bonds creates a very strong framework. This formation leads to the three main properties of diamond: hardness, incompressibility (density) and thermal conductivity. Diamonds have extreme values for these properties.

[handwritten: I think I'm reading this to learn about the use of diamonds in industry]

Hardness of Diamond

The Moh's scale of hardness is on a continuum from 1 to 10. The hardest substance on the scale is diamond at 10. To understand the hardness this represents, it is important to know that the Moh's scale of hardness does not have even intervals. Corundum is a mineral and the hardness scale is considered to be level 9, and diamond is five times harder than corundum . This is unlike graphite, the other polymorph of carbon, which is soft and has a Moh's scale of hardness of 1 or 2. The hardness of diamond makes it useful in industry. It is often used as a cutting tool, as in diamond studded drill bits and saws because the diamond is the hardest substance in the world.

[handwritten: this is an industry use]

Incompressibility

Diamond has the lowest molar entropy at room temperature of any mineral. This indicates a high degree of internal order. Diamond is not easily compressed, as it is formed, and withstands the incredible force of the pressure in the mantle of Earth. The standard molar entropy of diamond is 2.377, which is less than graphite. This makes the internal energy of diamond lower as it has a more compact structure and the volume is smaller, therefore diamond doesn't compress at high pressures.

[handwritten: I get a picture of the hardness of diamonds]

Thermal Conductivity

Diamond has excellent thermal conductivity, with 5 to 25 watts per centimeter. This thermal conductivity level is 4 times greater than copper and 6 times than silver. This makes diamond very useful in industry. For example, in saws, there is a lot of friction between the saw and the materials being cut, diamond in diamond saws quickly carry the heat away. While diamond has excellent thermal

[handwritten: again, a use for diamonds in industry]

Diamond Text With Callouts

conductivity, it is a poor conductor of electricity. This is unusual as most solids that conduct heat aren't poor conductors of electricity. This is unlike graphite, the other polymorph of carbon, which is a good conductor of electricity. Diamond has a high melting point, which is 3550 degrees Celsius.

Types of Diamonds

There are natural and synthetic diamonds. Natural diamonds are formed deep within the Earth's mantle, whereas synthetic diamonds are created in a lab. The process that forms natural diamonds is extensively studies, but is mostly unknown.

[handwritten: I wonder if synthetic diamonds are used in industry?]

Natural diamonds are old and formed in the ancient lithosphere. Diamonds we find today were formed about 3 billion years ago at a depth of 140-200 km beneath the Earth's crust. The areas where they formed were underneath ancient continents in locations call keels. Keels are the oldest parts of the continents; this is the base, or the cartons of the continents. Diamonds form from high pressure and high temperatures. The pressure that forms diamonds is considered to be about 45 thousand times that of the Earth's atmosphere. The temperature that formed diamonds is estimated to be above 950 degrees.

There are several types of natural diamonds. In addition to the diamond minerals found on continents and formed in the interior of the earth, there are natural polycrystalline diamonds called carbonado and framesite. Polycrystalline diamonds are formed on the Earth's crust from ultra-high pressure conditions. Carbonado is the term for the multigranular diamond aggregates from Central African Republic and Brazil. Framesite is a broader term to describe the

[handwritten: Wow! I had no idea there were types of diamonds]

Diamond Text With Annotations After Reading

about the reading. Try modeling all of these steps for your students, while stating your process aloud.

Reading Daily Duo Step 1: Preparing to Read

In preparing to read "The Wonder of Diamonds," I began by scanning the text and asking myself, "So, why am I reading this?" During the scan, I focused on clues to what the text was about. See *Diamond Text With Callouts* for parts of the text that helped me notice things during my scan; the circles show which sections I considered, and the arrows point to my thoughts about the information in the text that prepared me to read. The note at the bottom of the first page shows my answer to the question, "So, why am I reading this?"

Reading Daily Duo Step 2: Reading

Because this text is within my reading zone (see Chapter 5), I can read it easily, but your students may need support to tackle a text. The best way to support them is to make sure the readings you present them with fall within their reading zone—the level at which they can read independently and maintain comprehension. Another way to help your students with independent reading is to equip them with fix-up strategies to use when comprehension breaks down (see sidebar).

Fix-Up Strategies to Use When a Student Can't Figure Out a Word

1. Reread the sentence without the word. Think about what information is provided that would help you understand the meaning of the word.

2. Read the sentences before and after the problem sentence for clues to the word's meaning.

3. Look for prefixes or suffixes in the word that can give clues to meaning.

4. Break the word apart and look for smaller words you know.

Source: From Klinger & Vaughn (1998, p. 34).

Fix-Up Strategies to Use When a Student Gets Lost, or When Comprehension Breaks Down

1. Make a connection—connect what you are reading to something you already know.

2. Stop and think—check what is important about what you read, and think about what you are reading.

3. Check the print conventions—look at bold print, italicized words, and punctuation to get a clue about the meaning of the text.

4. Reread—reread the part you don't understand.

5. Reread a little slower—slow down when the reading is hard.

6. Retell what you've read—if you can say it to yourself, it will help you understand the next chunk of text.

7. Check the video in your head—if you can see it, you can understand it better.

Source: Adapted from Tovani (2000).

Reading Daily Duo Step 3: Noticing

After reading "The Wonder of Diamonds," I stopped and thought about what I had read. This is the third step: asking what matters about a text, paying attention to your thinking about the text, and then annotating in the margin things you wonder about, recognize from your prior knowledge, connect to other information or texts, and find interesting. *Diamond Text With Annotations After Reading* shows the annotations I made in the margin of the text, as well as sections I circled while reading; the notes and circles helped me as I moved into the second part of the Daily Duo—writing about the text. See also the second page of *Diamond Text With Callouts*.

Writing Daily Duo Step 4: Taking Notes

My notes about "The Wonder of Diamonds" focused on identifying key ideas and details and questioning the text. Notice in *Nancy's Noticings From Her Reading of "The Wonder of Diamonds"* that some of my notes start with the word *Important* as a clue to key information. A few of my notes also give details under a header; for example, check out "Diamonds Transportation to Earth's Crust." My focus in note taking was to record a few really important things about the text, and to ask myself a few great questions about it, which you can see at the bottom of *Nancy's Noticings*.

Writing Daily Duo
Step 5: Brief Writing Tasks

To illustrate a brief writing task for this text, I chose to do a one-minute paper. Using a 3 × 5 index card, I set a timer for one minute and began writing about "The Wonder of Diamonds." Interesting things popped up in my writing: I connected the industrial production of diamonds to their use for record needles, and reading the text made me curious about other possible uses for diamonds, as discovered in my one-minute writing. Notice that most of it is a recount of the key ideas and details in the text (see *Nancy's One-Minute Paper From Her Reading of "The Wonder of Diamonds"*).

Writing Daily Duo
Step 6: Writing About Reading

When writing about reading, students can write summaries, short informational essays, or even rough-draft opinion pieces or arguments. In *Nancy's Opinion Writing of "The Wonder of Diamonds,"* you can see the extended writing that I completed after reading the text. I spent only a little time on this exercise, about 15 minutes, and the writing certainly isn't perfect or even great. What it did do, however, is help me remember interesting facts—much to my husband's chagrin, as I informed him all about diamonds the next time we walked past the jewelry display at Costco! I focused on one genre in my writing about reading: I clearly stated my *opinion* early on, and then provided a few backup claims.

The Daily Duo
in Action Over a Week

We have considered the Daily Duo in action with a text, and the sequences you might choose for your students to follow, and now we turn to fitting the Daily Duo into your teaching week.

I know that you are squeezed for time during your English language arts block, so I designed this layout with time—or lack thereof—in mind.

The focus on the weeklong Daily Duo layout is to infuse your curriculum with reading and writing, and the teaching of reading comprehension strategies using nonfiction texts, and also to provide you with a handy reference guide for accomplishing this smoothly and easily. The sample layout is only one example of how to focus instruction on both reading of and writing

Notes : The Wonder of Diamonds

Important points
- Diamond is hardest substance on earth
- Diamond is used now in medical equipment — like scalpels that cut & cauterize
- Diamonds also form in space
Important The structure of diamonds allows many uses for the gem
Interesting dictions
"Diamonds transporation to Earth's crust."
- Its amazing diamonds make it to Earth's crust without changing to a different mineral
- I had no idea there was diamond in space?
- Its hard to imagine the diamond in my ring is 47 million years old & came up in a volcanic eruption
Questions
- Did the mining of diamonds in ancient times rely on slave labor?
- Are today's diamond mines safe for the miners? How does industry protect miners & the environment when retreiving diamonds?

Nancy's Noticings From Her Reading of "The Wonder of Diamonds"

One-minute Paper - Diamonds

I learned a lot about diamonds, I had never considered their industrial uses before. I knew record needles were made of diamonds but I didn't know about saws or surgical tools. Recently I found that beauty products for smoothing skin is made of diamonds too.
I knew diamonds were hard - my diamond wedding ring nicely scraped the front of my oven one day. I wonder what else diamond is used for? Jewelry, beauty products, surgical tools, saws ???

Nancy's One-Minute Paper From Her Reading of "The Wonder of Diamonds"

Opinion Papers
Diamonds

Diamonds are the most useful minerals known to man. Diamond is not only used for decorative purposes but also useful purposes.

Diamond use in art and jewelry began during the Medieval times, before that few diamonds were found in archeological digs and these were rough, unworked stones. Today, diamond is the preferred stone in engagement rings and an industry has grown from selling diamond rings to couples of all types and socioeconomic levels.

Archeological evidence suggests that diamonds were used for cutting and polish stone axes as far back as 2500 BC. Today, diamonds are used for cutting objects from the human body, to concrete in construction work. Because diamonds are so hard, they have many uses.

Since diamonds are found in space material that came to Earth, diamond could prove to be a mineral that is found on other planets. The formation of diamonds in space is thought to be different than diamond formation on Earth. Diamond can't be transformed to other minerals when being transported to Earth's surface.

Diamond will continue to be used in innovative ways in the future. Today it is used for both decorative purposes but also industrial purposes. Overall, diamonds are highly prized by many people.

Nancy's Opinion Writing of "The Wonder of Diamonds"

about texts. This is not the only layout you could use—it is only a suggestion—so modify the example and make it your own when you plan your lessons.

Early in the chapter, I suggested that you organize your reading time into three phases: the lesson, the practice, and the share. The weeklong Daily Duo layout is organized in this manner, suggesting objectives, teaching moves, and student practice focus for the lesson (L), practice (P), and share (S).

Weeklong Daily Duo Layout

On Day 1, students will read one short text, or part of a longer piece of text. If I were modeling this with "The Wonder of Diamonds," depending on my students' reading ability, I might read only the first few sections of the text on Day 1 and stop before the section on types.

DAY 1

READING

L: Notice by circling.

Objective: Teach students to call out what they notice in the text by circling, boxing, or underlining words, phrases, and sentences. You might say:

> "Today in our reading, let's pay close attention to what we notice about the text while we read. We are going to record those noticings by circling words and phrases in the text. Let me show you some examples."

P: Students prepare to read, read, notice, reread, and circle to note.

S: Discuss and chart what students noticed about their reading. You might ask:

> "What did you notice? What did you circle?"

WRITING

There is no writing activity on Day 1. Students only prepare to write by noticing.

On Day 2, no new text is introduced. Students refer to the text they read the day before. On this day, the students will read and write.

DAY 2

READING

L: Notice important points.

Objective: Teach students how to use stickies to take short notes called jots. You might say:

> "Sometimes you want to take notes on a text that you have read, and you don't have a lot of room to take the notes. In that case, you can use jots. Jots are short bullet points, or short phrases about thoughts you have about the reading."

P: Students prepare to read, read, notice, and take notes. A key point here is that, when they prepare to reread a text, they can remind themselves to find the important parts in order to write a few jots.

S: Discuss what students wrote about in their jots. You might ask:

> "What did you write down? How do your jots relate to the text?"

WRITING

L: Use notes to write a short piece.

Objective: Teach students to use their jots to write a short piece. You might say:

> "We just finished working on writing notes about what we read. Sometimes when we write about what we read, it helps us to understand what we read better. A short piece can be just a paragraph or two about the text we read."

P: Students write independently to produce a short text from the stickies and other notes they wrote while reading.

S: Have students share their writing with one another—especially how it relates to the article—using text-dependent references.

DAY 3

On Day 3, students read a second short text, or part of a longer piece of text. If I were modeling this with "The Wonder of Diamonds," I would use only the middle to last sections of the text on Day 3, having students read from the section on types to the end of the article.

READING

L: Notice by circling.

Objective: Teach students to call out what they notice in the text by circling, boxing, or underlining words, phrases, and sentences. You might say:

> "Today in our reading, let's pay close attention to what we notice about the text while we read. We are going to read a text that relates to (or is the reminder of) what we read two days ago. Again, we are going to record our noticings by circling words and phrases in the text."

P: Students prepare to read, read, notice, reread, and circle to note.

S: Discuss and chart what students noticed about their reading. You might ask:

> "What did you notice? What did you circle?"

WRITING

There is no writing activity on Day 3. Students only prepare to write by noticing.

DAY 4

On Day 4, no new text is introduced. Students refer to the text they read the day before.

READING

L: Notice important points.

Objective: Teach students to check in on their comprehension of the text. You might say:

> "Yesterday we finished reading a long article on diamonds (or a new article on a given topic). It's a good time to check in and make sure we are understanding what we read. Let's pull the article out and write a few notes together about the article. Let's think . . . What could we say about the text? What's important? What's interesting? What doesn't make sense?"

P: Students prepare to read, read, notice, and take notes. A key point here is that, when they prepare to reread a text, they can remind themselves to find the important parts in order to write down a few notes in their notebooks.

S: Discuss what students wrote about in their notebooks. You might ask:

> "What did you write down? How do your notes relate to the text?"

WRITING

L: Use notes to write a short piece.

Objective: Teach students to use the notes they wrote today, and the jots they wrote previously, to compose a short piece on what they learned by reading the text. You might say:

> "We just finished working on writing notes about what we read, and a couple of days ago we wrote jots down about the text. Let's look at the notes and the jots and think about what we learned. We are going to write a few paragraphs about what we learned. Make sure you state one or two things you learned, and it can be just a paragraph or two about the text we read."

P: Students write independently to produce a short text from the stickies and other notes they wrote while reading. The focus of this writing is to share what they learned.

S: Have students share their writing with one another—especially how it relates to the article—using text-dependent references.

On Day 5, students write about reading, creating a longer response based on their notes and sentence writing completed on Days 2 and 4.

DAY 5

READING

There is no reading lesson on Day 5. Students concentrate on writing.

WRITING

L: Write a summary.

Objective: Teach students how to use their notes and short writings from the previous days to write a summary. (For a few summary writing lessons, see the "Summarizing to Comprehend" section of Part III.) You might say:

> "Today we are going to use our notes, and our thinking about what we learned that we wrote down yesterday, to write a summary of the text we've been reading this week."

> Then follow one of the summary writing lessons from Part III.

P: Students write independently with coaching from the teacher. The students focus on writing a summary.

S: Highlight the work of a few students by sharing the draft of their summaries. Students can also share their summaries with one another. Remind students to focus on sharing how they put ideas together and collapsed information to create a summary about the text.

Next Steps to Consider

You might notice how smoothly and easily the Daily Duo fits together, allowing students to practice reading and writing about reading each day. Now you can teach the Daily Duo with a different text. Remember to make the teaching your own and use the Daily Duo sequences as they fit. You might also embark upon a writing unit of study—on opinion, argument, response to literature, a feature article, a book, or an informational report—as a next step. No matter what genre you choose, the sequences support you every step of the way toward student independence.

Planning Instruction for Student Success

In the digital age, we all know what it's like to zoom in to see an image close up, and zoom out to see the larger view. In Chapter 6, we zoomed in on the three phases of a reading class period:

- Focus lesson
- Practice
- Share

The phases tilt toward the goal of student independence and pretty much adhere to the gradual release model, which is that tried-and-true teaching and learning framework that helps you find a good balance of I Do It/We Do It/You Do It within each school day. Now, in this chapter, we zoom out. We take a step back to view our teaching plans from a greater distance so we can see the scale of the day-to-day lessons, the relationships between them, and how we might paint a wider canvas of planning across not just days or a single week, but several weeks.

I know, I know. If you are like me, you're itching to try the nonfiction comprehension lessons in Part III of this book, and go ahead if you like! But I promise your students will learn to read nonfiction to a greater degree—and learn to *learn from* nonfiction to a greater degree—if you see in the pages that follow how to plan lessons that span a longer period of time, and that are part of a bigger instructional goal. Great learning starts with good planning.

All of the nonfiction lessons in Part III can be used for virtually any unit you develop; you'll just need to adapt the lessons in a way that structures the learning for your students, based on the topic and the students' needs.

Planning Using Units of Study

One popular, research-based way to plan over time is by developing units of study (Ainsworth, 2011). A unit of study is a group of lessons that are taught over a period of a few weeks. The lessons focus on a central theme, or focus of study. If you are teaching an English language arts unit, you focus on a theme. If you are teaching a content unit, you think in terms of a focus for study. Some teachers and school departments organize all their instruction around units of study; some only teach one or two overarching units a year.

What is on your front burner to teach this year in terms of content? Planning with a unit-of-study model might resolve a lot of your questions. It might also help you as you work to ensure students learn from your teaching. For example, perhaps you want to teach students how to write an argument, or write in a specific content area like science, or you want to deeply teach a content area, such as ancient civilizations. Whether the goal for students is a writing outcome or content-area knowledge, pouring your teaching plans into a two- to four-week unit of study is practical.

With a unit of study, each lesson builds upon the previous one toward a key understanding, called an outcome (Tuchman Glass, 2012). Before you begin teaching the unit, you'll want to decide how students will show what they are learning along the way. This might include a culminating activity where students demonstrate what they've learned with a final project or performance. The key is to know what you expect students to know and be able to do at the end of the unit, *before* you start teaching the unit, so you can plan lessons that build student independence and competence to that outcome. Just remember that your role is to coach students along the way so that they own the learning!

The Unit's Arc Toward Independence

To exploit the zoom-in/zoom-out analogy once again, notice how a single, three-phase instructional block has the same trajectory as the three phases of a unit of study, shown below. That is, while there are no hard-and-fast lines between each phase, all teaching and learning needs to foster students' independence—early on. One of the biggest obstacles in American education is that, as a profession, we have clung to teacher-centric/teacher-controlled models of instruction.

Frontload: *The beginning* of the unit presents lessons that frontload the skills and strategies that you are focusing on in the study.

Practice: *The middle* of the unit builds students' independence in the skills and strategies you have been coaching and modeling.

Apply: *The end* of the unit is a wrap-up where the students apply their learning to a culminating activity. The activity could be a test, but is better set up as an applied project, like a piece of writing or another project a student can take on to show learning.

Got Your Calendar Out? Backward Planning

To begin planning any unit, start by examining standards and landing on the key final outcome you want students to learn. Then, literally sitting with a big desk calendar or a digital calendar, work backward from the last day of the unit (when students polish their final performance) to the first day of the unit, planning each day's Daily Duo and other lessons. Obviously, the early lessons start with an assumption of little or no ability with the new skills, and the later lessons are based on the premise that students can now use the strategies and skills independently.

Begin by Choosing a Focus

State and national standards in content areas, and the Common Core State Standards (National Governors Association Center for Best Practices & Council of Chief State School Officers, 2010), are the best sources for selecting outcomes that are grade-level aligned and focused on 21st century learner outcomes. Standards documents can also help you develop a final assessment, or project, the students will complete at the end of the unit. Mucking around with standards, thinking about what they mean for instruction and how they would look if students really learned them, helps you to plan.

So again, when you structure the learning, start with your outcome for the unit. Consider what you want students to know and do at the end of the unit. Is it to write a summary? Then have students work with a variety of texts while learning to write effective summaries. Is it to learn about the courses and consequences of the American Revolution? Then have students use the Daily Duo routines to read texts related to the American Revolution and take notes on the content to learn the concepts and ideas about the revolution and how it changed America.

As I mentioned, all units have a beginning, a middle, and an end. At the beginning of a unit, you immerse students in the concept of the unit, exploring the topic and texts that help students learn that topic. In the middle of the unit, you are intent on modeling and coaching students through the skills and strategies of the unit, gradually moving the responsibility of the learning to the students. At the end of the unit, students work on a project or paper that shows what they learned, and you culminate the unit with some sort of final assessment.

Let's Get Our Hands on Planning

Now I'm going to show you a sample unit on cells so you can have a concrete example in front of you. Then we'll look at where I drew my ideas from and the decisions that go into the day-to-day mapping across 10 days.

Cell Unit

	Day 1	Day 2	Day 3	Day 4	Day 5
Content	Teacher: Frontload information on cell structures through exploration of textbook, teacher-made Powerpoint, video, or other media.	Students: Observe cells and classify based on observations.	Students: Explore types and functions of organelles.	Students: Identify organelle and provide its structure and function.	Students: Compare and contrast plant and animal cells.
Activity	Students will: Read textbook section utilizing a lesson from Part III, Lessons for Getting Main Idea by Understanding Text Structures, and Prereading and Think-Aloud Lessons for Main Idea and Details.	Students will: Complete lab, take notes, and write a short summary on lab. Choose and utilize lesson from Part III, Summarizing to Comprehend.	Students will: Read textbook section utilizing a lesson from Part III, Lessons That Support Students While Reading for Main Idea and Details.	Students will: Read textbook section utilizing a lesson from Part III, Lessons That Support Students While Reading for Main Idea and Details, and Understanding Key Vocabulary.	Students will: Read textbook section utilizing a lesson from Part III, Lessons for Getting Main Idea by Understanding Text Structures, After-Reading Engagements: Exploring the Main Ideas and Details in Texts, and/or Understanding Key Vocabulary, and write a compare/contrast chart and supporting paragraph.

Daily Duo Reading Component

Daily Duo Writing Component

Daily Duo Reading Component

Daily Duo Reading Component

Daily Duo Reading Component

Daily Duo Writing Component

(Continued)

(Continued)

Day 6	Day 7	Day 8	Day 9	Day 10
Content	*Content*	*Content*	*Content*	*Content*
Teacher: Frontload functions of osmosis and diffusion.	Teacher: Explain further detail—osmosis and diffusion.	Teacher: Frontload information on cell reproduction, respiration and photosynthesis.	Students: Explain cell reproduction.	Students: Explain cellular respiration and photosynthesis.
Activity	*Activity*	*Activity*	*Activity*	*Activity*
Students will:	Students will:	Students will:	Students will:	Students will:
Read textbook section utilizing a lesson from Part III, Lessons That Support Students While Reading for Main Idea and Details.	Complete group activity utilizing lessons from Part III, Writing About Reading.	Read science article utilizing a lesson from Part III, Lessons That Support Students While Reading for Main Idea and Detail.	Complete group activity utilizing lessons from Part III, Summarizing to Comprehend, or Writing About Reading.	Complete group activity utilizing lessons from Part III, Writing About Reading.

Daily Duo Reading Component

Daily Duo Writing Component

Daily Duo Reading Component

Daily Duo Writing Component

Daily Duo Writing Component

Give survey assessment

Sample Unit of Study: Types of Cells

This unit on types of cells is a seventh-grade unit based on content standards (Achieve, 2013). A two-week unit, it begins with an introduction to cells and moves to students owning the information by applying what they have learned. Notice how I have incorporated the standards and the Daily Duo of reading and writing.

Focus/Outcomes: Students will learn that the cell is the smallest independent unit of life and that all living things are made up of cells.

Students will learn that cells contain smaller units called organelles, and they will be able to explain the function of major organelles.

Day 1	Day 2	Day 3	Day 4	Day 5
Frontload information on cell structures.	Observe cells and classify based on observations.	Explore types and functions of organelles.	Identify organelle and provide its structure and function.	Compare and contrast plant and animal cells.
Read textbook section utilizing a lesson from the "Lessons That Support Students While Reading for Main Idea and Details" and "Lessons for Getting Main Idea by Understanding Text Structures" sections of Part III.	Complete lab, take notes, and write a short summary on lab. Utilize a lesson from the "Summarizing to Comprehend" section of Part III.	Read textbook section utilizing the lesson *Ask Great Questions* in Part III.	Read textbook section utilizing a lesson from the "Understanding Key Vocabulary" section of Part III.	Read textbook section utilizing a lesson from the "Lessons That Support Students While Reading for Main Idea and Details" and "Understanding Key Vocabulary" sections of Part III.

Day 6	Day 7	Day 8	Day 9	Day 10
Frontload functions osmosis and diffusion.	Explain osmosis and diffusion.	Frontload cell reproduction, respiration, and photosynthesis.	Explain cell reproduction respiration and photosynthesis.	Set up investigation for describing how living things are made up of cells, which can be many different types of cells.
Read textbook section utilizing a lesson from the "Lessons That Support Students While Reading for Main Idea and Details" section of Part III.	Complete group activity and lab utilizing lessons from the "Writing About Reading" section of Part III.	Read science article utilizing a lesson from the "Lessons That Support Students While Reading for Main Idea and Details" section of Part III.	Complete group activity utilizing lessons from the "Writing About Reading" section of Part III.	Complete lab and coach student writing to prove their learning, utilizing lessons from the "Writing About Reading" section of Part III.
Give survey assessment				

How I Select the Daily Skills and Practice

OK, so the cell unit is pretty straightforward, and as the saying goes, it isn't rocket science to write such a unit. But it reflects a hefty amount of learning theory and education research—and standards sleuthing. In particular, you can see a lot of Common Core State Standards in it. Even though the CCSS explain what students need to know, they don't tell *how* to teach the skills and strategies. You make these decisions based on what will work best for your students.

Sample Nonfiction Unit of Study: Writing an Argument

Now let's look at another sample unit. Notice in *Argument Writing Unit* how the unit begins—by outlining a content objective and a literacy objective for each day. The outcome is writing an argument; for students, however, learning oral presentation of an argument can be just as effective. The literacy objective is based on the CCSS and utilizes the standards for reading informational texts and writing.

A central idea in the CCSS for Grades 6–12 is developing student ability to form an argument and base it on research with text-related references. Forming and presenting an effective argument is a skill needed by college students, but newer for us to teach as previous standards mostly focused on persuasive writing. Twenty-first century skills demand different levels of communication, collaboration, and critical analysis than students have developed in the past (Pacific Policy Research Center, 2010; Partnership for 21st Century Skills, 2009). The skills of communication and critical analysis are rolled into student ability to develop arguments. The learning progression for argument appears in the writing standards at the end of this chapter (see *Learning Progression: Writing, Common Core State Standards*). You can see by examining the learning progression that the expectations for student ability in argument move from Grades 6–8, when students are expected to introduce claims and a topic or issue and support them with logical reasoning, to Grades 11–12, where students are expected to introduce precise and knowledgeable claims and counterclaims and develop them fairly and thoroughly with relevant evidence.

As you consider this unit as an example, think about how to adapt it to your grade level. Adapting the unit to the grade level you teach can be accomplished by pulling the correct writing standards from the Common Core. For example, if you teach Grade 4 or 5, you can adapt it from an argument unit to an opinion writing unit. You can also refer to the learning progression for this standard, presented at the end of the chapter (see *Learning Progression: Writing, Common Core State Standards*), to see the expected level of engagement and rigor for your grade level, and to see what expectations come before or after to help you differentiate based on student need and ability.

Argument Unit

Time Frame: Three weeks.

Guiding Question: What do good writers include when writing about a topic? How do they decide on a point of view and use concepts and short quotes from a reading to support their point?

Materials You Will Need: A variety of texts and books from your specific content area of focus so that students can quote from their reading as textual evidence.

Outcomes:

- Write an argument that includes at least one claim and evidence supporting the claim.
- Support the claim with relevant information and credible sources.

Argument Writing Unit

Standards listed are the Common Core State Standards.

Day 1

Standards: W.1a, W.1b, W.1c

Lesson: Argumentative Writing in Part III, page 235

Content: Students learn the components of an argument: claim, reason, evidence,

Daily Duo: Writing Component

Day 2

Standards: W.7, W.8, W.9

Could also include RH/SS.1, RH/SS.2, RH/SS.8, or RS/TS.1, RS/TS.2, RS/TS.6

Lesson: Inquiry Charts in Part III, page 146

Content: Students learn to conduct an inquiry on a chosen topic. Students are involved in asking questions about a topic based on reading.

Daily Duo: Reading Component

Day 3

Standards: W.7, W.8, W.9

Could also include RH/SS.1, RH/SS.2, RH/SS.8, or RS/TS.1, RS/TS.2, RS/TS.6

Lesson: Inquiry Charts in Part III, page 146

Content: Students read one or two sources to fill in information on the inquiry chart. Students are collecting notes and information on the topic.

Daily Duo: Reading Component

Day 4

Standards: W.1a, W.1b, W.1c, W.1d, W.4

Lesson: Guided Writing in Part III, page 230

Content: Students learn how to write an introduction to an argument.

Daily Duo: Writing Component

Day 5

Standards: LS1 a-d, LS4, W.1a, W1b, W1c, W1d, W4, W10

Lesson: Say Something to Develop Understanding in Part III, page 176

Content: Students work in groups to make claims regarding a topic from their reading. Groups record thoughts and ideas produced in the group.

Daily Duo: Writing Component

Day 6

Standards: SL.1a-d, SL.4, W.1a, W.1b, W.1c, W.1d, W.4 and also RH/SS.1, RH/SS.2, RH/SS.8, or RS/TS.1, RS/TS.2, RS/TS.6

Lesson: Say Something to Develop Understanding in Part III, page 176

Content: Students work in groups to provide evidence for the claims they made on the previous day. Students use the group brainstorm to write their own summary of the information.

Daily Duo: Writing Component

Day 7

Standards: W.1a-e

Lessons: Guided Writing, page 230, and *Argumentative Writing,* page 235, in Part III

Content: Teacher models how to write the body of an argument, and students write short arguments on their own.

Daily Duo: Writing Component

Day 8

Standards: W.7, W.8, W.9

Could also include RH/SS.1, RH/SS.2, RH/SS 8, or RS/TS.1, RS/TS.2, RS/TS.6

Lessons: Partner Reading, page 150, and *ABC Graffiti,* page 166, in Part III

Content: Students partner up to read articles assigned based on their group topic. Students work in small groups to fill out the graffiti sheet on a topic of common interest.

Daily Duo: Reading Component

Day 9

Standards: W.1f

Lessons: Guided Writing, page 230, and *Argumentative Writing,* page 235, in Part III

Content: Teacher models how to write a conclusion to an argument, and students write a conclusion to the argument they wrote on Day 7.

Daily Duo: Writing Component

Day 10

Standards: W1a–f, W10

Lesson:

Argumentative Writing in Part III, page 235

Content: Students write a short argument in pairs including a claim, evidence, and conclusion.

Daily Duo: Writing Component

(Continued)

(Continued)

Day 11	Day 12	Day 13	Day 14	Day 15
The unit now shifts from collaborative work to independent work. The students will work on their own using what they learned about reading, writing, and thinking of arguments during Days 1–10.	*Standards:* W.7, W.8, W.9 Could also include RH/SS.1, RH/SS.2, RH/SS.8, or RS/TS.1, RS/TS.2, RS/TS.6	Standards: W.1a–f *Lesson: Argumentative Writing* in Part III, page 235	*Standards:* W.1a–f, W.5, W.6 *Lesson: Argumentative Writing* in Part III, page 235	Standards: W.1a–f, W.5, W.6, W.10 *Lesson: Argumentative Writing* in Part III, page 235
Standards: W.7, W.8, W.9	*Lesson: Looking for Important Information,* page 140, and *Learning Logs,* page 226, in Part III, continued from Day 11.	*Content:* Students draft argument essays.	*Content:* Students revise argument essays.	*Content:* Students polish and turn in argument essays.
Could also include RH/SS.1, RH/SS.2, RH/SS.8, or RS/TS.1, RS/TS.2, RS/TS.6	*Content:* Students check logs and continue reading and researching to gather information to close any gaps in supporting evidence for the claim.	*Daily Duo:* Writing Component	*Daily Duo:* Writing Component	*Daily Duo:* Writing Component
Lesson: Looking for Important Information, page 140, and *Learning Logs,* page 226, Part III	*Daily Duo:* Reading Component			
Content: Students research their topic of interest and record important information in their notebooks.				
Daily Duo: Reading Component				

Key: W = Writing; R H/SS = Reading: History/Social Studies; R S/TS = Reading: Science and Technical Subjects; SL = Speaking and Listening

80

- Organize evidence to support the claim logically.
- Provide a concluding section that follows the argument.

Performance Assessment: Students will create a fully developed argument piece with a thesis, supporting details from reading, and a conclusion reiterating the position. See *Sample of Student Argument Writing* for a sample of student writing based on this unit.

Planning Resources for Dynamic Daily Teaching

The CCSS are carefully designed as a cumulative progression of expectations from grade to grade. It helps to be able to see the cumulative progression of a standard at a glance, as the standards don't stand alone, but grow from previous grade levels' focus and expectations. This section presents a general outline of the standards and learning progressions, which organize the standards over time. You can access the CCSS online at www.corestandards.org. The learning progressions are available at the end of this chapter.

Planning Resource: The Common Core State Standards

There are four standard strands in the CCSS: Reading, Writing, Speaking and Listening, and Language. The standards for the primary grades also have a standard strand for Reading: Foundational Skills. Each strand, except for Reading: Foundational Skills is unified by a set of College and Career Readiness Anchor Standards that are identical across all grade levels and content areas. For example, the Anchor Standards for Reading and the grade-level reading content standards are organized into four topic areas:

- Key Ideas and Details: R.1, R.2, R.3
- Craft and Structure: R.4, R.5, R.6
- Integration of Knowledge and Ideas: R.7, R.8, R.9
- Range of Reading and Level of Text Complexity: R.10

The Writing standards differ slightly from the Reading standards. The Writing standards are also unified by a set of College and Career Readiness Anchor Standards, but the four topic areas are different from those of the Reading standards:

- Text Types and Purposes: W.1, W.2, W.3
- Production and Distribution of Writing: W.4, W.5, W.6

The invisible bike helmet could be the new way to prevent major head injuries caused by bicycle accidents. Since some people believe that helmets make them look uncool, the invisible bike helmet would be a great option incase of an accident. This is because of its inflating airbag with the ability to prevent any part of your head from getting hurt. The invisible bicycle helmet uses accelerometers and gyroscopes which are inside the bag. Also, the comfort of the "helmet" can be tested without causing pain, extreme force, or injury because of its fit around your head. Actual bike helmets were proven to not protect you as much as they should. Some may think, "I'm not going to spend 600 dollars on an air bag you can only use once" but that "air bag" you spent 600 dollars on can save you from spending thousands of dollars on surgery because you weren't wearing this product. The invisible bike helmet is a definite option for those who want to look good and stay safe.

Sample of Student Argument Writing

- Research to Build and Present Knowledge: W.7, W.8, W.9
- Range of Writing: W.10

The Speaking and Listening standards also have different topic areas. However, for this strand, there are only two:

- Comprehension and Collaboration: SL.1, SL.2, SL.3
- Presentation of Knowledge and Ideas: SL.4, SL.5, SL.6

The last strand of standards, Language, has three topic areas:

- Conventions of Standard English: L.1, L.2
- Knowledge of Language: L.3
- Vocabulary Acquisition and Use: L.4, L.5, L.6

Nonfiction-Related Standards

The standards that relate most closely to units of study in nonfiction reading and writing include the following:

- Reading Standards for Informational Text
  - All topics and all standards: RI.1–RI.10

- Writing Standards
  - Text Types and Purposes: W.1, W.2
  - Production and Distribution of Writing: W.4, W.5, W.6
  - Research to Build and Present Knowledge: W.7, W.8, W.9
  - Range of Writing: W.10

- Speaking and Listening Standards
  - Comprehension and Collaboration: SL.1, SL.2
  - Presentation of Knowledge and Ideas: SL.4, SL.5, SL.6

- Language Standards
  - Vocabulary Acquisition and Use: L.4, L.6

For teachers of Grades 6–12, additional content-area standards exist that can guide your planning work. These appear in the Literacy for History/Social Studies standards and the Literacy for Science and Technical Subjects standards. All of these standards closely align to appropriate units of study in your specific content areas. You would use the following standards for planning only when teaching in these specific subject areas:

- Reading Standards for Literacy in History/Social Studies, Grades 6–12; Reading Standards for Literacy in Science and Technical Subjects, Grades 6–12
  - Key Ideas and Details: RH.1, RH.2, RH.3; RST.1, RST.2, RST.3
  - Craft and Structure: RH.4, RH.5, RH.6; RST.4, RST.5, RST.6
  - Integration of Knowledge and Ideas: RH.7, RH.8, RH.9; RST.7, RST.8, RST.9
  - Range of Reading and Level of Text Complexity: RH.10; RST.10

- Writing Standards for Literacy in History/Social Studies, Science, and Technical Subjects, Grades 6–12
  - Text Types and Purposes: WHST.1, WHST.2
  - Production and Distribution of Writing: WHST.4, WHST.5, WHST.6

o   Research to Build and Present Knowledge: WHST.7, WHST.8, WHST.9
o   Range of Writing: WHST.10

Planning Resource: The Learning Progressions

The standards are organized so you can see all of the standards in a given area *for your grade level*. However, you cannot see what the progression of these standards looks like over time as students develop the skills and strategies. This look over time at student development is a learning progression. A learning progression is defined by James Popham (2008) as "the carefully sequenced sets of subskills and enabling knowledge that students need to master on their way to mastering a more distant curricular aim" (p. 83). When you can easily access the learning that comes before and after your grade level with a specific standard, you can reflect on your lessons to make sure you work within the correct level of rigor for your grade level and also have tools for differentiation at your fingertips.

Consider the learning progression of the standard for Reading: Informational Text (RI). When you look at the 10 standards in this area over time, you can see how the expectations grow and change from kindergarten through 12th grade. *Learning Progression: Reading: Informational Text, Common Core State Standards* is a table of the standard laid out as a learning progression. Notice how each year of learning builds upon the previous year. For example, the standard RI.4.1 for fourth grade states, "Refer to details and examples in a text when explaining what the text says explicitly and when drawing inferences from the text," and just three years later, in seventh grade, the standard RI.7.1 states, "Cite several pieces of textual evidence to support analysis of what the text says explicitly as well as inferences drawn from the text." Added to the standard in seventh grade is citing several pieces of textual evidence; this shows how the expectations of the standard grow over time.

The other standards (Writing, Language, Speaking and Listening, History/Social Studies, and Science and Technical Subjects) are also laid out in learning progressions, as shown in the pages that follow. Note that the Literacy in History/Social Studies and Science and Technical Subjects learning progressions start in Grade 6 and go through Grade 12. I've included these progressions here even though I am focusing on instruction for Grades 4–8 because I want you to see what the standards expect of students beyond middle school. Additionally, I have outlined the Writing standards for History/Social Studies, Science, and Technical Subjects for Grades 6–8.

In calling this chapter "Planning Instruction for Student Success," I'm aware that all kinds of things go into whether or not students achieve to the best of their abilities within any given time frame. But from my many years of teaching, I can say that the better I got at planning, the more my students learned. Maybe part of it is that all the planning work freed me up as a teacher to then *respond* to how my students received, reacted, and learned from the instruction. In any event, read and return to the ideas of this chapter as you immerse yourself in the specific lessons that begin in the next section, looking for ways to anchor them into your units.

Learning Progression: Reading: Informational Text, Common Core State Standards

Grade	Standard 1	Standard 2	Standard 3	Standard 4	Standard 5
Fourth	Refer to details and examples in a text when explaining what the text says explicitly and when drawing inferences from the text.	Determine the main idea of a text and explain how it is supported by key details; summarize the text.	Explain events, procedures, ideas, or concepts in a historical, scientific, or technical text, including what happened and why, based on specific information in the text.	Determine the meaning of general academic and domain-specific words or phrases in a text relevant to a grade 4 topic or subject area.	Describe the overall structure (e.g., chronology, comparison, cause/effect, problem/solution) of events, ideas, concepts, or information in a text or part of a text.
Fifth	Quote accurately from a text when explaining what the text says explicitly and when drawing inferences from the text.	Determine two or more main ideas of a text and explain how they are supported by key details; summarize the text.	Explain the relationships or interactions between two or more individuals, events, ideas, or concepts in a historical, scientific, or technical text based on specific information in the text.	Determine the meaning of general academic and domain-specific words and phrases in a text relevant to a grade 5 topic or subject area.	Compare and contrast the overall structure (e.g., chronology, comparison, cause/effect, problem/solution) of events, ideas, concepts, or information in two or more texts.
Sixth	Cite textual evidence to support analysis of what the text says explicitly as well as inferences drawn from the text.	Determine a central idea of a text and how it is conveyed through particular details; provide a summary of the text distinct from personal opinions or judgments.	Analyze in detail how a key individual, event, or idea is introduced, illustrated, and elaborated in a text (e.g., through examples or anecdotes).	Determine the meaning of words and phrases as they are used in a text, including figurative, connotative, and technical meanings.	Analyze how a particular sentence, paragraph, chapter, or section fits into the overall structure of a text and contributes to the development of the ideas.
Seventh	Cite several pieces of textual evidence to support analysis of what the text says explicitly as well as inferences drawn from the text.	Determine two or more central ideas in a text and analyze their development over the course of the text; provide an objective summary of the text.	Analyze the interactions between individuals, events, and ideas in a text (e.g., how ideas influence individuals or events, or how individuals influence ideas or events).	Determine the meaning of words and phrases as they are used in a text, including figurative, connotative, and technical meanings; analyze the impact of a specific word choice on meaning and tone.	Analyze the structure an author uses to organize a text, including how the major sections contribute to the whole and to the development of the ideas.
Eighth	Cite the textual evidence that most strongly supports an analysis of what the text says explicitly as well as inferences drawn from the text.	Determine a central idea of a text and analyze its development over the course of the text, including its relationship to supporting ideas; provide an objective summary of the text.	Analyze how a text makes connections among and distinctions between individuals, ideas, or events (e.g., through comparisons, analogies, or categories).	Determine the meaning of words and phrases as they are used in a text, including figurative, connotative, and technical meanings; analyze the impact of specific word choices on meaning and tone, including analogies or allusions to other texts.	Analyze in detail the structure of a specific paragraph in a text, including the role of particular sentences in developing and refining a key concept.

(Continued)

(Continued)

Grade	Standard 6	Standard 7	Standard 8	Standard 9	Standard 10
Fourth	Compare and contrast a firsthand and secondhand account of the same event or topic; describe the differences in focus and the information provided.	Interpret information presented visually, orally, or quantitatively (e.g., in charts, graphs, diagrams, time lines, animations, or interactive elements on Web pages) and explain how the information contributes to an understanding of the text in which it appears.	Explain how an author uses reasons and evidence to support particular points in a text.	Integrate information from two texts on the same topic in order to write or speak about the subject knowledgeably.	By the end of [the] year, read and comprehend informational texts, including history/social studies, science, and technical texts, in the grades 4–5 text complexity band proficiently, with scaffolding as needed at the high end of the range.
Fifth	Analyze multiple accounts of the same event or topic, noting important similarities and differences in the point of view they represent.	Draw on information from multiple print or digital sources, demonstrating the ability to locate an answer to a question quickly or to solve a problem efficiently.	Explain how an author uses reasons and evidence to support particular points in a text, identifying which reasons and evidence support which point(s).	Integrate information from several texts on the same topic in order to write or speak about the subject knowledgeably.	By the end of the year, read and comprehend informational texts, including history/social studies, science, and technical texts, at the high end of the grades 4–5 text complexity band independently and proficiently.
Sixth	Determine an author's point of view or purpose in a text and explain how it is conveyed in the text.	Integrate information presented in different media or formats (e.g., visually, quantitatively) as well as in words to develop a coherent understanding of a topic or issue.	Trace and evaluate the argument and specific claims in a text, distinguishing claims that are supported by reasons and evidence from claims that are not.	Compare and contrast one author's presentation of events with that of another (e.g., a memoir written by and a biography on the same person).	By the end of the year, read and comprehend literary nonfiction in the grades 6–8 text complexity band proficiently, with scaffolding as needed at the high end of the range.
Seventh	Determine an author's point of view or purpose in a text and analyze how the author distinguishes his or her position from that of others.	Compare and contrast a text to an audio, video, or multimedia version of the text, analyzing each medium's portrayal of the subject (e.g., how the delivery of a speech affects the impact of the words).	Trace and evaluate the argument and specific claims in a text, assessing whether the reasoning is sound and the evidence is relevant and sufficient to support the claims.	Analyze how two or more authors writing about the same topic shape their presentations of key information by emphasizing different evidence or advancing different interpretations of facts.	By the end of the year, read and comprehend literary nonfiction in the grades 6–8 text complexity band proficiently, with scaffolding as needed at the high end of the range.
Eighth	Determine an author's point of view or purpose in a text and analyze how the author acknowledges and responds to conflicting evidence or viewpoints.	Evaluate the advantages and disadvantages of using different mediums (e.g., print or digital text, video, multimedia) to present a particular topic or idea.	Delineate and evaluate the argument and specific claims in a text, assessing whether the reasoning is sound and the evidence is relevant and sufficient; recognize when irrelevant evidence is introduced.	Analyze a case in which two or more texts provide conflicting information on the same topic and identify where the texts disagree on matters of fact or interpretation.	By the end of the year, read and comprehend literary nonfiction at the high end of the grades 6–8 text complexity band independently and proficiently.

Source: Copyright 2010. National Governors Association Center for Best Practices and Council of Chief State School Officers. All rights reserved.

Learning Progression: Writing, Common Core State Standards

Grade	Standard 1	Standard 2	Standard 3	Standard 4	Standard 5
Fourth	Write opinion pieces on topics or texts, supporting a point of view with reasons and information.	Write informative/explanatory texts to examine a topic and convey ideas and information clearly.	Write narratives to develop real or imagined experiences or events using effective technique, descriptive details, and clear event sequences.	Produce clear and coherent writing in which the development and organization are appropriate to task, purpose, and audience. (Grade-specific expectations for writing types are defined in standards 1–3.)	With guidance and support from peers and adults, develop and strengthen writing as needed by planning, revising, and editing. (Editing for conventions should demonstrate command of Language standards 1–3 up to and including grade 4 on page 29.)
	a. Introduce a topic or text clearly, state an opinion, and create an organizational structure in which related ideas are grouped to support the writer's purpose.	a. Introduce a topic clearly and group related information in paragraphs and sections; include formatting (e.g., headings), illustrations, and multimedia when useful to aiding comprehension.	a. Orient the reader by establishing a situation and introducing a narrator and/or characters; organize an event sequence that unfolds naturally.		
	b. Provide reasons that are supported by facts and details.	b. Develop the topic with facts, definitions, concrete details, quotations, or other information and examples related to the topic.	b. Use dialogue and description to develop experiences and events or show the responses of characters to situations.		
	c. Link opinion and reasons using words and phrases (e.g., *for instance, in order to, in addition*).	c. Link ideas within categories of information using words and phrases (e.g., *another, for example, also, because*).	c. Use a variety of transitional words and phrases to manage the sequence of events.		
	d. Provide a concluding statement or section related to the opinion presented.	d. Use precise language and domain-specific vocabulary to inform about or explain the topic.	d. Use concrete words and phrases and sensory details to convey experiences and events precisely.		
		e. Provide a concluding statement or section related to the information or explanation presented.	e. Provide a conclusion that follows from the narrated experiences or events.		

(Continued)

Grade	Standard 1	Standard 2	Standard 3	Standard 4	Standard 5
Fifth	Write opinion pieces on topics or texts, supporting a point of view with reasons and information. a. Introduce a topic or text clearly, state an opinion, and create an organizational structure in which ideas are logically grouped to support the writer's purpose. b. Provide logically ordered reasons that are supported by facts and details. c. Link opinion and reasons using words, phrases, and clauses (e.g., *consequently, specifically*). d. Provide a concluding statement or section related to the opinion presented.	Write informative/explanatory texts to examine a topic and convey ideas and information clearly. a. Introduce a topic clearly, provide a general observation and focus, and group related information logically; include formatting (e.g., headings), illustrations, and multimedia when useful to aiding comprehension. b. Develop the topic with facts, definitions, concrete details, quotations, or other information and examples related to the topic. c. Link ideas within and across categories of information using words, phrases, and clauses (e.g., *in contrast, especially*). d. Use precise language and domain-specific vocabulary to inform about or explain the topic. e. Provide a concluding statement or section related to the information or explanation presented.	Write narratives to develop real or imagined experiences or events using effective technique, descriptive details, and clear event sequences. a. Orient the reader by establishing a situation and introducing a narrator and/or characters; organize an event sequence that unfolds naturally. b. Use narrative techniques, such as dialogue, description, and pacing, to develop experiences and events or show the responses of characters to situations. c. Use a variety of transitional words, phrases, and clauses to manage the sequence of events. d. Use concrete words and phrases and sensory details to convey experiences and events precisely. e. Provide a conclusion that follows from the narrated experiences or events.	Produce clear and coherent writing in which the development and organization are appropriate to task, purpose, and audience. (Grade-specific expectations for writing types are defined in standards 1–3.) Sufficient command of keyboarding skills to type a minimum of one page in a single sitting.	With guidance and support from peers and adults, develop and strengthen writing as needed by planning, revising, editing, rewriting, or trying new approach. (Editing for conventions should demonstrate command of Language standards 1–3 up to and including grade 5 on page 29.)

(Continued)

Grade	Standard 1	Standard 2	Standard 3	Standard 4	Standard 5
Sixth	Write arguments to support claims with clear reasons and relevant evidence. a. Introduce claim(s) and organize the reasons and evidence clearly. b. Support claim(s) with clear reasons and relevant evidence, using credible sources and demonstrating an understanding of the topic or text. c. Use words, phrases, and clauses to clarify the relationships among claim(s) and reasons. d. Establish and maintain a formal style. e. Provide a concluding statement or section that follows from the argument presented.	Write informative/explanatory texts to examine a topic and convey ideas, concepts, and information through the selection, organization, and analysis of relevant content. a. Introduce a topic; organize ideas, concepts, and information, using strategies such as definition, classification, comparison/contrast, and cause/effect; include formatting (e.g., headings), graphics (e.g., charts, tables), and multimedia when useful to aiding comprehension. b. Develop the topic with relevant facts, definitions, concrete details, quotations, or other information and examples. c. Use appropriate transitions to clarify the relationships among ideas and concepts. d. Use precise language and domain-specific vocabulary to inform about or explain the topic. e. Establish and maintain a formal style. f. Provide a concluding statement or section that follows from the information or explanation presented.	Write narratives to develop real or imagined experiences or events using effective technique, relevant descriptive details, and well-structured event sequences. a. Engage and orient the reader by establishing a context and introducing a narrator and/or characters; organize an event sequence that unfolds naturally and logically. b. Use narrative techniques, such as dialogue, pacing, and description, to develop experiences, events, and/or characters. c. Use a variety of transition words, phrases, and clauses to convey sequence and signal shifts from one time frame or setting to another. d. Use precise words and phrases, relevant descriptive details, and sensory language to convey experiences and events. e. Provide a conclusion that follows from the narrated experiences or events.	Produce clear and coherent writing in which the development, organization, and style are appropriate to task, purpose, and audience. (Grade-specific expectations for writing types are defined in standards 1–3.)	With some guidance and support from peers and adults, develop and strengthen writing as needed by planning, revising, editing, rewriting, or trying a new approach. (Editing for conventions should demonstrate command of Language standards 1–3 up to and including grade 6 on page 53.)

(Continued)

Grade	Standard 1	Standard 2	Standard 3	Standard 4	Standard 5
Seventh	Write arguments to support claims with clear reasons and relevant evidence. a. Introduce claim(s), acknowledge alternate or opposing claims, and organize the reasons and evidence logically. b. Support claim(s) with logical reasoning and relevant evidence, using accurate, credible sources and demonstrating an understanding of the topic or text. c. Use words, phrases, and clauses to create cohesion and clarify the relationships among claim(s), reasons, and evidence. d. Establish and maintain a formal style. e. Provide a concluding statement or section that follows from and supports the argument presented.	Write informative/explanatory texts to examine a topic and convey ideas, concepts, and information through the selection, organization, and analysis of relevant content. a. Introduce a topic clearly, previewing what is to follow; organize ideas, concepts, and information, using strategies such as definition, classification, comparison/contrast, and cause/effect; include formatting (e.g., headings), graphics (e.g., charts, tables), and multimedia when useful to aiding comprehension. b. Develop the topic with relevant facts, definitions, concrete details, quotations, or other information and examples. c. Use appropriate transitions to create cohesion and clarify the relationships among ideas and concepts. d. Use precise language and domain-specific vocabulary to inform about or explain the topic. e. Establish and maintain a formal style. f. Provide a concluding statement or section that follows from and supports the information or explanation presented.	Write narratives to develop real or imagined experiences or events using effective technique, relevant descriptive details, and well-structured event sequences. a. Engage and orient the reader by establishing a context and point of view and introducing a narrator and/or characters; organize an event sequence that unfolds naturally and logically. b. Use narrative techniques, such as dialogue, pacing, and description, to develop experiences, events, and/or characters. c. Use a variety of transition words, phrases, and clauses to convey sequence and signal shifts from one time frame or setting to another. d. Use precise words and phrases, relevant descriptive details, and sensory language to capture the action and convey experiences and events. e. Provide a conclusion that follows from and reflects on the narrated experiences or events.	Produce clear and coherent writing in which the development, organization, and style are appropriate to task, purpose, and audience. (Grade-specific expectations for writing types are defined in standards 1–3.)	With some guidance and support from peers and adults, develop and strengthen writing as needed by planning, revising, editing, rewriting, or trying a new approach, focusing on how well purpose and audience have been addressed. (Editing for conventions should demonstrate command of Language standards 1–3 up to and including grade 7 on page 53.)

(Continued)

(Continued)

Grade	Standard 1	Standard 2	Standard 3	Standard 4	Standard 5
Eighth	Write arguments to support claims with clear reasons and relevant evidence. a. Introduce claim(s), acknowledge and distinguish the claim(s) from alternate or opposing claims, and organize the reasons and evidence logically. b. Support claim(s) with logical reasoning and relevant evidence, using accurate, credible sources and demonstrating an understanding of the topic or text. c. Use words, phrases, and clauses to create cohesion and clarify the relationships among claim(s), counterclaims, reasons, and evidence. d. Establish and maintain a formal style. e. Provide a concluding statement or section that follows from and supports the argument presented.	Write informative/explanatory texts to examine a topic and convey ideas, concepts, and information through the selection, organization, and analysis of relevant content. a. Introduce a topic clearly, previewing what is to follow; organize ideas, concepts, and information into broader categories; include formatting (e.g., headings), graphics (e.g., charts, tables), and multimedia when useful to aiding comprehension. b. Develop the topic with relevant, well-chosen facts, definitions, concrete details, quotations, or other information and examples. c. Use appropriate and varied transitions to create cohesion and clarify the relationships among ideas and concepts. d. Use precise language and domain-specific vocabulary to inform about or explain the topic. e. Establish and maintain a formal style. f. Provide a concluding statement or section that follows from and supports the information or explanation presented.	Write narratives to develop real or imagined experiences or events using effective technique, relevant descriptive details, and well-structured event sequences. a. Engage and orient the reader by establishing a context and point of view and introducing a narrator and/or characters; organize an event sequence that unfolds naturally and logically. b. Use narrative techniques, such as dialogue, pacing, description, and reflection, to develop experiences, events, and/or characters. c. Use a variety of transition words, phrases, and clauses to convey sequence, signal shifts from one time frame or setting to another, and show the relationships among experiences and events. d. Use precise words and phrases, relevant descriptive details, and sensory language to capture the action and convey experiences and events. e. Provide a conclusion that follows from and reflects on the narrated experiences or events.	Produce clear and coherent writing in which the development, organization, and style are appropriate to task, purpose, and audience. (Grade-specific expectations for writing types are defined in standards 1–3.)	With some guidance and support from peers and adults, develop and strengthen writing as needed by planning, revising, editing, rewriting, or trying a new approach, focusing on how well purpose and audience have been addressed. (Editing for conventions should demonstrate command of Language standards 1–3 up to and including grade 8 on page 53.)

Learning Progression: Writing, Common Core State Standards

Grade	Standard 6	Standard 7	Standard 8	Standard 9	Standard 10
Fourth	With some guidance and support from adults, use technology, including the Internet, to produce and publish writing as well as to interact and collaborate with others; demonstrate sufficient command of keyboarding skills to type a minimum of one page in a single sitting.	Conduct short research projects that build knowledge through investigation of different aspects of a topic.	Recall relevant information from experiences or gather relevant information from print and digital sources; take notes and categorize information, and provide a list of sources.	Draw evidence from literary or informational texts to support analysis, reflection, and research. a. Apply grade 4 Reading standards to literature (e.g., "Describe in depth a character, setting, or event in a story or drama, drawing on specific details in the text [e.g., a character's thoughts, words, or actions]."). b. Apply grade 4 Reading standards to informational texts (e.g., "Explain how an author uses reasons and evidence to support particular points in a text").	Write routinely over extended time frames (time for research, reflection, and revision) and shorter time frames (a single sitting or a day or two) for a range of discipline-specific tasks, purposes, and audiences.
Fifth	With some guidance and support from adults, use technology, including the Internet, to produce and publish writing as well as to interact and collaborate with others; demonstrate sufficient command of keyboarding skills to type a minimum of two pages in a single sitting.	Conduct short research projects that use several sources to build knowledge through investigation of different aspects of a topic.	Recall relevant information from experiences or gather relevant information from print and digital sources; summarize or paraphrase information in notes and finished work, and provide a list of sources.	Draw evidence from literary or informational texts to support analysis, reflection, and research. a. Apply grade 5 Reading standards to literature (e.g., "Compare and contrast two or more characters, settings, or events in a story or a drama, drawing on specific details in the text [e.g., how characters interact]"). b. Apply grade 5 Reading standards to informational texts (e.g., "Explain how an author uses reasons and evidence to support particular points in a text, identifying which reasons and evidence support which point[s]").	Write routinely over extended time frames (time for research, reflection, and revision) and shorter time frames (a single sitting or a day or two) for a range of discipline-specific tasks, purposes, and audiences.

(Continued)

Grade	Standard 6	Standard 7	Standard 8	Standard 9	Standard 10
Sixth	Use technology, including the Internet, to produce and publish writing as well as to interact and collaborate with others; demonstrate sufficient command of keyboarding skills to type a minimum of three pages in a single sitting.	Conduct short research projects to answer a question, drawing on several sources and refocusing the inquiry when appropriate.	Gather relevant information from multiple print and digital sources; assess the credibility of each source; and quote or paraphrase the data and conclusions of others while avoiding plagiarism and providing basic bibliographic information for sources.	Draw evidence from literary or informational texts to support analysis, reflection, and research. a. Apply grade 6 Reading standards to literature (e.g., "Compare and contrast texts in different forms or genres [e.g., stories and poems; historical novels and fantasy stories] in terms of their approaches to similar themes and topics"). b. Apply grade 6 Reading standards to literary nonfiction (e.g., "Trace and evaluate the argument and specific claims in a text, distinguishing claims that are supported by reasons and evidence from claims that are not").	Write routinely over extended time frames (time for research, reflection, and revision) and shorter time frames (a single sitting or a day or two) for a range of discipline-specific tasks, purposes, and audiences.
Seventh	Use technology, including the Internet, to produce and publish writing and link to and cite sources as well as to interact and collaborate with others, including linking to and citing sources.	Conduct short research projects to answer a question, drawing on several sources and generating additional related, focused questions for further research and investigation.	Gather relevant information from multiple print and digital sources, using search terms effectively; assess the credibility and accuracy of each source; and quote or paraphrase the data and conclusions of others while avoiding plagiarism and following a standard format for citation.	Draw evidence from literary or informational texts to support analysis, reflection, and research. a. Apply grade 7 Reading standards to literature (e.g., "Compare and contrast a fictional portrayal of a time, place, or character and a historical account of the same period as a means of understanding how authors of fiction use or alter history"). b. Apply grade 7 Reading standards to literary nonfiction (e.g. "Trace and evaluate the argument and specific claims in a text, assessing whether the reasoning is sound and the evidence is relevant and sufficient to support the claims").	Write routinely over extended time frames (time for research, reflection, and revision) and shorter time frames (a single sitting or a day or two) for a range of discipline-specific tasks, purposes, and audiences.

(Continued)

(Continued)

Grade	Standard 6	Standard 7	Standard 8	Standard 9	Standard 10
Eighth	Use technology, including the Internet, to produce and publish writing and present the relationships between information and ideas efficiently as well as to interact and collaborate with others.	Conduct short research projects to answer a question (including a self-generated question), drawing on several sources and generating additional related, focused questions that allow for multiple avenues of exploration.	Gather relevant information from multiple print and digital sources, using search terms effectively; assess the credibility and accuracy of each source; and quote or paraphrase the data and conclusions of others while avoiding plagiarism and following a standard format for citation.	Draw evidence from literary or informational texts to support analysis, reflection, and research. a. Apply grade 8 Reading standards to literature (e.g., "Analyze how a modern work of fiction draws on themes, patterns of events, or character types from myths, traditional stories, or religious works such as the Bible, including describing how the material is rendered new"). b. Apply grade 8 Reading standards to literary nonfiction (e.g., "Delineate and evaluate the argument and specific claims in a text, assessing whether the reasoning is sound and the evidence is relevant and sufficient; recognize when irrelevant evidence is introduced").	Write routinely over extended time frames (time for research, reflection, and revision) and shorter time frames (a single sitting or a day or two) for a range of discipline-specific tasks, purposes, and audiences.

Learning Progression: Language, Common Core State Standards

Grade	Standard 1	Standard 2	Standard 3	Standard 4	Standard 5	Standard 6
Fourth	Demonstrate command of the conventions of standard English grammar and usage when writing or speaking. a. Use relative pronouns (*who, whose, whom, which, that*) and relative adverbs (*where, when, why*). b. Form and use the progressive (e.g., *I was walking; I am walking; I will be walking*) verb tenses. c. Use modal auxiliaries (e.g., *can, may, must*) to convey various conditions. d. Order adjectives within sentences according to conventional patterns (e.g., *a small red bag* rather than a *red small bag*). e. Form and use prepositional phrases. f. Produce complete sentences, recognizing and correcting inappropriate fragments and run-ons.* g. Correctly use frequently confused words (e.g., *to, too, two; there, their*).*	Demonstrate command of the conventions of standard English capitalization, punctuation, and spelling when writing. a. Use correct capitalization. b. Use commas and quotation marks to mark direct speech and quotations from a text. c. Use a comma before a coordinating conjunction in a compound sentence. d. Spell grade-appropriate words correctly, consulting references as needed.	Use knowledge of language and its conventions when writing, speaking, reading, or listening. a. Choose words and phrases to convey ideas precisely.* b. Choose punctuation for effect.* c. Differentiate between contexts that call for formal English (e.g., presenting ideas) and situations where informal discourse is appropriate (e.g., small-group discussion).	Determine or clarify the meaning of unknown and multiple-meaning words and phrases based on grade 4 reading and content, choosing flexibly from a range of strategies. a. Use context (e.g., definitions, examples, or restatements in text) as a clue to the meaning of a word or phrase. b. Use common, grade-appropriate Greek and Latin affixes and roots as clues to the meaning of a word (e.g., *telegraph, photograph, autograph*). c. Consult reference materials (e.g., dictionaries, glossaries, thesauruses), both print and digital, to find the pronunciation and determine or clarify the precise meaning of key words and phrases.	Demonstrate understanding of figurative language, word relationships, and nuances in word meanings. a. Explain the meaning of simple similes and metaphors (e.g., *as pretty as a picture*) in context. b. Recognize and explain the meaning of common idioms, adages, and proverbs. c. Demonstrate understanding of words by relating them to their opposites (antonyms) and to words with similar but not identical meanings (synonyms).	Acquire and use accurately grade-appropriate general academic and domain-specific words and phrases, including those that signal precise actions, emotions, or states of being (e.g., *quizzed, whined, stammered*) and that are basic to a particular topic (e.g., *wildlife, conservation,* and *endangered* when discussing animal preservation).

(Continued)

Grade	Standard 1	Standard 2	Standard 3	Standard 4	Standard 5	Standard 6
Fifth	Demonstrate command of the conventions of standard English grammar and usage when writing or speaking. a. Explain the function of conjunctions, prepositions, and interjections in general and their function in particular sentences. b. Form and use the perfect (e.g., *I had walked; I have walked; I will have walked*) verb tenses. c. Use verb tense to convey various times, sequences, states, and conditions. d. Recognize and correct inappropriate shifts in verb tense.* e. Use correlative conjunctions (e.g., *either/or, neither/nor*).	Demonstrate command of the conventions of standard English capitalization, punctuation, and spelling when writing. a. Use punctuation to separate items in a series.* b. Use a comma to separate an introductory element from the rest of the sentence. c. Use a comma to set off the words yes and no (e.g., *Yes, thank you*), to set off a tag question from the rest of the sentence (e.g., *It's true, isn't it?*), and to indicate direct address (e.g., *Is that you, Steve?*). d. Use underlining, quotation marks, or italics to indicate titles of works. e. Spell grade-appropriate words correctly, consulting references as needed.	Use knowledge of language and its conventions when writing, speaking, reading, or listening. a. Expand, combine, and reduce sentences for meaning, reader/listener interest, and style. b. Compare and contrast the varieties of English (e.g., dialects, registers) used in stories, dramas, or poems.	Determine or clarify the meaning of unknown and multiple-meaning words and phrases based on grade 5 reading and content, choosing flexibly from a range of strategies. a. Use context (e.g., cause/effect relationships and comparisons in text) as a clue to the meaning of a word or phrase. b. Use common, grade-appropriate Greek and Latin affixes and roots as clues to the meaning of a word (e.g., *photograph, photosynthesis*). c. Consult reference materials (e.g., dictionaries, glossaries, thesauruses), both print and digital, to find the pronunciation and determine or clarify the precise meaning of key words and phrases.	Demonstrate understanding of figurative language, word relationships, and nuances in word meanings. a. Interpret figurative language, including similes and metaphors, in context. b. Recognize and explain the meaning of common idioms, adages, and proverbs. c. Use the relationship between particular words (e.g., synonyms, antonyms, homographs) to better understand each of the words.	Acquire and use accurately grade-appropriate general academic and domain-specific words and phrases, including those that signal contrast, addition, and other logical relationships (e.g., *however, although, nevertheless, similarly, moreover, in addition*).

(Continued)

Grade	Standard 1	Standard 2	Standard 3	Standard 4	Standard 5	Standard 6
Sixth	Demonstrate command of the conventions of standard English grammar and usage when writing or speaking. a. Ensure that pronouns are in the proper case (subjective, objective, possessive). b. Use intensive pronouns (e.g., *myself, ourselves*). c. Recognize and correct inappropriate shifts in pronoun number and person.* d. Recognize and correct vague pronouns (i.e., ones with unclear or ambiguous antecedents).* e. Recognize variations from standard English in their own and others' writing and speaking, and identify and use strategies to improve expression in conventional language.*	Demonstrate command of the conventions of standard English capitalization, punctuation, and spelling when writing. a. Use punctuation (commas, parentheses, dashes) to set off nonrestrictive/parenthetical elements.* b. Spell correctly.	Use knowledge of language and its conventions when writing, speaking, reading, or listening. a. Vary sentence patterns for meaning, reader/listener interest, and style.* b. Maintain consistency in style and tone.*	Determine or clarify the meaning of unknown and multiple-meaning words and phrases based on grade 6 reading and content, choosing flexibly from a range of strategies. a. Use context (e.g., the overall meaning of a sentence or paragraph; a word's position or function in a sentence) as a clue to the meaning of a word or phrase. b. Use common, grade-appropriate Greek or Latin affixes and roots as clues to the meaning of a word (e.g., *audience, auditory, audible*). c. Consult reference materials (e.g., dictionaries, glossaries, thesauruses), both print and digital, to find the pronunciation of a word or determine or clarify its precise meaning or its part of speech. d. Verify the preliminary determination of the meaning of a word or phrase (e.g., by checking the inferred meaning in context or in a dictionary).	Demonstrate understanding of figurative language, word relationships, and nuances in word meanings. a. Interpret figures of speech (e.g., personification) in context. b. Use the relationship between particular words (e.g., *cause/effect, part/whole, item/category*) to better understand each of the words. c. Distinguish among the connotations (associations) of words with similar denotations (definitions) (e.g., *stingy, scrimping, economical, unwasteful, thrifty*).	Acquire and use accurately grade-appropriate general academic and domain-specific words and phrases; gather vocabulary knowledge when considering a word or phrase important to comprehension or expression.

(Continued)

Grade	Standard 1	Standard 2	Standard 3	Standard 4	Standard 5	Standard 6
Seventh	Demonstrate command of the conventions of standard English grammar and usage when writing or speaking. a. Explain the function of phrases and clauses in general and their function in specific sentences. b. Choose among simple, compound, complex, and compound-complex sentences to signal differing relationships among ideas. c. Place phrases and clauses within a sentence, recognizing and correcting misplaced and dangling modifiers.*	Demonstrate command of the conventions of standard English capitalization, punctuation, and spelling when writing. a. Use a comma to separate coordinate adjectives (e.g., *It was a fascinating, enjoyable movie* but not *He wore an old [,] green shirt*). b. Spell correctly.	Use knowledge of language and its conventions when writing, speaking, reading, or listening. a. Choose language that expresses ideas precisely and concisely, recognizing and eliminating wordiness and redundancy.*	Determine or clarify the meaning of unknown and multiple-meaning words and phrases based on grade 7 reading and content, choosing flexibly from a range of strategies. a. Use context (e.g., the overall meaning of a sentence or paragraph; a word's position or function in a sentence) as a clue to the meaning of a word or phrase. b. Use common, grade-appropriate Greek or Latin affixes and roots as clues to the meaning of a word (e.g., *belligerent, bellicose, rebel*). c. Consult general and specialized reference materials (e.g., dictionaries, glossaries, thesauruses), both print and digital, to find the pronunciation of a word or determine or clarify its precise meaning or its part of speech. d. Verify the preliminary determination of the meaning of a word or phrase (e.g., by checking the inferred meaning in context or in a dictionary).	Demonstrate understanding of figurative language, word relationships, and nuances in word meanings. a. Interpret figures of speech (e.g., literary, biblical, and mythological allusions) in context. b. Use the relationship between particular words (e.g., *synonym/antonym, analogy*) to better understand each of the words. c. Distinguish among the connotations (associations) of words with similar denotations (definitions) (e.g., *refined, respectful, polite, diplomatic, condescending*).	Acquire and use accurately grade-appropriate general academic and domain-specific words and phrases; gather vocabulary knowledge when considering a word or phrase important to comprehension or expression.

(Continued)

(Continued)

Grade	Standard 1	Standard 2	Standard 3	Standard 4	Standard 5	Standard 6
Eighth	Demonstrate command of the conventions of standard English grammar and usage when writing or speaking. a. Explain the function of verbals (gerunds, participles, infinitives) in general and their function in particular sentences. b. Form and use verbs in the active and passive voice. c. Form and use verbs in the indicative, imperative, interrogative, conditional, and subjunctive mood. d. Recognize and correct inappropriate shifts in verb voice and mood.*	Demonstrate command of the conventions of standard English capitalization, punctuation, and spelling when writing. a. Use punctuation (comma, ellipsis, dash) to indicate a pause or break. b. Use an ellipsis to indicate an omission. c. Spell correctly.	Use knowledge of language and its conventions when writing, speaking, reading, or listening. a. Use verbs in the active and passive voice and in the conditional and subjunctive mood to achieve particular effects (e.g., emphasizing the actor or the action; expressing uncertainty or describing a state contrary to fact).	Determine or clarify the meaning of unknown and multiple-meaning words or phrases based on grade 8 reading and content, choosing flexibly from a range of strategies. a. Use context (e.g., the overall meaning of a sentence or paragraph; a word's position or function in a sentence) as a clue to the meaning of a word or phrase. b. Use common, grade-appropriate Greek or Latin affixes and roots as clues to the meaning of a word (e.g., precede, recede, secede). c. Consult general and specialized reference materials (e.g., dictionaries, glossaries, thesauruses), both print and digital, to find the pronunciation of a word or determine or clarify its precise meaning or its part of speech. d. Verify the preliminary determination of the meaning of a word or phrase (e.g., by checking the inferred meaning in context or in a dictionary).	Demonstrate understanding of figurative language, word relationships, and nuances in word meanings. a. Interpret figures of speech (e.g., verbal irony, puns) in context. b. Use the relationship between particular words to better understand each of the words. c. Distinguish among the connotations (associations) of words with similar denotations (definitions) (e.g., bullheaded, willful, firm, persistent, resolute).	Acquire and use accurately grade-appropriate general academic and domain-specific words and phrases; gather vocabulary knowledge when considering a word or phrase important to comprehension or expression.

Source: Copyright 2010. National Governors Association Center for Best Practices and Council of Chief State School Officers. All rights reserved.

Note: Beginning in grade 3, skills and understandings that are particularly likely to require continued attention in higher grades as they are applied to increasingly sophisticated writing and speaking are marked with an asterisk (*).

Learning Progression: Speaking and Listening, Common Core State Standards

Grade	Standard 1	Standard 2	Standard 3	Standard 4	Standard 5	Standard 6
Fourth	Engage effectively in a range of collaborative discussions (one-on-one, in groups, and teacher led) with diverse partners on grade 4 topics and texts, building on others' ideas and expressing their own clearly. a. Come to discussions prepared, having read or studied required material; explicitly draw on that preparation and other information known about the topic to explore ideas under discussion. b. Follow agreed-upon rules for discussions and carry out assigned roles. c. Pose and respond to specific questions to clarify or follow up on information, and make comments that contribute to the discussion and link to the remarks of others. d. Review the key ideas expressed and explain their own ideas and understanding in light of the discussion.	Paraphrase portions of a text read aloud or information presented in diverse media and formats, including visually, quantitatively, and orally.	Identify the reasons and evidence a speaker provides to support particular points.	Report on a topic or text, tell a story, or recount an experience in an organized manner, using appropriate facts and relevant, descriptive details to support main ideas or themes; speak clearly at an understandable pace.	Add audio recordings and visual displays to presentations when appropriate to enhance the development of main ideas or themes.	Differentiate between contexts that call for formal English (e.g., presenting ideas) and situations where informal discourse is appropriate (e.g., small-group discussion); use formal English when appropriate to task and situation. (See grade 4 Language standards 1 on page 28 for specific expectations.)
Fifth	Engage effectively in a range of collaborative discussions (one-on-one, in groups, and teacher led) with diverse partners on grade 5 topics and texts, building on others' ideas and expressing their own clearly. a. Come to discussions prepared, having read or studied required material; explicitly draw on that preparation and other information known about the topic to explore ideas under discussion. b. Follow agreed-upon rules for discussions and carry out assigned roles. c. Pose and respond to specific questions by making comments that contribute to the discussion and elaborate on the remarks of others. d. Review the key ideas expressed and draw conclusions in light of information and knowledge gained from the discussions.	Summarize a written text read aloud or information presented in diverse media and formats, including visually, quantitatively, and orally.	Ask and answer questions about what a speaker says in order to clarify comprehension, gather additional information, or deepen understanding of a topic or issue.	Tell a story or recount an experience with appropriate facts and relevant, descriptive details, speaking audibly in coherent sentences.	Create audio recordings of stories or poems; add drawings or other visual displays to stories or recounts of experiences when appropriate to clarify ideas, thoughts, and feelings.	Adapt speech to a variety of contexts and tasks, using formal English when appropriate to task and situation. (See grade 5 Language standards 1 and 3 on page 28 for specific expectations.)

(Continued)

Grade	Standard 1	Standard 2	Standard 3	Standard 4	Standard 5	Standard 6
Sixth	Engage effectively in a range of collaborative discussions (one-on-one, in groups, and teacher led) with diverse partners on grade 6 topics, texts, and issues, building on others' ideas and expressing their own clearly. a. Come to discussions prepared, having read or studied required material; explicitly draw on that preparation by referring to evidence on the topic, text, or issue to probe and reflect on ideas under discussion. b. Follow rules for collegial discussions, set specific goals and deadlines, and define individual roles as needed. c. Pose and respond to specific questions with elaboration and detail by making comments that contribute to the topic, text, or issue under discussion. d. Review the key ideas expressed and demonstrate understanding of multiple perspectives through reflection and paraphrasing.	Interpret information presented in diverse media and formats (e.g., visually, quantitatively, orally) and explain how it contributes to a topic, text, or issue under study.	Delineate a speaker's argument and specific claims, distinguishing claims that are supported by reasons and evidence from claims that are not.	Present claims and findings, sequencing ideas logically and using pertinent descriptions, facts, and details to accentuate main ideas or themes; use appropriate eye contact, adequate volume, and clear pronunciation.	Include multimedia components (e.g., graphics, images, music, sound) and visual displays in presentations to clarify information.	Adapt speech to a variety of contexts and tasks, demonstrating command of formal English when indicated or appropriate. (See grade 6 Language standards 1 and 3 on page 53 for specific expectations.)
Seventh	Engage effectively in a range of collaborative discussions (one-on-one, in groups, and teacher led) with diverse partners on grade 7 topics, texts, and issues, building on others' ideas and expressing their own clearly. a. Come to discussions prepared, having read or researched material under study; explicitly draw on that preparation by referring to evidence on the topic, text, or issue to probe and reflect on ideas under discussion. b. Follow rules for collegial discussions, track progress toward specific goals and deadlines, and define individual roles as needed. c. Pose questions that elicit elaboration and respond to others' questions and comments with relevant observations and ideas that bring the discussion back on topic as needed. d. Acknowledge new information expressed by others and, when warranted, modify their own views.	Analyze the main ideas and supporting details presented in diverse media and formats (e.g., visually, quantitatively, orally) and explain how the ideas clarify a topic, text, or issue under study.	Delineate a speaker's argument and specific claims, evaluating the soundness of the reasoning and the relevance and sufficiency of the evidence.	Present claims and findings, emphasizing salient points in a focused, coherent manner with pertinent descriptions, facts, details, and examples; use appropriate eye contact, adequate volume, and clear pronunciation.	Include multimedia components and visual displays in presentations to clarify claims and findings and emphasize salient points.	Adapt speech to a variety of contexts and tasks, demonstrating command of formal English when indicated or appropriate. (See grade 7 Language standards 1 and 3 on page 53 for specific expectations.)

(Continued)

(Continued)

Grade	Standard 1	Standard 2	Standard 3	Standard 4	Standard 5	Standard 6
Eighth	Engage effectively in a range of collaborative discussions (one-on-one, in groups, and teacher led) with diverse partners on grade 8 topics, texts, and issues, building on others' ideas and expressing their own clearly. a. Come to discussions prepared, having read or researched material under study; explicitly draw on that preparation by referring to evidence on the topic, text, or issue to probe and reflect on ideas under discussion. b. Follow rules for collegial discussions and decision-making, track progress toward specific goals and deadlines, and define individual roles as needed. c. Pose questions that connect the ideas of several speakers and respond to others' questions and comments with relevant evidence, observations, and ideas. d. Acknowledge new information expressed by others, and, when warranted, qualify or justify their own views in light of the evidence presented.	Analyze the purpose of information presented in diverse media and formats (e.g., visually, quantitatively, orally) and evaluate the motives (e.g., social, commercial, political) behind its presentation.	Delineate a speaker's argument and specific claims, evaluating the soundness of the reasoning and relevance and sufficiency of the evidence and identifying when irrelevant evidence is introduced.	Present claims and findings, emphasizing salient points in a focused, coherent manner with relevant evidence, sound valid reasoning, and well-chosen details; use appropriate eye contact, adequate volume, and clear pronunciation.	Integrate multimedia and visual displays into presentations to clarify information, strengthen claims and evidence, and add interest.	Adapt speech to a variety of contexts and tasks, demonstrating command of formal English when indicated or appropriate. (See grade 8 Language standards 1 and 3 on page 53 for specific expectations.)

Reading for Literacy: History/Social Studies, Common Core State Standards

Grade	Standard 1	Standard 2	Standard 3	Standard 4	Standard 5
Sixth–Eighth	Cite specific textual evidence to support analysis of primary and secondary sources.	Determine the central ideas or information of a primary or secondary source; provide an accurate summary of the source distinct from prior knowledge or opinions.	Identify key steps in a text's description of a process related to history/social studies (e.g., how a bill becomes law, how interest rates are raised or lowered).	Determine the meaning of words and phrases as they are used in a text, including vocabulary specific to domains related to history/social studies.	Describe how a text presents information (e.g., sequentially, comparatively, causally).
Ninth–Tenth	Cite specific textual evidence to support analysis of primary and secondary sources, attending to such features as the date and origin of the information.	Determine the central ideas or information of a primary or secondary source; provide an accurate summary of how key events or ideas develop over the course of the text.	Analyze in detail a series of events described in a text; determine whether earlier events caused later ones or simply preceded them.	Determine the meaning of words and phrases as they are used in a text, including vocabulary describing political, social, or economic aspects of history/social science.	Analyze how a text uses structure to emphasize key points or advance an explanation or analysis.
Eleventh–Twelfth	Cite specific textual evidence to support analysis of primary and secondary sources, connecting insights gained from specific details to an understanding of the text as a whole.	Determine the central ideas or information of a primary or secondary source; provide an accurate summary that makes clear the relationships among the key details and ideas.	Evaluate various explanations for actions or events and determine which explanation best accords with textual evidence, acknowledging where the text leaves matters uncertain.	Determine the meaning of words and phrases as they are used in a text, including analyzing how an author uses and refines the meaning of a key term over the course of a text (e.g., how Madison defines *faction* in *Federalist* No. 10).	Analyze in detail how a complex primary source is structured, including how key sentences, paragraphs, and larger portions of the text contribute to the whole.

(Continued)

(Continued)

Grade	Standard 6	Standard 7	Standard 8	Standard 9	Standard 10
Sixth–Eighth	Identify aspects of a text that reveal an author's point of view or purpose (e.g., loaded language, inclusion or avoidance of particular facts).	Integrate visual information (e.g., in charts, graphs, photographs, videos, or maps) with other information in print and digital texts.	Distinguish among fact, opinion, and reasoned judgment in a text.	Analyze the relationship between a primary and secondary source on the same topic.	By the end of grade 8, read and comprehend history/social studies texts in the grades 6–8 text complexity band independently and proficiently.
Ninth–Tenth	Compare the point of view of two or more authors for how they treat the same or similar topics, including which details they include and emphasize in their respective accounts.	Integrate quantitative or technical analysis (e.g., charts, research data) with qualitative analysis in print or digital text.	Assess the extent to which the reasoning and evidence in a text support the author's claims.	Compare and contrast treatments of the same topic in several primary and secondary sources.	By the end of grade 10, read and comprehend history/social studies texts in the grades 9–10 text complexity band independently and proficiently.
Eleventh–Twelfth	Evaluate authors' differing points of view on the same historical event or issue by assessing the authors' claims, reasoning, and evidence.	Integrate and evaluate multiple sources of information presented in diverse formats and media (e.g., visually, quantitatively, as well as in words) in order to address a question or solve a problem.	Evaluate an author's premises, claims, and evidence by corroborating or challenging them with other information.	Integrate information from diverse sources, both primary and secondary, into a coherent understanding of an idea or event, noting discrepancies among sources.	By the end of grade 12, read and comprehend history/social studies texts in the grades 11–CCR text complexity band independently and proficiently.

Reading for Literacy: Science and Technical Subjects, Common Core State Standards

Grade	Standard 1	Standard 2	Standard 3	Standard 4	Standard 5
Sixth–Eighth	Cite specific textual evidence to support analysis of science and technical texts.	Determine the central ideas or conclusions of a text; provide an accurate summary of the text distinct from prior knowledge or opinions.	Follow precisely a multistep procedure when carrying out experiments, taking measurements, or performing technical tasks.	Determine the meaning of symbols, key terms, and other domain-specific words and phrases as they are used in a specific scientific or technical context relevant to *grades 6–8 texts and topics*.	Analyze the structure an author uses to organize a text, including how the major sections contribute to the whole and to an understanding of the topic.
Ninth–Tenth	Cite specific textual evidence to support analysis of science and technical texts, attending to the precise details of explanations or descriptions.	Determine the central ideas or conclusions of a text; trace the text's explanation or depiction of a complex process, phenomenon, or concept; provide an accurate summary of the text.	Follow precisely a complex multistep procedure when carrying out experiments, taking measurements, or performing technical tasks, attending to special cases or exceptions defined in the text.	Determine the meaning of symbols, key terms, and other domain-specific words and phrases as they are used in a specific scientific or technical context relevant to *grades 9–10 texts and topics*.	Analyze the structure of the relationships among concepts in a text, including relationships among key terms (e.g., *force, friction, reaction force, energy*).
Eleventh–Twelfth	Cite specific textual evidence to support analysis of science and technical texts, attending to important distinctions the author makes and to any gaps or inconsistencies in the account.	Determine the central ideas or conclusions of a text; summarize complex concepts, processes, or information presented in a text by paraphrasing them in simpler but still accurate terms.	Follow precisely a complex multistep procedure when carrying out experiments, taking measurements, or performing technical tasks; analyze the specific results based on explanations in the text.	Determine the meaning of symbols, key terms, and other domain-specific words and phrases as they are used in a specific scientific or technical context relevant to *grades 11–12 texts and topics*.	Analyze how the text structures information or ideas into categories or hierarchies, demonstrating understanding of the information or ideas.

(Continued)

(Continued)

Grade	Standard 6	Standard 7	Standard 8	Standard 9	Standard 10
Sixth– Eighth	Analyze the author's purpose in providing an explanation, describing a procedure, or discussing an experiment in a text.	Integrate quantitative or technical information expressed in words in a text with a version of that information expressed visually (e.g., in a flowchart, diagram, model, graph, or table).	Distinguish among facts, reasoned judgment based on research findings, and speculation in a text.	Compare and contrast the information gained from experiments, simulations, video, or multimedia sources with that gained from reading a text on the same topic.	By the end of grade 8, read and comprehend science/technical texts in the grades 6–8 text complexity band independently and proficiently.
Ninth– Tenth	Analyze the author's purpose in providing an explanation, describing a procedure, or discussing an experiment in a text, defining the question the author seeks to address.	Translate quantitative or technical information expressed in words in a text into visual form (e.g., a table or chart) and translate information expressed visually or mathematically (e.g., in an equation) into words.	Assess the extent to which the reasoning and evidence in a text support the author's claim or a recommendation for solving a scientific or technical problem.	Compare and contrast findings presented in a text to those from other sources (including their own experiments), noting when the findings support or contradict previous explanations or accounts.	By the end of grade 10, read and comprehend science/technical texts in the grades 9–10 text complexity band independently and proficiently.
Eleventh– Twelfth	Analyze the author's purpose in providing an explanation, describing a procedure, or discussing an experiment in a text, identifying important issues that remain unresolved.	Integrate and evaluate multiple sources of information presented in diverse formats and media (e.g., quantitative data, video, multimedia) in order to address a question or solve a problem.	Evaluate the hypotheses, data, analysis, and conclusions in a science or technical text, verifying the data when possible and corroborating or challenging conclusions with other sources of information.	Synthesize information from a range of sources (e.g., texts, experiments, simulations) into a coherent understanding of a process, phenomenon, or concept, resolving conflicting information when possible.	By the end of grade 12, read and comprehend science/technical texts in the grades 11–CCR text complexity band independently and proficiently.

Writing for Literacy: History/Social Studies, Science, and Technical Subjects, Common Core State Standards, Grades 6–8

Grade	Standard 1	Standard 2	Standard 4	Standard 5
Sixth–Eighth	Write arguments focused on *discipline-specific content.* 1a. Introduce claim(s) about a topic or issue, acknowledge and distinguish the claim(s) from alternate or opposing claims, and organize the reasons and evidence logically. 1b. Support claim(s) with logical reasoning and relevant, accurate data and evidence that demonstrate an understanding of the topic or text, using credible sources. 1c. Use words, phrases, and clauses to create cohesion and clarify the relationships among claim(s), counterclaims, reasons, and evidence. 1d. Establish and maintain a formal style. 1e. Provide a concluding statement or section that follows from and supports the argument presented.	Write informative/explanatory texts, including the narration of historical events, scientific procedures/experiments, or technical processes. 2a. Introduce a topic clearly, previewing what is to follow; organize ideas, concepts, and information into broader categories as appropriate to achieving purpose; include formatting (e.g., headings), graphics (e.g., charts, tables), and multimedia when useful to aiding comprehension. 2b. Develop the topic with relevant, well-chosen facts, definitions, concrete details, quotations, or other information and examples. 2c. Use appropriate and varied transitions to create cohesion and clarify the relationships among ideas and concepts. 2d. Use precise language and domain-specific vocabulary to inform about or explain the topic. 2e. Establish and maintain a formal style and objective tone. 2f. Provide a concluding statement or section that follows from and supports the information or explanation presented.	Produce clear and coherent writing in which the development, organization, and style are appropriate to task, purpose, and audience.	With some guidance and support from peers and adults, develop and strengthen writing as needed by planning, revising, editing, rewriting, or trying a new approach, focusing on how well purpose and audience have been addressed.

(Continued)

(Continued)

	Standard 6	Standard 7	Standard 8	Standard 9	Standard 10
Sixth–Eighth	Use technology, including the Internet, to produce and publish writing and present the relationships between information and ideas clearly and efficiently.	Conduct short research projects to answer a question (including a self-generated question), drawing on several sources and generating additional related, focused questions that allow for multiple avenues of exploration and efficiently.	Gather relevant information from multiple print and digital sources, using search terms effectively; assess the credibility and accuracy of each source; and quote or paraphrase the data and conclusions of others while avoiding plagiarism and following a standard format for citation.	Draw evidence from informational texts to support analysis reflection, and research.	Write routinely over extended time frames (time for reflection and revision) and shorter time frames (a single sitting or a day or two) for a range of discipline-specific tasks, purposes, and audiences.

Source: Copyright 2010. National Governors Association Center for Best Practices and Council of Chief State School Officers. All rights reserved.

PART III

The Lessons and Texts

In Part II, we considered the Daily Duo, a framework that helps you integrate reading and writing into your teaching in a way that helps students engage deeply with ideas and information. In Chapters 5, 6, and 7, I referred to lessons that can help you in this quest. And here they are! Please see the Contents for a list of lesson titles.

Part III has four sections that cover key strategies. Whether you want to show your students how recognizing text structure can aid reading and writing (see "Lessons for Getting Main Idea by Understanding Text Structures" on page 110), improve their abilities to read for main ideas and details (see "Prereading and Think-Aloud Lessons for Main Idea and Details" on page 131, "Lessons That Support Students While Reading for Main Idea and Details" on page 145, and "After-Reading Engagements: Exploring the Main Ideas and Details in Texts" on page 164), help them summarize (see "Summarizing to Comprehend" on page 174), or help them tackle specific discipline or content-area vocabulary (see "Understanding Key Vocabulary" on page 207 and "Writing About Reading" on page 224), Part III is your go-to lesson vault. I want to give a special callout here to the final section, which showcases writing about reading, the gold standard we strive toward in developing readers with 21st century skills: critical thinking, communication, and creativity.

Here and there you'll come across my mantra, "Avoid round-robin reading!" When you see it, know that I want you to focus students on actually reading, *for*

*themselve*s, and not reading aloud for the class to hear the mistakes or pauses they make, or for another student to jump in and tell them a word. This is just stressful and embarrassing for students, and it doesn't further their ability to read well.

As you delve into the lessons, keep in mind that they are designed to help you pick up and teach. Each lesson outlines a focus, an objective, and steps, and will give you the background to understand the *why* behind the teaching. Each lesson is laid out in the same easy-to-follow format to help you focus on just the essence of the lesson and think about using it with your students. You can use the lessons by keeping the book close to you and follow it as you go, or you can glance through it, gleaning the ideas you need and crafting lessons on your own. Either way, you can make the lessons work for you.

The Texts to Support the Lessons

In the Appendix, you will find a variety of texts and articles for use with your students. There are 17 in all. Some are short and others long; some are written for younger students and others for older students. To help you as you teach the lessons, choose the articles that work for your students. Of course, once they learn the strategies, the idea is for you to choose the texts and articles that you normally use in your classroom, but the 17 texts available here can help you build that foundation.

Lessons for Getting Main Idea by Understanding Text Structures

Getting the main idea is the beginning of all real-world things a student can do with real-world text. I've been teaching main idea for years and years, and of course it's one of many attributes of good reading we want our students to master. When you think about it, if a reader gets the main idea of a text, the reader is prepped to analyze, evaluate, and respond to the piece. So in that sense, finding nonfiction's main idea might be the most important skill to teach. The thing is, it takes a whole lot of modeling and a whole lot of practice for readers to mine a piece of text for main idea with expertise.

In this section, I share four lessons and some shortcuts and secrets for helping students understand main idea. One secret: Discovering main idea is all about understanding text structures, and understanding text structures is all about understanding relationships. For students to get the main idea of nonfiction articles and texts, they need to understand the facts and information presented, *and* the relationships among the facts and information, because often the author's main idea is located in these relationships. As the *structures* that hold the information together, these relationships arrange information so that ideas become evident.

Good readers knit facts, information, and ideas into a whole understanding; weaker readers tend to tune in just to literal facts and information and struggle to see the relationships that create or enhance an author's main ideas. Authors use text structures on which to hang these relationships; at the end of this chapter you will find an explanation of the different text structures, including an example and a visual for each.

As you delve into the lessons, please note:

- Among the multitude of ways to teach text structure, these lessons are provided just to get you started.
- The last lesson in the chapter can be used over and over again as you teach the various text structures.
- Modify the lessons and examples with your own articles or texts.

Three Pieces of Advice From Me to You

As you delve into the lessons, keep these points in mind:

1. **Make the lessons your own.** The lessons are thorough enough for you to pick up and teach as is, but by all means, feel free to change them and do what works best for your objectives and your students.

2. **Teach for independence.** As you put the lessons into play, focus on *students doing* and not *teacher doing*. Set an egg timer, your iPhone alarm—whatever it takes to make sure you wrap up a demonstration on the spot if it exceeds 15 minutes. Really! Students learn by doing. Check out Part II, "The Daily Duo" (Chapter 5, page 50) for a refresher on planning lessons if needed.

3. **Experiment with different articles.** Use the articles in the Appendix to teach the lessons, but then roam! A lot of great articles are available online, in newspapers, and in magazines in bookstores—get in the habit of finding, filing, and using them. Remember, too, that you can do potent mini-lessons (under 5 minutes), for example reading aloud or projecting just a very small portion of the piece.

As you jump in and teach, remember to have fun!

Survey the Text

When to Use: When prepping to read. One suggestion is to use this as a lesson for Daily Duo Step 1, *Preparing to Read* (see Chapter 5, page 52).

Pressley (2002) suggests this activity as a way for students to get a sense of what they are going to read about, to determine a purpose for reading, and to identify important sections of the text based on their purpose for reading.

Lesson Objective: Read, examine, and think about the features of a text to set a purpose for reading and try to glean the main idea.

Materials Needed: A copy of the text you have chosen to use for the lesson (it needs to have an introduction, a conclusion, headings, and a couple of text features, e.g., graphs, tables, or pictures); or a projector to project the model text, chart paper and markers, and if you choose a chart created from one of the graphic organizers at the end of the chapter.

Grouping: Whole class.

Time: 15 minutes.

STEP 1. Pose Guiding Questions

Pose two or three guiding questions to the class to pique students' interest and get them thinking about why they are going to read; the questions for this sample lesson come from Neufeld (2005). The questions give students a reason for surveying the text, and hint at what to look for as they survey.

- What does this text appear to be about?
- What are some of the important topics/ideas covered in the text?
- How is the text organized?

To get the class started with the survey strategy, you might say,

"Good readers tend to look over a text before they read it to put their mind around what they are going to read and put their attention on the topic. This is called *surveying the text.* When you survey something, you are doing an assessment of it; we also call this an appraisal. People do surveys for all sorts of reasons, but mostly they are trying to gather information that will help them understand something. I am going to teach you to do a survey of a text before you read it."

Then show the students the text you have chosen to use for a model. Make sure it has headings and at least one other text feature, such as a table or graph.

STEP 2. Read the Title and Major Headings

Model for students how readers orient themselves to a text. You might say something like this:

"Now that we have some questions to think about and answer, let's start our survey. First, we are going to read the title and the major headings together.
    "Let's read together. What do you think the text is going to be about, based on the title and headings?"

Lead a brief discussion on this topic, making sure that the students do the talking, not you. Remember, you are working on the students' thinking and talking skills!

STEP 3. Read Only the Introduction and Conclusion

After getting students started with surveying the text by having them read and think about the title and headings, it is time to jump into reading part of the text. Say,

> "We are going to keep surveying the text—this time by reading part of it. We are going to read the first paragraph—the introduction—together. While we are reading, I want you to think about the questions we asked to get us started. What might the text be about? And what might some of the important topics be in the text?"

Once you have read the introduction together, lead a brief discussion about the first paragraph to see what students are thinking. Make notes of their remarks on a chart so you can come to consensus about what the text is about, and possible important topics. To do this, write down ideas the class suggests, and then discuss the group's thinking and decide what the beginning of the text is about. Writing these ideas down is important because it makes the conversation visual and also records the thoughts of students—this keeps the responsibility on them for both the conversation and the thinking. After you read and discuss the introduction, *repeat this step* by reading the conclusion.

Once you have read the introduction and the conclusion together, lead the class in thinking about the organization of the text. You might get across the idea that authors often reveal their most important ideas and purposes in the opening and closing, which is why these two sections are great to survey ahead of reading. Then move on to how the introduction and conclusion often provide clues to the text structure. Say,

See the next lesson, *Use Format Cues*, for a description of each type of text structure. Also see Chapter 4 (page 42).

> "Let's look at our third question: How is the text organized? This question addresses the text organization. The text organization refers to how the text is written. Ways to organize the text can include cause and effect, compare and contrast, descriptive, problem-solution, and sequence. *[Make notes of their remarks on a projection of the graphic organizer you choose; it is important to use the one that corresponds to the structure of the text you selected. The graphic organizers appear at the end of the chapter.]* Let's look for clues in the introduction and the conclusion that might give us an idea of the text organization."

Help the class identify the possible text organization from the introduction and conclusion.

STEP 4. Examine Text Features

The final step in surveying the text is for students to examine the text features for other details about the text topic. The text features can also give you a clue about how the text might be organized. Lead the students through the text, checking the text features and adding to their thoughts on the chart.

STEP 5. Make Conclusions and Decide on a Purpose for Reading

After you finish surveying the text with the class, return to that chart where you have been recording your students' thinking. Now it is time for the students to land on answers to the three questions posed at the beginning of the lesson. You can wrap up the lesson by posing a purpose for reading, and then read the entire text to or with the class.

Use Format Cues

When to Use: Right before students' independent reading of nonfiction articles.

This mini-lesson reinforces the previous lesson on surveying a text and gets students ready to independently read a nonfiction text.

Lesson Objective: Examine headings, subheadings, and paragraphs to figure out text structure.

Materials Needed: Copies of articles that interest students (they need to have at least one heading and subheadings).

Grouping: Individual or small group.

Time: 5–10 minutes.

STEP 1. Direct Students' Attention to Text Cues

At the beginning of the mini-lesson, cue students into what they will work on while reading, and remind them to use text cues to figure out the text. Say,

> "While you are reading today, I want to use a couple of strategies to help you figure out what the text is about. You can use these strategies before you read, and again while you are reading. First, look at the important headings for cues about the structure of the text; if you know the structure of the text [refer to something you have taught before on text structure], you can understand what you are reading better. Then, check out the subheadings and see if there are more clues to the text structure. I find it really helps me to read the major headings and the subheading together. This gives me a clue about the text structure, and then I have an idea about what I might read."

Model reading headings and subheadings and making a guess about the text structure.

STEP 2. Notice Format Cues in Paragraphs

Continue the mini-lesson by talking students through checking their hypothesis, or guess, about the text structure by checking the paragraphs for text structure. You might say,

> "So, we've made a hypothesis, an educated guess, about what we think the text structure is. Let's skim the first and second paragraphs to see if we are correct."

Model skimming the paragraphs, pointing out the sentences that indicate the type of text structure in place. Here are some clues:

Cause and Effect: First the cause is presented and discussed, and then the effect.

Chronology: Events are organized by time.

Compare and Contrast: Two or more ideas are discussed, with details showing how they are the same and different.

Definition and Illustration: A word or term is given, and information illustrating the concept of the word or term follows.

Descriptive: Information is given with descriptive details, beginning with general facts and moving to specific details. Can include **List**, **Matrix**, and **Web**.

Narrative Informational: Information is presented through elements of fiction: characters, setting, and plot.

Problem-Solution: A problem is presented in the text; the solution usually appears later in the text, after the problem is fully fleshed out.

Question-and-Answer: Author asks a question, then answers it. Sometimes the answer can easily be found in the text word for word. This text structure is common in science books.

Sequence: Information is provided in lists.

String: Steps in a process are discussed, often with details.

STEP 3. Encourage Students as They Work!

As you circulate, coaching and guiding your students, watch for a few pitfalls:

- Students get stuck and stop working. Remind them to check the headings and see if they can figure out the structure of the text. Refer them to a teacher-made chart outlining different text structures. Refer to Chapter 4 for text structures, and make a chart as needed to remind your students of the text structure types and attributes. You can also use the graphic organizers at the end of that chapter to help you in making a chart.
- Students race through the article without really reading. Remind them that reading practice helps them become better readers. Perhaps carry on a short conversation about the text they are reading to help motivate them.
- If students are working in groups, some students do the work, and others just sit. Remind students of your class guidelines about group work, and check in with any disengaged students to see what the problem is. Then remind the group how to work together.

Use Concept Maps for Problem-Solution Pieces

When to Use: When reading a problem-solution structured section; great for textbooks.

A concept map is a visual representation of the text organization. Problem-solution is described in Chapter 4 (page 42), and the *Problem-Solution Graphic Organizer* appears at the end of this chapter. Armbruster, Anderson and Meyer (1991) laid the groundwork for this thinking strategy to help students better comprehend what they read. These authors developed organization frames to help students recognize the text structure and then begin to summarize the text. This lesson focuses on problem-solution text structure using a textbook.

Lesson Objective: Create a visual representation of the organization of ideas in a text.

Materials Needed: An identified textbook section in a social studies or science textbook that discusses a problem and solution; a chart made from an enlarged printout of the textbook page or projector to project the textbook page.

Grouping: Whole class.

Time: 15 minutes to teach the Five Questions Frame; an additional 15 minutes for students to read and respond using the frame.

STEP 1. Introduce the Reason for Using the Textbook

Direct your students to the page or section in the textbook you want them to pay attention to during the lesson. Explain that textbooks often discuss lots of problems and solutions, and learning to see this text structure in a textbook will help them when they need to read a textbook chapter or section.

STEP 2. Introduce the Five Questions Associated With a Problem-Solution Text Structure

Convey to students that problem-solution texts often provide information, which can be understood by asking five simple questions (Armbruster, Anderson, & Ostertag, 1987):

Five Questions Frame

1. Who has a problem?

2. What is the problem?

3. What actions were taken to try and solve the problem?

4. What were the results of those actions?

5. Did any of the results solve the problem?

Discuss the questions with the class, read the text, and see if the text can answer any of the questions. Chart or record the students' answers.

STEP 3. Fill in the Frame

Demonstrate how to record the answers to the questions in the Five Questions Frame. To create a frame, draw a T-chart on a large piece of paper or on the board, and number the frame with the five questions. Help students see the progression in the frame from the problem, including its parts (who, what, how), to the solution (what, why). Fill in the Five Questions frame together as a class.

STEP 4. Give It a Go

Direct students to another section of the textbook. Have them work individually or in pairs to identify answers to the five questions and fill in the frame in their notebooks while reading the new section. Students can first read silently, then confer with one another about the questions and possible answers, and finally create a frame representing the problem-solution together. They can record the frame in notebooks or on a small chart (see an example in *Student-Created Frame for Problem-Solution*).

Elizabeth I

Problem	Solution
1. Anne Boleyn did not have heir to the throne.	1. Henry VIII (Anne Boleyn's husband) killed and beheaded her so he could later have a new wife with heir to the throne.
2. Mary I suspected that Elizabeth attempted treason.	Elizabeth was imprisoned in the Tower of London.
3. Elizabeth saw Mary, Queen of Scots as a threat.	She had Mary, Queen of Scots imprisoned, then executed.

Student-Created Frame for
Problem-Solution

Recognize Many Text Structures

When to Use: When you want to develop students' knowledge about text structures so they can quickly and independently recognize those they come across in their reading.

This lesson is actually a *list* of text structures that you can teach to help your students understand the existing types. I recommend that you use the suggested lesson format and then teach each text structure at a different time rather than all in one lesson. This lesson format focuses on *guided discovery*. Like guided practice in that the students work under the watchful eye and guidance of the teacher, guided discovery involves letting the students have a go at the work on their own, instead of breaking the learning down into steps. Guided discovery focuses on the students figuring out the text structure on their own as they work in groups to outline the text. In essence, the students conduct a text search to decide on the structure of a reading.

Lesson Objective: Learn and examine text structures and recognize text structures in articles, online reading, and textbooks.

Materials Needed: A copy of the article you have chosen to model the lesson, plus copies of additional articles for student practice; a chart created from an enlarged copy of the text or projector to project the model article.

Grouping: Whole class.

Time: 20 minutes.

STEP 1. Introduce the Text Structure (see Chapter 4, page 42, as well as the lesson *Use Format Cues* earlier in this chapter)

When you introduce each text structure, explain it and then show a diagram of the structure. This helps students "see" the structures while they think about the characteristics of each type. Graphic organizers showing the possible diagrams are listed at the end of this section, on pages 120–130.

STEP 2. Give Examples of the Text Structure

After talking about the characteristics of the text structure with students, show them what you mean with a real-world example. Do a think-aloud about the text structure in the book, article, or other text you are presenting and then fill in a graphic organizer to show them the design of the text. It also helps to teach students words that signal text structure:

> **Cause and Effect:** *as a result of, because, the cause, consequently, due to, for this reason, on account of, since, the outcome is, then . . . so, therefore, this leads to. Cause and Effect Graphic Organizers 1 and 2* at the end of the section are two ways of visualizing the organization of cause and effect.

> **Classification:** *categories, class, classifications, elements, features, groups, kinds, methods, types, varieties, ways.* The *Matrix Graphic Organizer* is one way of visualizing classification.

> **Compare and Contrast:** *as . . . as, as opposed to, compared to, either . . . or, in contrast to, instead of, less, more, on the other hand, rather than, similar to, similarly, unlike.* The *Compare and Contrast Graphic Organizer* is one way of visualizing classification.

Definition and Illustration: *define as, is stated as, is used to mean, known as, the term means; for example, for instance, specifically, such as, to illustrate.* The *Definition and Illustration Graphic Organizer* is one way of visualizing words/terms, definitions, and descriptions of concepts.

List: *also, and, as well as, besides, in addition, furthermore, moreover, or, plus, too.* The *List Graphic Organizer* is one way of visualizing list organization.

Order of Importance: *central, chief, principal, main, major, primary, significant; ending with, finally, finishing with, lastly, least.* The *Hierarchy Graphic Organizer* is one way of organizing order of importance.

Problem-Solution: *challenge, difficulty, dilemma, issue, need, problem; answer, improve, indicate, plan, propose, resolve, respond, solve, suggest.* The *Problem–Solution Graphic Organizer* is one way of visualizing problem-solution.

Question and Answer: *answer, estimate, how, it could be that, perhaps, question, solution, what, when, where, who, why.* The *Question and Answer Graphic Organizer* is one way of visualizing questions and answers.

Time Order: *after, at, before, during, finally, first (second, third, etc.), next, on, then, until, while.* The *Sequence Graphic Organizer* is one way of visualizing time order.

STEP 3. Have Students Discover Text Structure in Their Reading

Organize students into groups and have them examine an article or text to figure out the text structure. Student groups can create a chart of the text structure (see *Student-Made Chart on Text Structure* for an example). The students can also present their charts to one another, being careful to explain the text structure they decided was in the text and justify their ideas by pointing out parts of the book that back up their thinking.

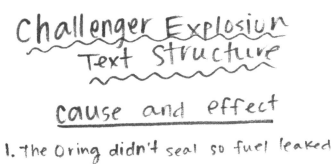

Challenger Explosion Text Structure

cause and effect

1. The O ring didn't seal so fuel leaked out.

2. They were neglient with safety and design so it blew up.

3. The explosion happened so Nasa had decreased funding and public disappointment.

Student-Made Chart on Text Structure

Cause and Effect Structure for a Chronological Event

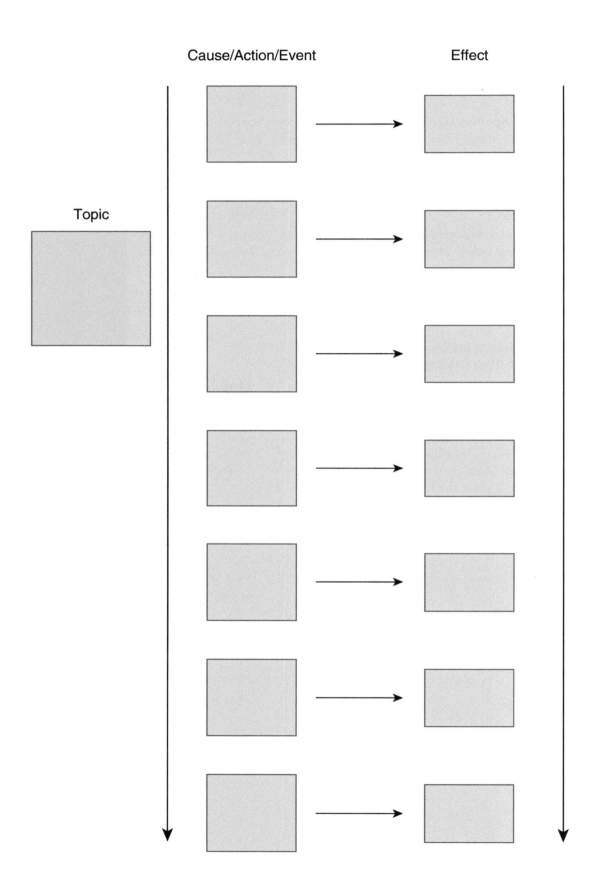

Cause/Action/Event

Effect

Topic

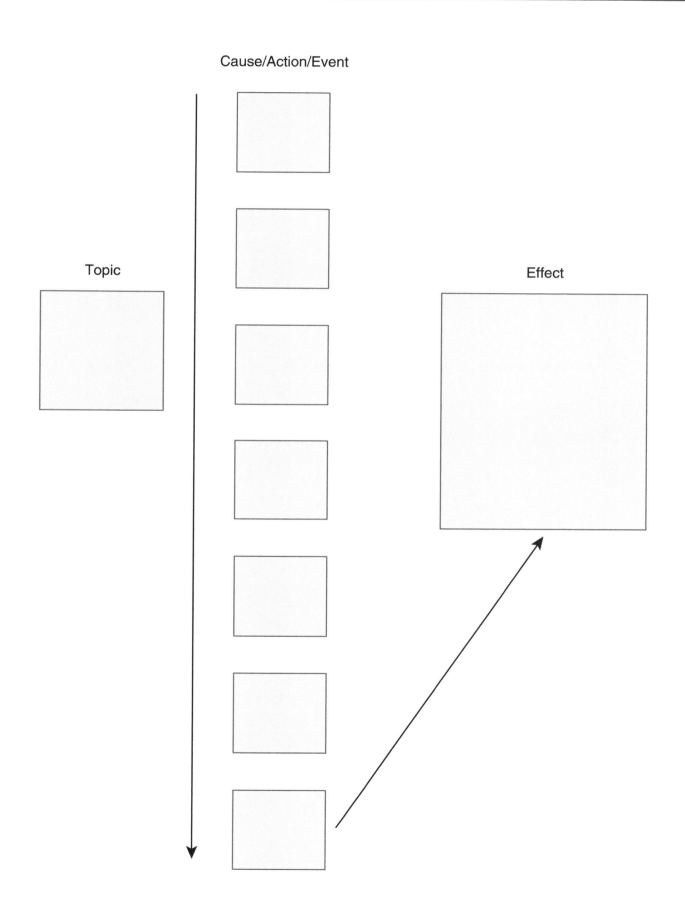

Cause/Action/Event

Topic

Effect

Matrix Graphic Organizer

Attributes → Item/Thing/Subject →				

Compare and Contrast Graphic Organizer

Same   **Different**

$$\longleftrightarrow$$

$$\longleftrightarrow$$

$$\longleftrightarrow$$

$$\longleftrightarrow$$

$$\longleftrightarrow$$

$$\longleftrightarrow$$

Definition and Illustration Graphic Organizer

Definition

=

Illustration

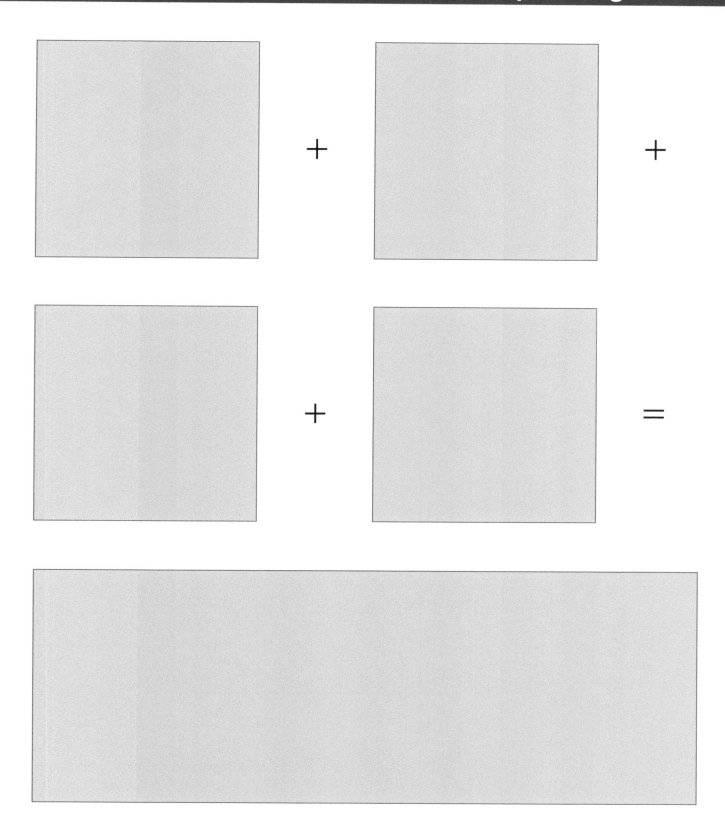

Problem		Solution
1.	→	1.
2.	→	2.
3.	→	3.

Question and Answer Graphic Organizer

Question	Answer
1.	1.
2.	2.
3.	3.
4.	4.
5.	5.

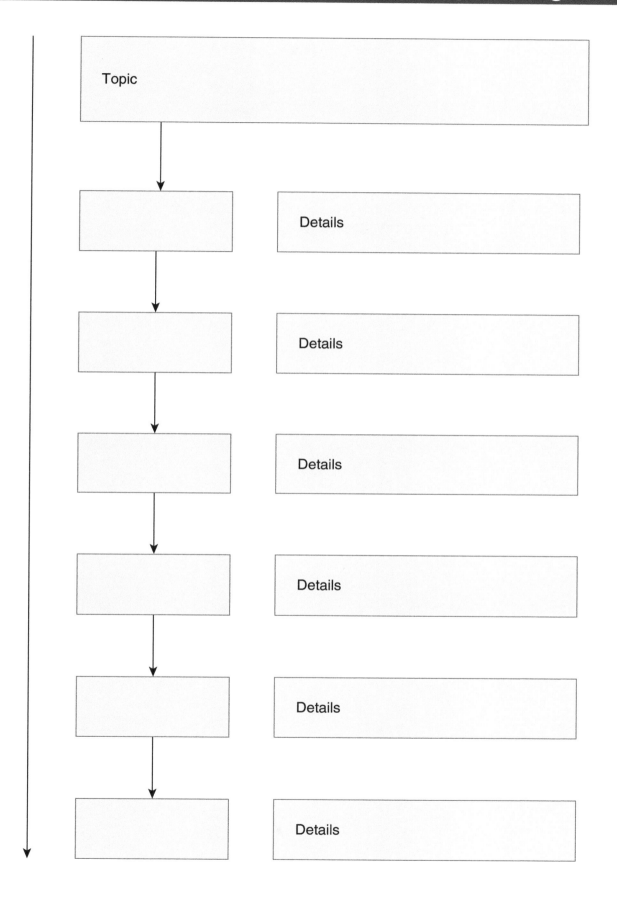

Topic

Details

Details

Details

Details

Details

Details

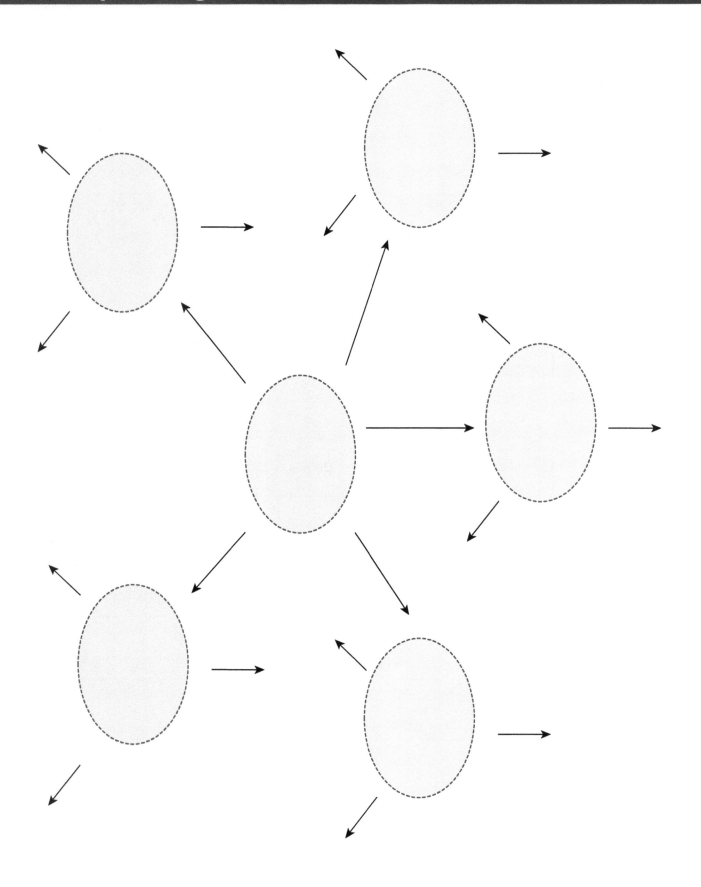

Prereading and Think-Aloud Lessons for Main Idea and Details

This section includes lessons on helping students prepare for reading (check the first step of the Daily Duo, *Preparing to Read*, in Chapter 5, page 52) by activating their thinking about what they know and might want to know about a topic, as well as the strategies they use as readers. When your students move from prereading to reading, the think-aloud lessons in this section will work well for Daily Duo Step 2, *Reading*; perhaps Step 3, *Noticing*; and Step 4, *Taking Notes* (see Chapter 5, pages 53–54). There is no hierarchical order to the lessons, and different lessons may work for your students at different times.

Three Pieces of Advice From Me to You

As you delve into the lessons, keep these points in mind:

1. **Make the lessons your own.** The lessons are thorough enough for you to pick up and teach as is, but by all means, feel free to change them and do what works best for your objectives and your students.

2. **Teach for independence.** As you put the lessons into play, focus on *students doing* and not *teacher doing*. Set an egg timer, your iPhone alarm—whatever it takes to make sure you wrap up a demonstration on the spot if it exceeds 15 minutes. Really! Students learn by doing.

3. **Experiment with different articles.** Use the articles in the Appendix to teach the lessons, but then roam! A lot of great articles are available online, in newspapers, and in magazines in bookstores—get in the habit of finding, filing, and using them. Remember, too, that you can do potent mini-lessons (under 5 minutes), for example reading aloud or projecting just a very small portion of the piece.

As you jump in and teach, remember to have fun!

Annotating Text

When to Use: When students are ready to read with a partner or independently. You can use this lesson with Daily Duo Step 2, *Reading,* and Daily Duo Step 3, *Noticing.*

Teaching students to mark up the text and make notes in the margins is a great way to ensure their comprehension, but annotating text can go far beyond comprehension to help students prepare to write about a text. When students summarize an article, they need to state clearly what the article is about, and they need notes to refer back to for help with writing. Few good writers write from thin air; most great writers use notes to help them formulate ideas. Summary writing is no exception just because it is short. Sometimes the shortest writing is the hardest writing to do!

Lesson Objective: Brainstorm symbols and markings to annotate text and use the annotations while reading.

Materials Needed: A copy of the article you have chosen for each student; a chart or projector to record notes and ideas; highlighters and pens.

Grouping: Whole class.

Time: 15–20 minutes depending on the length of the article.

STEP 1. Prepare

The first step involves brainstorming with students to create an annotation key or guide (see *Annotation Sample* for an example of a class-brainstormed annotation key). Say,

> "Today I want you to put your thinking caps on. We are going to create a 'key' to help us read this article. This key will be the markings we use to take notes on what we are reading. Good readers often annotate the text they are reading. That is what we are going to do, but first we are going to think about the notes we might take to help us think about the text while we are reading. Let me show you what I mean. *[With an image of the article projected, find a sentence in the article you think is important, underline the sentence, and then put an exclamation point (!) in the margin of the article next to where you underlined the sentence.]* See this sentence? I think it is really important in this article. Let me read it to you and tell you why. *[Go ahead and share your thinking.]* Now, I underlined the sentence so I can find it easily when I go back and review the article, and I also wrote an exclamation point in the margin right by it. I used the exclamation point because I think the sentence is important and the exclamation point reminds me of exciting or important things. Now, let's brainstorm a few symbols, or markings, we could use to help us mark up the text while we are reading."

Brainstorm markings with the class that the students can use to annotate the text. They can choose symbols that matter to them; the exact markings really don't matter, as long as they make sense to your class. The key idea is for the students to come up with things they might think of or notice while reading and associate that thinking with a symbol. Their ideas or thoughts might include "I'm stuck," "I don't understand," "This is important," "This is a key detail," "This is the main idea," and so on, and common symbols and markings to represent this thinking might include these:

- Question marks (?)
- Asterisks (*)
- Pound signs (#)
- At signs (@)
- Stars (☆)
- Happy faces (☺)
- Sad faces (☹)
- Text typing abbreviations, like *IDK* (for "I don't know")

STEP 2. Read the Article and Annotate the Text

Once the class comes up with a key for the annotations they will use, have students read the text and annotate in the margins. They can read independently or with a partner.

STEP 3. Debrief

After the class finishes reading, go back through the article and engage the students in a lively discussion about what symbols they used, as well as why and where in the article they used them. I encourage you to have a lively discussion! Let the students talk. This is not time for you to do a think-aloud. The power lies in students sharing their insights, the trouble spots in the reading, and even the sweet spots (the ideas or information in the text that they loved or connected with).

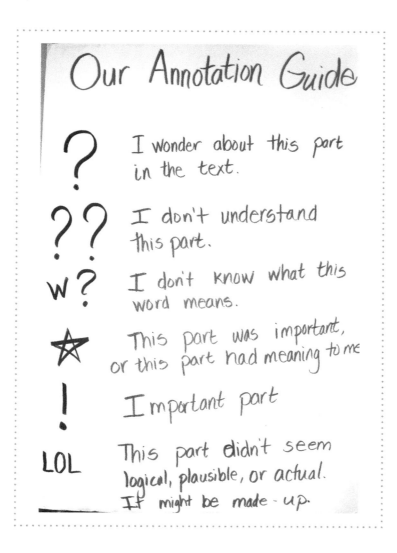

List, Group, Label

When to Use: When you want to tap prior knowledge before reading. You can use this lesson with Daily Duo Step 1, *Preparing to Read.*

This lesson is a prereading activity, to be taught before students read an article. Based on a technique called List, Group, Label, or LGL, developed by Taba way back in 1967, it is a still a great activity to do with students (Blachowicz & Fisher, 2002)!

Lesson Objective: Prepare for reading by thinking about prior knowledge.

The List, Group, Label method was originally designed only to introduce new vocabulary (we will revisit this method in the "Understanding Key Vocabulary" section of Part III); however, it works very well to help students focus on their relative background knowledge. We want students to remember and recognize what they know, or don't know, about the subject of a reading so they can focus on what they read and not tune out! LGL helps students recognize main ideas and details because it helps them "get" what they are reading.

Materials Needed: A copy of the article you have chosen for each student; a chart or projector to record notes and ideas. You can use the *List, Group, Label Graphic Organizer* provided at the end of this lesson, or have students use the organizer for independent work as a follow-up to this lesson.

Grouping: Whole class broken down into small work groups for discussion.

Time: 30 minutes.

STEP 1. List

Select a one- or two-word topic from the article the class is going to read. Write this topic on the board, chart, or projector. Give a short description of the topic you wrote down. Don't refer to the article, yet.

STEP 2. Get Students' Brain Muscles Working

Break students into smaller work groups. Working in groups, have the students brainstorm words or phrases related to the topic on the board and record their brainstorming on small-sized chart paper. Encourage all students to respond by using a sharing protocol. To implement, instruct students to share ideas one at a time, going around the group once before allowing anyone to share a second idea. Encourage students to brainstorm at least 20 things about the topic.

STEP 3. Group

With students working in the same small group, have them group their words into smaller categories. The students are responsible for coming up with the categories and choosing how to organize the words. They can have an "other" category for words that don't fit.

STEP 4. Label

Once students finish organizing their words, have them write labels for each category. It helps to have the students recopy the words with the labels on a fresh piece of paper.

STEP 5. Share

Working in groups, with one student designated as speaker, have the students justify their word and idea groupings and the labels they chose to describe the categories.

STEP 6. Read the Article

Distribute the article and have the students read it in groups. After they have read the article, in the same groups, have them add new words or phrases to their brainstorm categories.

STEP 7. Students Discuss What Details They Added to Their Charts

Using the student-created charts, have one student from each group share orally with the whole class what words and labels were added to the chart after they read the article.

List, Group, Label Graphic Organizer

NAME: _____   DATE: _____

List words in
this column.

Group similar words
together.

Label each group of
words. The label should
describe the grouping.

_____

_____

_____

_____

ABC Brainstorming

When to Use: When you want to develop student interest in the topic of an article or text. You can use this lesson with Daily Duo Step 1, *Preparing to Read.*

Tapping prior knowledge is a way of waking up students' brains to get their thinking juices flowing, and to prepare them to notice and retain new information. When you tap prior knowledge, you activate students' thinking muscles! A good lesson for activating students' thinking by conjuring up things they may already know about a topic, this activity is simple: Students work to think of words and phrases associated with the topic and matched to each letter of the alphabet. This strategy comes from Raymond Jones (1998).

Lesson Objective: Prepare for reading by tapping prior knowledge.

Materials Needed: A copy of the selected article for the teacher only; an ABC sheet for each student, or a sheet of paper for students to list the letters of the alphabet.

Grouping: Whole class or individual.

Time: 15 minutes.

STEP 1. Prepare the ABC Sheet

Pass out the ABC sheet, or if using student notebooks or sheet paper, have students list all the letters of the alphabet on the paper leaving room beside each letter to write out a word or phrase.

STEP 2. Identify the Topic

Checking the article you selected, identify the topic for the students. The topic should be broad and general to give lots of room for brainstorming. State the topic in one word or a simple phrase. I highly recommend that you write the topic down on a whiteboard, chart, or projectable so that the students can visualize it.

STEP 3. Guide the Brainstorm

Let your students loose with their pencils and the brainstorming sheets! In this step, the students start to fill in the ABC brainstorming sheet, in no particular order. Give them a solid 5 minutes to work on this alone.

STEP 4. Pair

When students seem to lose steam coming up with ideas for the ABC brainstorming sheet, pair them up. Together they can fill in the blanks for letters not yet completed.

STEP 5. Share

Once students have exhausted their bank of ideas to list beside the letters, have them share. Go around the room facilitating the sharing of words and phrases based on the topic and connected to the letters of the alphabet. Remember, be inclusive in your acceptance of the students' answers. The idea is to activate their prior knowledge, not to assess them on their knowledge of a topic. While their answers should be justifiable in connection to the topic, be flexible and have fun with the activity.

ABC Brainstorming

NAME: _____ DATE: _____

A	**N**
B	**O**
C	**P**
D	**Q**
E	**R**
F	**S**
G	**T**
H	**U**
I	**V**
J	**W**
K	**X**
L	**Y**
M	**Z**

Available for download at **www.corwin.com/nonfictionnow**

Source: Adapted from Jones (1998).

ABC Brainstorming

NAME: Oceania Group   DATE:

A	Australia	**N**	Nauru
B	Biodiversity	**O**	Oceania
C	Continent	**P**	Papua New Guinea
D	Descendants	**Q**	Equator
E	Ecotourism	**R**	Region
F	Fold Mountains	**S**	Solomon Islands
G	Guam	**T**	Tuvalu
H	Huge	**U**	Under water
I	Indonesia	**V**	Vanuatu
J	Fiji	**W**	Wellington
K	Kiribati	**X**	Exculsive maritime zones
L	Languages (817)	**Y**	Yams
M	Malay Acchipelago	**Z**	Zealandia

Source: Adapted from Jones (1998).

Looking for Important Information

When to Use: As a mini-lesson to develop a purpose for reading. You can use this lesson with Daily Duo Step 2, *Reading*, or Step 3, *Noticing*.

Before students practice a strategy on their own, it is highly effective for you to teach the strategy as a think-aloud. Block and Israel (2004) created a lesson to teach readers to allocate their attention while reading by using a think-aloud. In a think-aloud, you model each and every step by talking about your thinking and making your thoughts transparent for students. Often, we assume that students understand what goes on in our minds when we teach them steps in a lesson; in other words, we assume they know how to think about reading nonfiction text. Often, they don't, and a think-aloud is a great strategy to help students "see" the process of comprehension.

Lesson Objective: Demonstrate for students how to give their attention to important sentences and avoid distraction from unimportant details while reading.

Materials Needed: A projectable image of the article you wish to use for the think-aloud, or a content-area textbook. If using a textbook, ensure students have their textbooks out in front of them. Be certain to use an article students have not seen before, or a new section of the textbook.

Grouping: Whole group, large or small.

Time: 15 minutes.

STEP 1. Bring Student Attention to the Text

Project the article so all students can see it, or have them turn to the page in the textbook that you will use. Say,

> "When reading an article *[or chapter in the book]*, you will find clues to
> help you find the most important information in the article *[or section]*. The
> author does this on purpose to help us as readers. I'm going to read the
> beginning of this article aloud, and then I am going to walk you through
> how I find these clues for the most important information. I want you to
> follow along while I read."

STEP 2. Read the Text

Read the beginning of the article or the chapter in the textbook. Predetermine how much of the text you need to read to cover at least two important clues. This will differ depending on the article or section of the textbook you chose. Because this is a think-aloud, you do the reading, and students follow along. Remember, you are modeling for the students.

STEP 3. Pause and Think-Aloud

Say,

> "I noticed while I was reading that the author repeated some words and
> restated some ideas more often."

Then point to the repeated words and/or the restated ideas to demonstrate. Say,

"Look at this word *[or phrase]*. It is repeated several times in the text. The author uses it in this sentence *[read the sentence, or portion of the sentence]* and in this sentence *[read the sentence, or portion of the sentence]*. Because it is repeated, I know that this is important information.

"There is another clue that I can use to find the most important information in the text. The author often provides an example about the most important idea. So, we might see a sentence telling us some information, and that sentence is followed by another sentence containing the words 'for example,' or the author may put in a quote, or the author may follow the first sentence in a paragraph with another sentence providing detail about the important idea."

Now, point to the clues in the text that tell you the idea is important. This clue may be a signal phrase like *for example* or a nonexample of the idea signaled by a word like *although*. The clue may be a quote, or even a sentence immediately following the important idea, providing some specific information.

STEP 4. Read While Students Think About the Text

Read the next paragraph or section of the text that contains an important idea. This time, rather than modeling your "thinking" about the text clues, let the students describe what they see in the text. Remember to give them lots of wait time once you prompt them to find the textual clues, and don't rush in and answer the question yourself. Allow the students to think, talk with one another, and then respond with their thinking about the important ideas in the text section based on the textual clues. Try asking questions to prompt students' thinking:

- Do you see any clues in the text that point to the important information?
- Do you see any repeated words, or words with similar meanings?
- Do you see any repeated phrases?
- Do you notice any sentences appearing immediately after the one where you think the important idea is that provide detail about the idea?
- Do you see any sentences with examples or quotes? Check the sentence before it; does it have an important idea in it?

Continue the process until you have reached nearly the end of the selected text.

STEP 5. Have Students Read the Last Section of the Text Independently and Practice Finding Important Information With a Partner

Now it is time for students to give it a go on their own. Have them read the last part of the text individually and then practice one of the strategies for finding the important ideas in a text or article (try one of the "Lessons for Getting Main Idea by Understanding Text Structures" in Part III). Students should find this fairly straightforward as texts and articles often end with a summary of what has been presented.

Follow Up: Once you perform this think-aloud several times with different texts, encourage students to try it when they read. You may want to post the question prompts in your classroom to remind them to use the strategy when reading on their own.

Using Anticipation Guides to Practice Adjusting Understandings

When to Use: Before reading; when you want to pique students' interest in reading a text, and after reading; when you want students to practice looking to the text to support their assertions. You can use this lesson with Daily Duo Step 2, *Preparing to Read*, and Step 3, *Noticing*.

An anticipation guide is a prereading activity to help students access background knowledge about a text. However, anticipation guides do more than this—they set a purpose for reading and provide a framework for summarizing an article after reading.

Lesson Objective: Evaluate statements about a text before and after reading.

Materials Needed: A copy of the text or article you have chosen for each student; prepared statements on a chart (see *Sample Anticipation Guide*), handout, or projectable image; a chart or projector to record notes and ideas.

Grouping: Whole class.

Time: 25 minutes or longer depending on the length of the text.

STEP 1. Prepare the Statements

Select between five and eight statements from the text that focus on the theme or main idea; then falsify one or two statements (see *Sample Anticipation Guide*). You do this because you want students to make a judgment about the statements based on their prior knowledge and then, after they read, to evaluate their decisions about the truth of the statements to the text. Including a few false statements can pique students' interest in determining what is true and false and get them thinking beyond literal recall and focusing on evaluation. Students can circle *true* or *false* next to the statements.

When creating an anticipation guide, you write between 5 and 8 statements based on the text that students will read. You can pull these statements right from the text, or write them based on the Big Ideas in the text. To get students thinking about what they are going to read, add in a couple of statements that are false. You add in these false statements so that students can explore whether the statements presented are true or false. The idea is to pique the students' interest in reading the text.

This sample on the Declaration of Independence is created from the following website: www .constitutionfacts.com/us-declaration-of-independence/fascinating-facts. Remember, two of the facts are false.

Question	Circle *T* for true, and *F* for false
1. The original Declaration of Independence was signed in August, not July, 1776.	T F
2. Robert Livingston, a member of the committee who wrote the Declaration of Independence, never signed it.	T F
3. On the back of the Declaration of Independence are some handwritten words that say, "Original Declaration of Independence."	T F
4. Jefferson wrote the first draft, and the committee made hardly any revisions to his draft.	T F
5. In Jefferson's draft, he criticized the slave trade, but this criticism of the slave trade was removed in spite of Jefferson's objections.	T F
6. All of the signers of the Declaration were in their 40s and 50s in age.	T F
7. When the Declaration was signed, the population of the United States was estimated to be 2.5 million. Today the population is close to 300 million.	T F

STEP 2. Present the Statements

Say,

> "Today we are going to read *[insert article topic or title]*, but before we read, I want you to think about what you know about *[insert topic]*. Look at these statements. I want you to you to read each one on your own and think about it and decide if the statement is true or false based on what you know about the topic. If you don't know much about it, that's OK—take a guess or make a hypothesis, using your best thinking."

Give the class time to read the statements and make a prediction. Then lead the students in a discussion about what they think about the truth of the statements. Have students do the thinking (you are not modeling here, but facilitating a discussion), and encourage students to justify their answers by sharing specific details from their knowledge. Don't give away which statements are true or false! You want to give students a purpose to read (to find out the answers).

STEP 3. Read

Have the students read the text individually, or in pairs. If you choose to read the article out loud, make sure to do the reading yourself. Do not have students read out loud in a round-robin fashion (see my notes on round-robin reading at the beginning of Part III. It isn't an effective teaching tool!).

STEP 4. Revisit the Statements

After reading, revisit the statements. Let the students revise their original thinking about the statement.

STEP 5. Discuss Confirmation or Correction of Statements, Referencing the Text

Discuss with the class whether a statement is true or false. If a statement is true, have the students search the text to find the sentences, phrases, or words that prove it. Do the same thing with the false statements, having the students search the text to find the sentences, phrases, or words that disprove the statement. Poll the class as you go to see what the students thought about the statement and whether they changed their minds after reading the text.

Once you have repeatedly modeled this process with students, have them do Steps 1 through 4 on their own, and then discuss the validity of the statements together as a group.

STEP 6. Summarize and Share

Using the true statements, have the students orally summarize the text with a partner.

Lessons That Support Students While Reading for Main Idea and Details

In this section, you'll find lessons that help students identify the main idea and details in texts while they read. As you guide and support your students' reading, the lessons in this section will work well for Daily Duo Step 2, *Reading*, and Step 3, *Noticing*, and some lessons will build up to Step 4, *Taking Notes* (see Chapter 5, pages 53–54). There is no hierarchical order to the lessons, and different lessons may work for your students at different times. The lessons suggest that you use an article to model or practice the strategy; thus, the article you choose may influence which lesson fits best. Remember, recommended articles are available in the Appendix, or you can use any article you find on the Internet or in a print resource.

Three Pieces of Advice From Me to You

As you delve into the lessons, keep these points in mind:

1. **Make the lessons your own.** The lessons are thorough enough for you to pick up and teach as is, but by all means, feel free to change them and do what works best for your objectives and your students.

2. **Teach for independence.** As you put the lessons into play, focus on *students doing* and not *teacher doing*. Set an egg timer, your iPhone alarm—whatever it takes to make sure you wrap up a demonstration on the spot if it exceeds 15 minutes. Really! Students learn by doing.

3. **Experiment with different articles**. Use the articles in the Appendix to teach the lessons, but then roam! A lot of great articles are available online, in newspapers, and in magazines in bookstores—get in the habit of finding, filing, and using them. Remember, too, that you can do potent mini-lessons (under 5 minutes), for example reading aloud or projecting just a very small portion of the piece.

As you jump in and teach, remember to have fun!

Inquiry Charts

When to Use: Inquiry charts, or I-Charts (Hoffman, 1992), help students identify main ideas in a text. The I-Chart revs up students' thinking about what they are reading (see the lesson *Using Inquiry Chart Summaries to Scaffold Text-to-Text Learning on* page 184). An I-Chart is a during-reading activity, as students can fill out the chart while reading.

Working with the I-Chart can develop into a bank of multiple charts, if you choose to have students read more than one article or text to explore a topic. Students would use one *I-Chart* graphic organizer for each text they read. Once your students have fluency with the strategy and the organizer, you can teach them to create an I-Chart for multiple texts (such as "Disney Channel Stars Speak Out Against Cyberbullying" and "Text-Message Bullying Becoming More Common" in the Appendix).

Lesson Objective: Recognize and record key details in text.

Materials Needed: A copy of the article you have chosen for each student; an I-Chart created on a large piece of butcher paper (use the *I-Chart* reproducible on page 148 as a model), or an electronic version of the I-Chart and a projector; student notebooks to record their individual I-Charts, or copies of the I-Chart for each student.

Grouping: Whole class and individual, working cooperatively or independently.

Time: 45 minutes for one article or text. Working with the I-Chart can extend over several periods, and also move into homework depending on how many articles, texts, or multimedia sources students read and explore in relation to the topic.

STEP 1. Prepare to Teach

Using an I-Chart does require some preparation before teaching. This involves reading the text, or skimming multiple texts on the same subject, and thinking about questions that will guide students' purpose for reading and remembering. Notice the questions listed at the top of the I-Chart sample. I recommend that you focus the questions on facts and details and on important ideas that you want students to explore in their reading. Keep the number of questions relatively short; this example shows four questions, plus "Other Interesting (but Maybe Trivial) Facts" and "New Questions." Students can use these boxes to record things they notice and ask during the reading that are unrelated to the questions you have formulated.

STEP 2. Go Over the I-Chart With Students

Now that you have prepared the I-Chart, go over the columns and discuss the questions with the students. Help them grasp the ideas in the reading to answer the questions, and to think about new questions they might have about the reading. Show them how to record information in the boxes appropriately. You may notice the I-Chart is a matrix; to get a better grasp on developing a matrix, see the *Matrix Graphic Organizer* on page 122. Your students may not have experienced a matrix, and may need a little help filling it in.

STEP 3. Work on the "What We Know" Information

In the first row of the I-Chart, students record what they already know about the topic and the questions. See the end of this lesson for an example I-Chart filled out with students' responses. If they knew something about the topic or a question, they filled in the box; if they didn't (which is just fine because our goal for reading is to help students learn new information about the world), they just left the corresponding box blank.

STEP 4. Notice and Wonder

Call students' attention to the "Other Interesting (but Maybe Trivial) Facts" and "New Questions" boxes. Ask your students what they might wonder about, talk to them about stopping when something in the reading grabs their attention, and show them how to record their observations and questions in these boxes while reading. If they want to record an interesting fact, or a question, before they start reading, they may also record it in the appropriate box of the I-Chart.

STEP 5. Read and Work Through the I-Chart

Have students read an article. If you plan to teach more than one article in a text set, or to explore online resources on a topic, start your first lesson with just one article to familiarize your students with the ins and outs of I-Chart thinking.

Once students have read the article, discuss it. During discussion, students may start to make connections between the questions on the I-Chart and the information in the text. This is great! Have them record their thoughts, ideas, and questions, as well as any facts and details they retrieve from the text, in the corresponding boxes on the chart. If students don't make any connections during the discussion, that is just fine! They only need a little guidance and modeling from you. Work through each question running across the top of the I-Chart and talk about how students might answer the questions, referring to the text to justify answers. It is fine, and even desirable, to put direct quotes from the text in the boxes to back up an answer. Remember not to do the thinking for your students! Prompt them and guide them to what a question is asking and where they might find the answer. Don't just provide the answer for them. Remember, we want to build strong thinking muscles in our students!

STEP 6. Wrap Up or Continue!

Once students have read and answered the questions on the I-Chart, and have asked any new questions about the topic (great for further investigation), talk the class through any big learning or "aha" they had about the topic. Record the big learning or "aha" in one sentence across the bottom of the I-Chart; see the completed version for an example.

If students are working through a text set with the I-Chart, show them how to record the next resource in the subsequent row, and then repeat the process. Students can explore as many related texts as appropriate, or that make sense, for your classroom inquiry. The text set on cyberbullying in the Appendix ("Disney Channel Stars Speak Out Against Cyberbullying" and "Text-Message Bullying Becoming More Common") would make a great inquiry.

I-Chart

NAME: _____ DATE: _____

QUESTIONS TO ASK ABOUT THE TEXT: What is most important about what I read? What are the big ideas? What are the details supporting the big ideas? What else do I need to know?

Topic/Source: _____

ANSWERS TO QUESTIONS I ASKED ABOUT THE TEXT

What I Know	
Facts and Details	
Other Interesting Facts (even if they are minor/ trivial)	
New Questions I Have	

Available for download at **www.corwin.com/nonfictionnow**

Source: Adapted from Hoffman (1992).

I-Chart

NAME: Sample Student   DATE:

QUESTIONS TO ASK ABOUT THE TEXT: What is most important about what I read? What are the big ideas? What are the details supporting the big ideas? What else do I need to know?

Topic/Source: How to choose a checking account

ANSWERS TO QUESTIONS I ASKED ABOUT THE TEXT

What I Know	checking accounts hold money.
Facts and Details	Accounts with no extra fees are best. Accounts with no minimum balance requirement are best too. Need parent to open an account.
Other Interesting Facts (even if they are minor/trivial)	Not all accounts are the same. Some accounts have fees for almost everything.
New Questions I Have	Why do I need a checking account?

Source: Adapted from Hoffman (1992).

Partner Reading

When to Use: When your students need some reading practice, this is a great lesson for teaming them up and allowing them to help one another read (decode) and retell (a simple step in comprehension).

Lesson Objective: Work with a partner to retell key details from a text.

Materials Needed: Copies of an assortment of articles; a timer.

Grouping: Partners, two students paired together.

This is a great time to connect your students together to help one another. Try pairing a more fluent reader with a less proficient one. You can also pair students together based on language proficiency or, to push and stretch their thinking, pair students with equal reading ability.

Time: 20 minutes.

STEP 1. Pair and Prepare

Pair students together to select their articles. Allowing them to choose the article that most interests them helps to build their desire to read.

STEP 2. Students Begin Reading

Students take turns reading the article. First, one student (the more fluent reader if you have paired the students together in this way) reads for 5 minutes. Then, the second student reads *the same passage* for 5 minutes. Your job during this step is to monitor students' reading, helping them fix up their thinking if they get stuck decoding a word. You can also monitor the activity for time.

STEP 3. Students Do a Retell

Once both students have read the same passage for 5 minutes each, with one student echoing the other student's reading, they stop to do a retelling of the text. First, one student retells what was read for 2 minutes, and the other student listens. Then both students confer, checking back with the text, to see if the retelling captured the main points or details from the passage they read. Your job during this step is to monitor students' retelling, encouraging them to think about what they read and to check the text as needed to recall key details.

STEP 4. Students Continue Reading and Retelling

Students continue to read the article taking turns. Again, the first student reads for 5 minutes, and then the second student reads *the same passage* for 5 minutes. After both students have read for 5 minutes, they stop reading and retell the text to each other. The students can alternate who goes first to retell the text.

Your job is to continue monitoring students' reading and retelling, keeping them on track and encouraging them to stick with the task!

Paragraph Shrinking

When to Use: When students identify main ideas and details from a text, they tap into their short-term memories to reconnect with their reading. This helps improve comprehension. This lesson is based on the research by Fuchs, Fuchs, and Kazdan, as cited by Sporer and Brunstein (2009).

Lesson Objective: Identify main idea in single paragraphs.

Materials Needed: Copies of an assortment of articles; highlighters.

Grouping: Partners, two students paired together.

This is a great time to connect your students together to help one another. Try pairing a more fluent reader with a less proficient one. You can also pair students together based on language proficiency or, to push and stretch their thinking, pair students with equal reading ability.

Time: 30 minutes.

STEP 1. Pair and Prepare

Pair students together and have them select their articles. Allowing them to choose the article that most interests them helps to build their desire to read.

STEP 2. Students Begin Reading

Students read the article aloud to each other. One student reads the first paragraph while the other student listens. Your job is to monitor the partners and help them fix up their thinking if they get stuck. Students stop at the end of the first paragraph.

STEP 3. Students Recall the Main Idea

Once students have read the first paragraph, they talk together, referring to the text, and decide on the main idea of the paragraph.

STEP 4. Students Highlight the Main Idea in the Text

After students have talked together to identify the main idea in the text, they highlight the phrase or sentence that contains the main idea of the paragraph. Your job is to help the students correctly identify the main idea, and then guide their highlighting skills. Too often, students cannot discriminate what is most important, and they will highlight almost every word in the paragraph.

STEP 4. Students Continue Reading and Noting

Once students have finished highlighting the main idea in the first paragraph, they go on to read the second paragraph. They continue the sequence, with the second student reading (and from here on reading every other paragraph). After either student reads a paragraph, together the pair decides on the main idea and highlights the phrase or sentence that contains it.

STEP 5. Continuing the Paired Reading

Students continue reading the entire text in this manner: reading one paragraph, identifying its main idea, and highlighting the important part. The students take turns assuming the role of the reader.

Prediction Relay

When to Use: Making predictions about a reading *based on facts in the text* helps students comprehend what they are reading. When students make their own predictions about text while reading and test their predictions against what they have read, they are testing their own reading comprehension. Strategic readers do this often, and struggling readers rarely engage in this type of thinking (Fuchs, Fuchs, Mathies, & Martinez, 2002; Sporer & Brunstein, 2009).

Lesson Objective: Make a prediction about text and confirm or disconfirm the prediction after reading.

Materials Needed: Copies of an assortment of articles (a longer article, 500–700 words or so, works best for this lesson. You can look through the Appendix to choose articles for your students, and you can also use magazine articles or texts from the Internet); student notebooks.

Grouping: A small group of 3 or 4 students, paired partners, or individuals.

Time: 30 minutes.

STEP 1. Prepare

Organize students for reading. Pair students together, or if they are working in small groups, assign who will make the first prediction, the next prediction, and so on. Make sure students have a copy of article they chose to read and a notebook to record their predictions. Allowing them to choose the article that most interests them helps to build their desire to read.

STEP 2. Students Begin Reading

Students read the beginning of the article to themselves. A good reference is to have students read the first 75–100 words of an article, the first couple of paragraphs, or the first half-page if the text is in a book.

STEP 3. Students Make a Prediction

Once students have read the beginning of the article, they predict what the next hundred words, couple of paragraphs, or half-page will be about. They must make these predictions based on the key ideas and details from the first part of the article. If students are working in pairs or small groups, they can talk together, referring to the text, and decide on the key ideas.

STEP 4. Students Record Their Predictions

After students have come up with a prediction, they write it down in their notebooks. Using a sentence frame may help them start writing (for examples, see *Prediction Sentence Frames*). Your job is to help the students accurately identify the key ideas in the first part of their reading so that their predictions are plausible and related to the text. Some students may need some help thinking through their predictions as struggling readers tend to make a prediction, just to make a prediction, and don't consider if their predictions match the details in the text in any way.

STEP 4. Students Continue Reading, Thinking About Their Predictions

Now students read the next portion of the text—the next 100 words or so, the next half-page, or the next couple of paragraphs. After reading this section, they decide if their predictions were true.

STEP 5. Students Evaluate Their Predictions

The students need to reread their predictions and think: Was the next part of the text about what they thought it might be about? If the students decide that their predictions were true, they can go on. If the predictions weren't true, the students need to go back and check their understanding of the first few paragraphs. This step can be difficult for struggling students who tend to give up if they made a false prediction, unsure of how to reread and make a new prediction. Sometimes struggling students will go through the motions of checking their prediction, continuing to read without evaluating whether their predictions were true or false. Your job is to help readers with this step. Check in with them to see how they are thinking about their predictions. Ask them why they think a prediction is correct and encourage them to point out text that backs up the confirmation. If they make an incorrect prediction, encourage them to reread the passage, looking for key details to clue them in to what might come next in the article.

STEP 6. Students Continue Making Predictions and Reading

If students are working in a small group, or in pairs, they can switch roles as they continue to read as well as make and confirm or disconfirm their predictions. They can take turns not only reading to one another but also making the prediction.

Prediction Sentence Frames

From reading the first part of _____ I predict that this article is going to be about _____.

The section of the article I read was about _____

_____

_____.

Based on this information, I think the next part of the article is going to be about _____

_____.

The first section of the article I read was about _____

_____

_____.

I noticed the text features of the next section and I think it is going to be about _____

_____

_____.

I have read most of the article. The article includes this information: _____

_____

_____.

I think the end of the article will discuss _____

_____

_____.

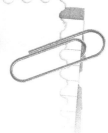

Connecting to the Author's Big Idea

When to Use: Here is another lesson employing a think-aloud to engage students in learning a strategy. In a think-aloud, you model each and every step by talking about your thinking and making your thinking transparent for students. See *Looking for Important Information* in the previous section of Part III for another lesson involving a think-aloud. Block and Israel (2004) created several think-aloud lessons to teach readers comprehension strategies. This lesson focuses on connecting ideas in a text to the author's central theme.

Lesson Objective: Link main idea sentences to the big idea in a book or article.

Materials Needed: A projectable image of the article or page from your selected nonfiction book.

Grouping: Whole group, small or large.

Time: 20 minutes.

STEP 1. Bring Students' Attention to the Text

Project the article or first page in the book so all students can see it. Say,

> "When reading an article *[or a book]*, you need to think about the author's big idea for writing the article *[or book]*. The author always has a big idea. The big idea is the theme of the article *[or book]*. I can get some idea of what the big idea, or theme, of the article *[or book]* is by reading the beginning of the article *[or first couple of pages of the book]*. I'm going to read the beginning of this article *[or book]* aloud, and then I am going to walk you through my thinking about what the big idea might be."

STEP 2. Read the Text

Read the beginning of the article or the first couple of pages in the book. Predetermine how much of the text you will need to read to find the big idea. This will differ depending on the article or book you chose. Because this is a think-aloud, you do the reading, and students follow along. Remember, you are modeling for the students.

STEP 3. Pause and Think-Aloud

Say,

> "I noticed while I was reading that the author seems to be going in a direction with this article *[or book]*. I think that I am on the same train of thought as the author."

Then point to the sentences that give you a clue about the big idea in the text. Say,

> "Look at this section of the text. The author is talking a lot about the same idea. *[State the idea, which depends on the book or article you are reading.]*"

STEP 4. Make a Prediction About the Big Idea

Say,

> "I think the author is leading me to the big idea; I think the big idea is *[state the big idea you pointed out in Step 3]*. Now I am going to read the next section *[or page]* and see if I am right."

Read the next section of the text.

STEP 5. Confirm or Disconfirm the Prediction

Say,

> "OK, I was thinking that the big idea was *[state the big idea]*, and now I am thinking that I am correct because *[point out the sentences or ideas that support your thinking]*."

Or say,

> "I was thinking that the big idea was *[state your thoughts on the big idea]*, and now I am thinking that I am wrong because *[point out the sentences or ideas that show why your thinking was incorrect]*."

STEP 6. Continue Reading and Pause to Connect to the Author's Big Idea

Read another large section of the article or four or five pages in the book. Say,

> "Once I read a big part of the article *[or four or five pages in the book]*, I can figure out why the author wrote this article *[or book]*. He *[or she]* wanted to give us information about *[state the big idea or theme of the text]*. I know I am correct in my thinking because these sentences and paragraphs repeat the idea presented at the beginning of the text *[point to the appropriate places in the text]*. I can also double-check against the title of the article." *[Point out how the title gives clues about the big idea.]*

STEP 7. Summarize the Steps You Took in Connecting to the Big Idea

Say,

> "It is really important for us to figure out the big idea, or theme, of an article *[or a book]*. Doing this helps us understand what we are reading. I just showed you the way that I connect ideas from the text together to find the big idea. I read a bit, then I made a prediction, and then I read some more to see if I was right or wrong. Then, after I read a big part of the article *[or book]*, I could see why the author wrote the article. The big idea popped out at me because I connected ideas from the paragraphs together."

Follow Up: Once you perform this think-aloud several times with different texts, encourage students to try it when they read. You may want to post the question prompts (see *Questions to Prompt for Big Ideas*) in your classroom to remind them to use the strategy when reading on their own.

Questions to Prompt for Big Ideas

- What direction is the author going in the article?
- If so, what part of the text backs up your thinking?

- What are the ideas the author is discussing?
- If you were wrong about the Big Idea, how could you revise your thinking about the Big Idea?

- What do you predict the author's Big Idea is?

- What part of the text could help you?

- Were you correct in your thinking about the Big Idea?

Pause, Describe, and Infer

When to Use: Good readers pause when reading and double-check their understanding. Often, they do this by quickly remembering the important facts and details in the part of the text they have just read. For readers who are familiar with the information in a text, this process may occur quickly. Readers who are unfamiliar with the information presented, however, may slow down their reading and take longer pauses to make sure they understand the text.

When readers pause and review what they have just read, they also infer the topic likely presented in the next sentence or paragraph. Good readers do this by confirming their understanding of what they have read, and focusing on what might come next. To do this, they tap into their prior knowledge about the topic presented in the text. An inference is a type of conclusion you reach by using text clues and background knowledge.

Lesson Objective: Check for understanding and infer upcoming topics.

Materials Needed: A projectable image of the selected article or page of the nonfiction book. If using an article, you will need copies of the article for pairs of students to use.

Grouping: Whole group, small or large.

Time: 30 minutes.

STEP 1. Bring Students' Attention to the Text

Project the article or first page of the book so all students can see it. Say,

> "When reading an article *[or a book]*, you need to check your understanding while you are reading. You can do this by pausing for a moment after reading a paragraph or a difficult sentence and think, 'What did this just say?' and 'What is the main idea of what I just read?' *[Each sentence and paragraph always has a point, and often struggling readers read without checking their understanding.]* I'm going to read the beginning of this article aloud, and then I am going to walk you through my thinking about what I am understanding while I read."

STEP 2. Read the Text

Read the first couple of paragraphs in the text. Predetermine how much of the text you will need to read to ensure enough information is presented to allow you to check for understanding. This will differ depending on the article or book you chose. Because this is a think-aloud, you do the reading, and students follow along. Remember, you are modeling for the students.

STEP 3. Pause and Think Aloud

Say,

> "When I read, I automatically check my understanding. I want to show you my thinking so you can think about how you check your understanding while you read. Look at this sentence *[point to the first sentence that has some meaning in the text]*. I think this sentence means *[fill in with what you read about]*.
>
> "Now, I'm going to read a couple more sentences and stop to check my understanding. *[Read a few more sentences and repeat the think-aloud process of checking understanding as described.]* Now, this article isn't too hard

for me to read. Sometimes, when I read something hard for me, I have to slow down and stop more often to check that I am understanding what I am reading. It is a good idea for you to stop and check your understanding. When I don't get what I'm reading, I reread the sentence or paragraph. You can do that too. When you are reading and you stop and realize you just don't get it, reread."

STEP 4. Read and Repeat

Read a few more sentences or a paragraph, with pauses to think aloud about your understanding of the text. Explain your thinking about the meaning of the sentences to the class. Also, share any connections you are making to the text or topic based on what you already know.

STEP 4. Infer

Say,

> "When good readers read, they think about what the next part of the text might be about. They make accurate inferences based on what they read. Doing this helps them continue to figure out what they are reading about and check that they understand the reading."

Before reading the next paragraph of the article or book, wonder aloud about what you think it will present. To do this, you think about what you already know about the topic or subject of the text, and you think about what you've already read. When you do this, you make an inference. You think, "What might the next part of the text be about, based on what I know and from what I've read so far?" Say,

> "I'm going to make an inference now before I read the next section of the article *[or book].* So far the article is talking about *[fill in the blank with information from the article you are reading],* so I am thinking the next part is going to tell about *[state what you are thinking, such as additional details, specific information about the details presented so far, another aspect of the idea, or, based on text features, another main idea in the text].* Remember, an inference is not a prediction. I am using what I know about the topic and deciding what might be discussed next in the article *[or book]."*

STEP 5. Read and Check the Inference

Read the section of text that you made the inference about, and note whether your inference was correct. Talk about this out loud to model for students how you check your thinking. The inference won't be answered "right there" in the text, but the information presented in the text will help you determine if your thinking was on track or not.

STEP 6. Continue Reading, Pausing, Checking, and Making Inferences

Read a few more sections of text, pause, check, and make inferences, modeling the process for the students. Then prepare the students to do this on their own.

STEP 7. Students Read and Practice the Process

Assign students to groups of two and pass out the article to the student pairs. Say,

> "Now I want you to work with a partner to continue reading the text. After each paragraph, I want you to pause and check that you understand what

you just read. Tell each other what you think the paragraph was about. After you do that, make an inference—predict what the next paragraph might be about. Then read and see if your thinking was close to what was presented. You won't find your answer "right there" in the text—you will have to think about the topic, and the gist, of what the author wrote to determine if you are on track. I want you to continue reading this way until you get to the end of the article."

Once the class finishes reading the article, talk with the students about how they did in checking their understanding and making inferences.

Follow Up: Once you perform this think-aloud several times and have students practice with you, encourage them to try it when they read. You may want to post the question prompts (see *Questions to Prompt for Making Inferences*) in your classroom to remind them to use the strategy when reading on their own.

Questions to Prompt for Making Inferences

• What did the text say?	• Based on what you know, and what you read, what do you think the remainder (or next section) of the text will be about?
• Why do you think the author wrote this?	
• What do you already know about this topic?	• What is a statement you could make about the text/topic/article?

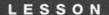

Ask Great Questions

When to Use: Students whose comprehension breaks down while reading need fix-up strategies (see sidebar in Chapter 6, page 66) to help them repair their comprehension. Fix-up strategies—for example, learning to ask questions of a text—help students become independent readers of all types of texts at multiple levels of complexity. Asking questions is like talking to the text. Students think about their thinking while reading, or in other words, they employ a metacognitive strategy. The questions students can ask to keep their comprehension on track are endless; however, this lesson focuses on two types of questions that help students track their comprehension of facts and details. The first type of questions focus on the students' general understanding of the text, and include "Do I get what I just read?" "Does this make sense?" and "Is this clear?" The second type of questions are about details—who, what, when, where, why, and how. This lesson teaches students to ask both types of questions.

Lesson Objective: Ask questions of text to make sure it makes sense, and to understand details about a reading.

Materials Needed: Copies of the article you have chosen for each student; sticky notes; a chart or projector to record questions. See Step 3 of this lesson for types of questions to ask in creating a chart.

Grouping: Whole class or small group.

Time: 20–30 minutes.

STEP 1. Organize for Reading

Pass out the article and sticky notes. Say,

> "Class, today we are going to practice asking questions while we are reading. Asking questions can help us make sure we understand what we are reading, and asking questions can also help us figure out the main ideas in a text. We are going to practice together while reading this article. *[Explain the article a bit.]* When we stop to ask a question, I want you to record your questions on a sticky note. I'm going to keep track of our questions here on the board *[or chart]*."

If needed, model for the students how to write a question on a sticky note.

STEP 2. Read the Text

Read the first couple of paragraphs in the text. Predetermine how much of the text you will need to read to ensure enough information is presented to allow you to ask a question. This will differ depending on the article you chose. Then pause.

STEP 3. Practice Asking "Do I Get It?" Questions

Say,

> "I don't know if it happens to you, but sometimes when I'm reading, I just don't get it. I mean, I don't understand what I'm reading. This is the first type of question we can ask ourselves: 'Do I get it?' So, now that we have read the beginning of this article, let's ask a question. Think for a moment to yourselves. What is a question you can ask to see if you understand the text?"

Guide students to think of questions. You might look for questions like these:

- Do I get what I just read?
- Is this clear?
- What parts of the text do I just not get?
- What's fuzzy in my head about the reading?

Give students time to decide if they have a question about the reading, and if they do, give them time to write it down on a sticky note. Elicit from the students a few questions and record them on the board or chart.

STEP 4. Practice Detail Questions

Read a few more paragraphs in the text. Make sure you read enough of the article to present at least one main idea. Say,

> "There are other types of questions we can ask also. We can ask questions that help us understand what the ideas in the text are. I call these the 'who, what, when, why, where, and how' questions. Let's think for a moment about this part of the article we just read. Can we ask a question?"

Elicit question ideas from the class and record them on the board or chart. Questions might include:

- Who is the focus in this article?
- What happened? or What seems to be really important?
- When did the main events take place?
- Where did the things occur?
- Why did the people in the text do what they did?
- How did the people make things happen?
- How do I think this issue is going to end?

At the end of the question brainstorming, have students read a couple of paragraphs on their own and write their own "who, what, why, when, where, or how" question on a sticky note. Students may have several questions. Remember, your job is to coach them through the process. Let the students do the thinking. You can provide gentle thinking prompts, but don't come up with the questions for them. Keep their thinking muscles active!

STEP 5. Continue Reading the Article and Asking Questions

Make sure that by the time the students finish reading the article, they have three or four sticky notes with questions. Have them put the sticky notes on top of their article and turn in the papers as an *exit ticket* (see the writing activity *Admit and Exit Tickets* in the "Writing About Reading" section of Part III). Then, you can scan the sticky notes for students' questions. What you see on the sticky notes will tell you your next steps. You may find your students need more modeling and practice asking great questions while reading.

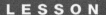

Relate to the Reading

When to Use: When students relate to a reading, they do more than make text-to-self connections. They also relate new information to something they already know, or something they have read or experienced. When students relate a reading to something they already know, they create neural pathways in their brains to retain the new information. We want students to strengthen the synaptic pathway between neurons (where information is stored)—the connection between known and new information. We can provide experiences with the new information to strengthen these neural pathways, and the first step is to "wake up" the brain and bring to students' awareness what they may already know, or have read or experienced, about the subject of a text.

Lesson Objective: Connect information read to things students already know about the subject, or something related to the subject.

Materials Needed: A copy of the article you have chosen for each student; a large sheet of chart paper or a projector to record notes and ideas.

Grouping: Whole class.

Time: 30–40 minutes.

STEP 1. Identify the Topic

To prepare students to relate and connect to their reading, a few "road signs" can help you along the way as you work with students to read a text. "Road signs" are what I call the little notes I write in the margins of text to remind me how to connect it to my students. Sometimes I need the road signs to be bigger so I write them on sticky notes and place them strategically on the text so I remember to stop and chat with the class about an idea or information. You really cannot wing this if you want to do it well, so prep a few notes for yourself before you start reading an article with the class.

STEP 2. Prep for Reading

Pass out the article and have the students scan it quickly, circling things they notice or words that pop out at them. (For a lesson on teaching how to use the text structure to connect to the text before reading, see *Annotating Text* in the "Prereading and Think-Aloud Lessons for Main Idea and Details" section of Part III). Elicit from the students the sentences, words, or phrases that they circled or underlined. Talk with the class about forming a prediction about the text based on their noticings. Write the prediction on an enlarged piece of chart paper or a projectable image.

STEP 3. Read the Article To, or With, the Class

This step is a cross between a think-aloud (see the lessons earlier in this chapter utilizing think-alouds, *Connecting to the Author's Big Idea* and *Pause, Describe, and Infer*) and student-led, independent reading. Your job is to orchestrate the reading, stopping students where you have placed your road signs in the text. While you move students through the text along these predesignated stopping places, the students can read on their own, or if the text is too hard, you can read it out loud to them as they follow along. The idea is not for the students to just blast their way through the text and then after reading discuss the questions you have formulated; they need to participate in this stopping, thinking, and talking *during* the reading.

STEP 4. Stopping for the Road Signs

You will stop reading the text periodically according to your notes. When you stop, your purpose is for the students to connect the new information to something they already know, or have read or experienced. An important action here is that *all* the students need to be thinking and talking about the text, not just one or two students. So, rather than ask your question and call on students with hands raised, have students talk with a partner about the question you posed. If a pair is stuck and has no idea, or no previous knowledge, about the information just read, combine two pairs to make a small group of four who can bounce ideas off one another. Remember, your students will be reluctant to talk with each other until this learning technique becomes routine in your classroom.

Here is a list of questions to get you started with your road signs. They focus on connecting the main ideas and details from an article to what students already know. Among the infinite amount of questions you could ask, these few are just ideas:

- Have you ever heard or read about *[information from the article]* before?
- Do you know anything about *[information from the article]*?
- What was the big idea in that sentence? What do you think about that big idea?
- Do the details in the sentence that talk about *[information from the article]* remind you of anything you know (or have read or experienced)?
- How would you connect what you know to what you think this article is about?
- How does what you know connect to the big idea in this paragraph (or sentence)?
- Does this paragraph (or sentence) say anything that gives you details about something you already know (or have read or experienced)?

STEP 5. Revisiting Road Signs After Reading

After you finish reading the article, go back and discuss the points in the texts that you discussed with the students, prompting them to do the talking about the text, what was discussed, and how they relate to the information in the article. Take notes on what the students say on a chart or projectable image. Remember, your job is to facilitate the conversation, not do the talking for the students.

STEP 6. List the Big Ideas From the Text

After the class has finished with the discussion after reading, ask the students to recall the big ideas from the text and write them down on a chart or projectable image. It is good for students to check the text once in a while, and it is *great* if they can do this from memory. When they recall the big ideas of a reading from memory, it shows that some of the new information is wiring to things they already know, and they can retrieve that information, at least on a short-term basis.

After-Reading Engagements

Exploring the Main Ideas and Details in Texts

This is the final of the three lesson clusters on main idea and key details. This batch of lessons addresses how to develop students' ability to think about texts after they read them. There are some lessons that will also help students with brief writing tasks, as in the Daily Duo, Step 4, *Note Taking*, and Step 5, *Brief Writing Tasks*. There is no hierarchical order to the lessons, and different lessons may work for your students at different times.

Three Pieces of Advice From Me to You

As you delve into the lessons, keep these points in mind:

1. **Make the lessons your own.** The lessons are thorough enough for you to pick up and teach as is, but by all means, feel free to change them and do what works best for your objectives and your students.

2. **Teach for independence.** As you put the lessons into play, focus on *students doing* and not *teacher doing*. Set an egg timer, your iPhone alarm—whatever it takes to make sure you wrap up a demonstration on the spot if it exceeds 15 minutes. Really! Students learn by doing.

3. **Experiment with different articles.** Use the articles in the Appendix to teach the lessons, but then roam! A lot of great articles are available online, in newspapers, and in magazines in bookstores—get in the habit of finding, filing, and using them. Remember, too, that you can do potent mini-lessons (under 5 minutes), for example reading aloud or projecting just a very small portion of the piece.

As you jump in and teach, remember to have fun!

Graffiti

When to Use: To engage students in a fun way about the content they learned while reading.

Sometimes students need to step back from a reading to think about the topic and the information they know, or have read, about the topic. Graffiti is a comprehension activity that helps them do just that—step back and write, but on the walls and with markers!

Lesson Objective: Identify and record main idea and details in an article.

Materials Needed: 7–8 pieces of large chart paper or butcher paper posted around the classroom; markers; a copy of the article you have chosen for each student.

Grouping: Whole class.

Time: 30 minutes.

STEP 1. Prepare the Graffiti Charts

Skim the selected article for 7–8 subtopics. Write one subtopic at the top of each paper. Post the charts around the room.

STEP 2. Have Students Read the Article

Hand out the article and have students read. Before they begin reading, remind them to read for the main idea and supporting details. Also remind them that they can annotate the text (see the lesson *Annotating Text* in the "Prereading and Think-Aloud Lessons for Main Idea and Details" section of Part III) while they read.

STEP 3. Explain the Rules of "Graffiti"

Point out the charts posted on the walls around the room. Explain to students that they will be moving around the room adding words, ideas, and phrases from their reading to the charts using markers. Explain that they need to check out the subtopic written at the top of the page, and then they will have 30 seconds to write down all the terms, ideas, and phrases from their reading related to the topic.

STEP 4. Divide the Class Into Groups and Start Writing!

Assign students to groups of 7 or 8 (you will have the same number of groups as you have chart papers posted). Give each group a particular color marker. Have the students go around the room in groups, from chart to chart, posting their ideas about the subtopic on the charts. Keep time, and move students to the next chart paper every 30 seconds.

ABC Graffiti

When to Use: To engage students after reading and prepare them to think deeply about the content they explored in the text.

ABC Graffiti was created by Massey and Heafner (2004) as a great marriage of two lessons: *ABC Brainstorming* (see the "Prereading and Think-Aloud Lessons for Main Idea and Details" section of Part III) and *Graffiti* (see above).

Lesson Objective: Synthesize ideas about a topic by brainstorming words and phrases.

This lesson focuses on students brainstorming words and ideas about a topic. Students may need a way to organize the ideas about a single topic that come up from multiple text sources in different content areas, and this activity provides exactly that opportunity—to synthesize ideas and information across texts. Now, I don't suggest you dive in with this activity once students have read broadly about an idea or a topic. Nope, I suggest you teach it *first* with one of the texts in the Appendix (for example, "The Wonder of Diamonds" or "Disney Channel Stars Speak Out Against Cyberbullying." That way your students can learn the basics of the activity before they use it to organize their learning from other class reading like textbooks, feature articles, or primary sources.

Materials Needed: A copy of the article you have chosen for each student; *ABC Graffiti* sheet for each student.

Grouping: Whole class, small group, and individual.

Time: 45 minutes.

STEP 1. Read the Text

Students read selected text on their own or with a partner. For struggling readers, it helps to read with a partner, or to listen to a partner read while they follow along.

STEP 2. Students Brainstorm the ABC Graffiti Sheets

Students complete the ABC Graffiti sheets on their own, filling in as much as they can alone. In the next step, they will work in groups, so if a student gets stuck, encourage him or her to keep thinking, but not to worry as the group can help out.

Students brainstorm words, concepts, and ideas from the reading that begin with the letters of the alphabet. They can record single words or phrases. Allow students to refer back to the text as much as necessary to complete the brainstorming activity, but stop them after 3 or 4 minutes.

STEP 3. Students Meet in Groups to Compare Notes

Break the class into groups of 3 or 4 students. Keep the groups small so that all students must participate in the discussion and thinking. Using their individual ABC Graffiti sheets as support, students collaborate to create a group ABC Graffiti sheet. Students cannot refer back to the article this time. They will use their notes, and they will have to do some talking to come to agreement on what word or phrase will represent each letter of the alphabet. Give the students 5 minutes only! It is OK if they have blank spots on their sheet, but make sure they write their group's name on it!

STEP 4. Share ABC Graffiti Sheet With Another Group

Have each group swap the group-generated ABC Graffiti sheet with another group. Once organized, each group continues to brainstorm on another group's ABC Graffiti sheet.

Again, students cannot refer back to the article. They will use their notes, and they will have to do some talking to come to agreement on what word or phrase will represent each letter of the alphabet. Give the students 5 minutes only! It is OK if they have blank spots on their sheet.

STEP 5. Share ABC Graffiti Sheet With Another Group One More Time!

Have each group swap the group-generated ABC Graffiti sheet with a different group. Groups cannot have their own sheets back yet. Once organized, each group continues to brainstorm on another group's ABC Graffiti sheet. This time students *can* refer back to the article. They will use their notes, and they will have to do some talking to come to agreement on what word or phrase will represent each letter of the alphabet. Give the students enough time to finish the task—it may take 10–15 minutes. Have students "call for a lifeline" if they get stuck and need help; they can ask you or another group for ideas. All the letters will need a word or phrase written down before groups go on to the next step.

STEP 6. Students Write a Thesis Statement

Once they have completed the ABC Graffiti sheets, the students return the sheets to the original group. Group members should read their sheet and see what ideas the other students came up with to describe the main ideas and details in the article using the alphabet. The students then work together to write a thesis statement that captures the essence of the article; see the example of a completed ABC Graffiti sheet. Give the groups 10 minutes to finish up.

STEP 7. Share

Each group quickly shares its thesis statement.

ABC Graffiti

NAME: _____   DATE: _____

A		N	
B		O	
C		P	
D		Q	
E		R	
F		S	
G		T	
H		U	
I		V	
J		W	
K		X	
L		Y	
M		Z	

OUR SUMMARY

Thesis Statement From Our Summary

Available for download at **www.corwin.com/nonfictionnow**

Source: Adapted from Massey & Heafner (2004).

ABC Graffiti

NAME: Group B   Solar System   DATE:

A Astronomy	**N** Neptune
B Belt (asteroid)	**O** Oxygen
C Copernicus	**P** Planets
D Dwarf Planet	**Q** Quiet
E Earth	**R** Recycled Stardust
F Formed	**S** Supernova
G Gas	**T** Terrestrial
H Hydrogen	**U** Uranus
I Ice balls	**V** Venus
J Jupiter	**W** Water
K Kuiper Belt	**X** Axis
L Life	**Y** System
M Mars	**Z** Zigzag

OUR SUMMARY

Our sun is a third-generation star that holds 13 planets plus countless asteriods and comets. The solar system is made of different worlds: rocky, dwarf, gaseous, and giant. The solar system is a type of space neighborhood.

Thesis Statement From Our Summary

The solar system is filled with planets and space objects that are diverse.

Source: Adapted from Massey & Heafner (2004).

LESSON

Informing Others About the Reading

When to Use: To have students summarize a text after reading.

There are different purposes for writing summaries about reading. Most of the summary lessons in the "Summarizing to Comprehend" section of Part III help the writer learn, remember, or connect to articles and texts read. Another type of summary is a reader-based summary, or one written for another person. This type of summary informs a reader about a topic, an information point, or a text. Examples of reader-based summaries are book reviews and abstracts. Learning how to write a summary for an audience is a good practice for students because it helps them learn to review their writing for clarity, and polish their writing so that it makes sense to others. When a student writes to inform, or to develop a reader's interest in a book, article, or text, the student needs to become an expert at the information, or very familiar with the text he or she is summarizing.

Lesson Objective: Write a summary to interest another person in a topic, article, or text.

Materials Needed: Copies of an assortment of articles; paper and pencils or computers for writing.

Because each student is going to write a summary for another student in class to read, the class needs to work with different texts. A large amount of short articles might be available from your local newspaper or an online news source.

Grouping: Whole class or small group.

Time: 10 minutes for the lesson, and an unspecified amount of time for students to read their articles and write the summaries. These tasks can be broken into chunks and completed in class over a few days with you as the students' writing coach, or done outside of class as homework.

STEP 1. Prepare, and Ground Your Teaching

A short, 10- to 15-minute reminder of what to do when writing for an audience, this lesson should be taught after the students have had considerable practice writing summaries and only need a reminder of how to summarize. The lesson also helps students remember to set a purpose for reading (to understand a text in depth in order to summarize it for another person). Modeling this through a think-aloud is helpful (see the lessons *Connecting to the Author's Big Idea* and *Pause, Describe, and Infer* in the "Lessons That Support Students While Reading for Main Idea and Details" section of Part III). To prepare for the think-aloud, choose an article of interest to you, read it, and make sure you know what it is about before you start teaching.

STEP 2. Launch the Lesson

Say,

"Today we are going to read and summarize what we are reading in a different way. We have practiced some summarizing to make sure we understand what we are reading, but today we are going to write a summary and publish it. We are going to be writing summaries for each other. I want you to get excited about what you are reading in your article, and your goal is to write a short summary getting another student interested in reading the article too."

Then go into an explanation of the process the students need to follow. Say,

"Because you are going to be working on this on your own, I want to remind you of the process to follow that can help you stay on track and not get stuck. Look at the steps in the chart *[or projected image]* of Rules for Summary Writing *[see Chapter 4, page 47]*. Remember, you are writing for someone else, so you will want to be very clear at the beginning of your summary of what you read, including the title and the author's name. Also, as you finish your summary, remember to check your spelling!"

Then continue with the lesson by reviewing each step in the process through a think-aloud. Discuss your thinking about the process using a text with which you are comfortable. The process is as follows:

- **Choose a goal for reading.** Students decide why they will read a text before they begin reading it. Because they are writing to share their summaries to interest another student in reading what they have read, this can be a purpose for reading.
- **Get really comfortable with the text.** Remind students to read, reread, annotate (see the lesson *Annotating Text* in the "Prereading and Think-Aloud Lessons for Main Idea and Details" section of Part III), and reread the text or article. The students must be very confident that they understand what they have read because they are going to inform someone else about the article or topic. Remind them if they are having trouble understanding to use their fix-up strategies (see the sidebar in Chapter 6 on page 66), ask a friend, or ask you for help.
- **Chunk the text.** Students can chunk the text to prepare to write a summary. They might chunk it by beginning, middle, and end, or by important information like topic sentences and details.
- **Write.** You can use any of the summary steps presented in the book in Chapter 4, pages 45–47, or the "Summarizing to Comprehend" section of Part III (e.g., *Teaching the Four Rules of Summary Writing*) to remind students of the steps to take in summary writing. Keep the students focused on combining ideas and information into a single statement and paraphrasing main ideas and details into their own words.
- **Check for content.** Often, getting swept up in the details, students who are learning to write summaries write about the unimportant parts of the text. Remind your students to double-check their summaries against the article, and to review their notes to make sure they've captured the important parts and ideas in the article or text.
- **Edit for grammar, punctuation, sentence form, and length.** As a final step, students edit. They need to double-check that their summaries are polished and "reader friendly"!

Paragraph Shrinking Plus

When to Use: When students need to focus only on identifying main idea.

In the *Paragraph Shrinking* lesson from the "Lessons That Support Students While Reading for Main Idea and Details" section of Part III, students focused on identifying the main idea in paragraphs. This lesson extends that activity to have students orally create a short summary, and is based on the research by Fuchs, Fuchs, and Kazdan, as cited by Sporer and Brunstein (2009).

Lesson Objective: Identify main idea in single paragraphs, and use main ideas to summarize an article or text.

Materials Needed: Copies of an assortment of articles; highlighters; notebooks.

Grouping: Partners, two students paired together.

This is a great time to connect your students together to help one another. Try pairing a more fluent reader with a less proficient one. You can also pair students together based on language proficiency or, to push and stretch their thinking, pair students with equal reading ability.

Time: 20–30 minutes for the paired reading, and 15 minutes for the summary writing. These two steps can be completed on two different days.

STEP 1. Pair and Prepare

Pair students together and have them select their articles. Allowing them to choose the article that most interests them helps to build their desire to read.

STEP 2. Have Students Begin Reading

Students read the article aloud to each other. One student reads the first paragraph while the other student listens. Your job is to monitor the partners and help them fix up their thinking if they get stuck. Students stop at the end of the first paragraph.

STEP 3. Have Students Recall the Main Idea

Once students have read the article, have them reread the text paragraph by paragraph. They read the first paragraph; talk together, referring to the text; and decide on the main idea of the paragraph.

STEP 4. Have Students Highlight the Main Idea in the Text

After students have identified the main idea in the text by talking together, they highlight the phrase or sentence that contains the main idea of the paragraph. Your job is to help the students correctly identify the main idea, and then guide their highlighting skills. Too often, students cannot discriminate what is most important, and they will highlight almost every word in the paragraph.

STEP 5. Have Students Continue Reading and Noting

Once students have finished highlighting the main idea in the first paragraph, they go on to read the second paragraph. They continue the sequence, with the second student reading (and from here on reading every other paragraph). After either student reads a paragraph, together the pair decides on the main idea in the paragraph and highlights the phrase or sentence containing it.

STEP 6. Continue the Paired Reading

Students continue reading the entire text in this manner: reading one paragraph, identifying its main idea, and highlighting the important part. The students take turns assuming the role of the reader until they finish reading the text.

STEP 7. Write the Summary

Next, the students examine the topic sentences they have highlighted and write a summary together. Say,

> "We've been working hard to write good summaries. Today we are going to take the articles you highlighted with your partner, and you are going to work with your partner to write a summary of the article. I want you to only use the topic sentences that you highlighted to write this summary. Remember the steps to writing a good summary."

Refer the students to the *Four Rules for Summary Writing*, either posted in the classroom or projected for everyone to see. In the "Summarizing to Comprehend" section of Part III, see also the lesson *Teaching the Four Rules for Summary Writing*.

Four Rules for Summary Writing

1.	**Collapse lists:** If you see a list of things, think of a word or phrase that can be a name for the whole list.	**3.**	**Get rid of unnecessary detail:** Some information can be repeated, or the same thing is said in different ways. Other information may be trivial.
2.	**Use topic sentences:** Look for a sentence that summarizes the whole paragraph. If you don't see one, make one up for yourself.	**4.**	**Collapse paragraphs:** Some paragraphs explain others, and some expand a beginning paragraph. Keep the necessary paragraphs and join together information from paragraphs that connect.

Source: Brown, Day, & Jones (1983); Hare & Borchardt (1984).

Summarizing
to Comprehend

"Go ahead and write your summaries." I heard a science teacher say recently to her students after they had finished taking notes on a chapter on Darwin and evolution. At first glance, it looked like the kids knew what to do. They were working in groups, using a "foldable" to record their notes, but translating those notes into a group-written summary was something that stumped them. Mostly, all the students sat in their groups, trying to look busy, but in the end, they didn't write summaries. In the end, the teacher had to go around the classroom and help each group individually. Condensing many facts of a text, or life, or learning takes time and skill. Too often, we assume our students can easily do what we have taught them. This is not an assumption I think we should make (Chou, 2012). Learning to write summaries includes teaching the points expected in a good summary, and also teaching the processes of how to write a good summary. Part of the problem has been that we haven't explicitly named for students the distinct processes involved in summarizing, and we haven't given sufficient instructional time in the school day to allow students to practice summary writing. Therefore, the lessons in this chapter focus on the *processes* of how to distill texts to their important essences and how to scaffold students' efforts so they can become good at summary writing, and confident in writing their ideas down—even when we aren't around!

Summarizing to comprehend requires the reader to make judgments about what is the most vital information in the text, and what information isn't vital and doesn't need to be recorded. It requires students to be able to succinctly put the ideas of the text into their own words after reading, whether verbally or in writing.

There are two purposes to summarizing:

- The reader is involved in a meaningful task that also helps him or her comprehend the text.
- The reader writes a summary to inform others.

The lessons in this chapter get at each distinct purpose and are designed to really nudge students toward independence, so no matter whether they are doing it for themselves as an unconscious way of understanding or for the express purpose of sharing a text with others, they will capture the essence of the text well.

Three Pieces of Advice From Me to You

As you delve into the lessons, keep these points in mind:

1. **Make the lessons your own.** The lessons are thorough enough for you to pick up and teach as is, but by all means, feel free to change them and do what works best for your objectives and your students.

2. **Teach for independence.** As you put the lessons into play, focus on *students doing and not teacher doing.* Set an egg timer, your iPhone alarm—whatever it takes to make sure you wrap up a demonstration on the spot if it exceeds 15 minutes. Really! Students learn by doing.

3. **Experiment with different articles.** Use the articles in the Appendix to teach the lessons, but then roam! A lot of great articles are available online, in newspapers, and in magazines in bookstores—get in the habit of finding, filing, and using them. Remember, too, that you can do potent mini-lessons (under 5 minutes), for example reading aloud or projecting just a very small portion of the piece.

As you jump in and teach, remember to have fun!

Say Something to Develop Understanding

When to Use: During reading to give students confidence in talking about their thinking. You can use this lesson with Daily Duo Step 2, *Reading*; Daily Duo Step 3, *Noticing*; and Daily Duo Step 4, *Taking Notes.*

Harste, Short, and Burke developed this teaching strategy in 1988, and it has stood the test of time! An effective method to encourage students to think while reading, *Say Something* helps students prepare to write a summary if they record what they, or other students, are saying about a reading (Harste & Short, 1995).

Lesson Objective: Students respond to a section of text, checking their understanding of the reading and stating their ideas succinctly.

Materials Needed: A copy of the article you have chosen for each student; student notebooks; a chart or paper for recording and a projector to project images.

Grouping: Whole class broken into groups of 4 or 5, or small group.

Time: 20 minutes.

STEP 1. Prepare the Article for Reading

Skim the selected article for stopping points.

Mark stopping points on student copies of articles, and write these marks on one copy before reproducing the article. Or post the stopping points and have students copy them down on the article. Display the *Say Something Directions* to guide students' interaction.

Use a symbol—for example, an arrow ➔ or another mark ✖—to make the marks on students' copies of the article.

STEP 2. Have Students Read the Article and Stop at the Stopping Points

Working in small groups, students read to the first stopping point.

STEP 3. Have Students "Say Something"

At the predetermined stopping point, the students "say something," using the *Say Something Directions* and *Say Something Idea Starters*, about what they just read. Have the students share in a designated order around the group, or in a popcorn fashion. All students must respond to the text and need to listen to one another. If you allow the students to run the groups, make sure to designate group leaders and that these students can facilitate the taking-turns process, and remind the group to listen to each other's thoughts and ideas. For prompts to help students' thinking, see *Say Something Idea Starters.*

STEP 4. Have Students Jot Notes

After everyone in the group has a turn to say something, the students should jot down what they noted was important about the article. A jot is a very short bullet point about the text. The students can jot in a notebook, on sticky notes, or in the margin of the article. (See the "Weeklong Daily Duo" section of Chapter 6 for an example lesson about teaching jots for both reading and writing.)

STEP 5. Have Students Write a Summary (Optional)

Students can use their jots to write a summary of the article, either as a group or individually.

Say Something Directions

1. Decide in your group who is going to say something first and who will be next.
2. Read to the first stopping point marked in the text.
3. When you say something, focus on one or more of these ideas:
   - Make a comment.
   - Make a prediction.
   - Ask a question (using detail from the article).
   - Make a connection to text or information.
   - Ask about what is confusing.
   - Clarify something from the text.

If you cannot do one of six ideas, reread!

Say Something Idea Starters

Make a Comment

I noticed . . .
I think . . .
This part is interesting because . . .
This part is boring because . . .

Make a Prediction

I predict that . . .
I guess that . . .
I think the next part is going to be about . . . because . . .
I wonder if . . .

Ask a Question (using detail from the article)

Why . . . ?
Who . . . ?
What . . . ?
When . . . ?
Where . . . ?
What does this part mean?
Can you help me understand . . . ?

Make a Connection to Text or Information

This part . . . [explain in detail] is related to . . .
This information . . . [explain in detail] reminds me of . . . [connect to information or another text].
The differences between . . . and this article are . . . [explain in detail].
The similarities between . . . and this article are . . . [explain in detail].

(Continued)

(Continued)

Ask About What Is Confusing

I don't get . . .
Do you understand . . . ?
This doesn't make sense because . . .
Can you help me get . . . ?

Clarify Something From the Text

Now I get it! This means . . . [explain in detail from the article].
This makes sense now because . . .
I think it means . . .
This part is telling us . . .

Using 3-2-1 Exit Cards to Assess Students' Understanding

When to Use: When you want to quickly assess students' understanding of a lesson or a reading in order to provide feedback or adjust your teaching, or to gauge students' understanding as an "exit ticket" at the end of a lesson.

An exit card is a quickly written response to a prompt that helps you give formative feedback to students about their comprehension and ability to write key details. It also helps you see if students can write succinctly in preparation to summarize a text.

Although it is more of a quick activity to assess students' understanding than a full-blown lesson, I recommend you teach the process explicitly before using the 3-2-1 exit card to assess students' understanding. You wouldn't want a student to misinterpret the directions and then not be able to respond. This adaptation of exit cards was created by Rick Wormeli (2005).

Lesson Objective: Write a short statement about what you understood about the reading.

Materials Needed: A copy of the selected article for each student; a half-sheet of 8½ × 11–inch paper for each student.

Grouping: Whole class or small group.

Time: 5 minutes.

STEP 1. Pass and Prep

Pass out the half-sheets of paper to all students and prep them for the activity. Say,

> "We are going to do some quick writing called a 3-2-1 exit card. I want you to write 3 important details from the article, 2 thoughts you have about the article, and 1 topic sentence."

Then go over with the class your definition of an important detail, a topic sentence, and a statement of their thinking—students need to know what you expect.

STEP 2. Give Students Time to Write

Give the students 3–4 minutes to write the exit card. Meander around the class and support students who are having trouble thinking of what to write.

STEP 3. Collect the Card and Analyze

At the end of the lesson, or class period, collect the exit cards. Later in the day, when you have a few moments, look through the cards to note what students wrote down. This exercise is a formative assessment so you can learn the level of each individual student's comprehension of the article. You can use the information you glean to design a follow-up lesson on the article topic if needed. If your students are not comprehending (you will note this because the cards will be blank or have little written in them, or the information will be incorrect), then plan a comprehension lesson. You can use any of the lessons in the "Lessons for Getting Main Idea by Understanding Text Structures," "Prereading and Think-Aloud Lessons for Main Idea and Details," "Lessons That Support Students While Reading for Main Idea and Details," and "After-Reading Engagements" sections of Part III

Extensions: You can vary the prompt for the 3-2-1 exit card in any purposeful fashion. Just remember you are assessing students' understanding of an article, so examine the article you are using with the exit card and come up with prompts. For more ideas of prompts for exit cards, see the *Admit and Exit Tickets* activity in Chapter 12. Below, you can also see an exit card completed by a student for the article "Disney Channel Stars Speak Out Against Cyberbullying" provided in the Appendix.

3-2-1 Exit Card

With this exit card, you have students write 3 things they learned from the lesson, 2 things they found interesting and want to know more about, and 1 question they have.

Exit Card

Write down:

3 things you learned from the article
2 things you found interesting in the article
1 question you have about the article

3
· lots of kids get bullied
· Stars are helping out so kids feel better if they were bullied
· kids get bullied online too
2
· I don't think its right to hurt someone on Facebook
· We need a law to stop it
1
→ Kids get bullied online.

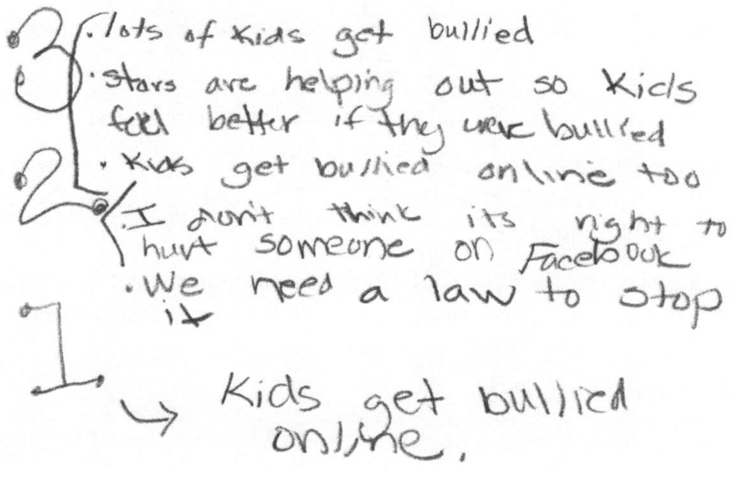

3-2-1 Exit Card for "Disney Channel Stars Speak Out Against Cyberbullying" Article

Using Response Logs to Track Information and Understandings

When to Use: During reading/partner work.

Response logs help students comprehend what they are reading. The logs are also really helpful tools for students to refer to when they are going to write a summary of a text. Response logs can be very open-ended, where the students write down things they find interesting in the text, or they can be more structured. I like using three-column notes to help students organize their thinking about their reading and prepare them to write a summary of an article.

Lesson Objective: Students respond to and record specific information while reading.

Materials Needed: Copies of an assortment of articles, student notebooks, or copies of the *Student Response Log* (see page 183).

Grouping: Partners, two students paired together.

This is a great time to connect your students together to help one another. Try pairing a more fluent reader with a less proficient one. You can also pair students together based on language proficiency or, to push and stretch their thinking, pair students with equal reading ability.

Time: 20 minutes.

STEP 1. Pair and Prepare

Pair students together to select their articles. Allowing them to choose the article that most interests them helps to build their desire to read.

STEP 2. Have Students Begin Reading

Students take turns reading the article. Have them stop at the end of the first paragraph so you can model how to think about whether or not to note something important or interesting in their response logs.

STEP 3. Have Students Stop and Take Notes

Say,

> "Now we are going to practice taking notes in our response logs. In the first column, write down the paragraph number you are responding to. The paragraph we just read is Paragraph One, so I am going to write '1' in the column. Did anyone find something interesting in the paragraph? *[Choose a student to share his or her response.]* So, *[insert student's name]* thought this detail in the paragraph was interesting: *[repeat the detail that the student has shared]*. I am going to write a note about what was interesting in Column Two, and then in Column Three I am going to write *[insert student's name]* thoughts about that interesting detail."

Encourage students to stop at the end of each paragraph and discuss whether they found anything interesting in the text to note.

Text-message Bullying

P 2		•24% of 1,000 middle schoolers surveyed have been harassed by texting.	•It's revolting to know how many people are bullied and hurt.
P 4		•There is a growing number of people being bullied via texting.	• This makes me curious why people are becoming decieving and hurtful.
P 10		•People are upset by the way they are bullied.	•Was their bully wanting to hurt them? why?
P 13		•Bullying is much more likely to happen face to face.	• Is this because the bully wants to see there reaction? This is still very sad.

STEP 4. Have Students Continue Reading and Note Taking

Students continue to read the article, taking turns and stopping at the end of each paragraph to talk about what they find interesting. The students add to their response logs if they find something interesting in the paragraph, but they are not obligated to write about each paragraph in the text (this is an authentic activity—it isn't about writing something if there isn't anything to note!). For an example of a student's response log, see the notes on the left. Your job is to monitor students' reading and note taking, keeping them on track and encouraging them to stick with the task!

STEP 5. Have Students Write a Summary of the Article Together

Once students finish reading the article and recording their notes in the response logs, they can write a joint summary of the article in the response log on a new page. Have students review their notes, recheck the paragraphs where they made the notes, and write a summary of the article incorporating their thoughts about the important ideas and using the topic sentences in the article.

Student Response Log

NAME: _____   DATE: _____

Paragraph	What Was Interesting From the Text	My Thoughts

Using Inquiry Chart Summaries to Scaffold Text-to-Text Learning

When to Use: When you want students to synthesize and summarize two or more texts.

The "Lessons That Support Students While Reading for Main Idea and Details" section of Part III includes a lesson on using I-Charts to help students identify main ideas and details while reading. A great way to wrap up using an I-Chart is to have students write a summary about the inquiry and what they discovered based on their reading. This will require students to summarize two or more articles or texts together. In essence, they will be summarizing the results of their inquiry. Expanding on the *Inquiry Charts* lesson presented in "Lessons That Support Students While Reading for Main Idea and Details," this lesson shows you how to use an I-Chart with two or more texts and have the students summarize what they learned from the inquiry.

Lesson Objective: Summarize information collected about an inquiry question.

Materials Needed: Copies of articles or texts on a given subject (which you can choose, but you will develop more buy-in on the part of students if they choose the subject); an I-Chart created on a large piece of butcher paper, or an electronic version of the I-Chart and a projector to project the image on the board; student notebooks to record their individual I-Charts, or a copy of the I-Chart for each student.

Grouping: Whole class and individual, working cooperatively or independently.

Time: 20 minutes for the first article (assuming you taught the *Inquiry Charts* lesson in the "Lessons That Support Students While Reading for Main Idea and Details" section of Part III as a precursor and the students know how to use the I-Chart graphic organizer on their own). Working with the I-Chart can extend over several periods, and also move into homework depending on how many articles, texts, or multimedia sources students read and explore in relation to the topic.

STEP 1. Prepare to Teach

Follow these steps, but teach the *Inquiry Charts* lesson in "Lessons That Support Students While Reading for Main Idea and Details" first.

Using an I-Chart does require some preparation before teaching. This involves reading the text, or skimming multiple texts on the same subject, and thinking about questions that will guide students' purpose for reading and remembering. Notice the questions listed at the top of the I-Chart sample. I recommend that you focus the questions on facts and details and on important ideas that you want students to explore in their reading. Keep the number of questions relatively short; this example shows four questions, plus "Other Interesting (but Maybe Trivial) Facts" and "New Questions." Students can use these boxes to record things they notice and ask during the reading that are unrelated to the questions you have formulated.

Now that you have the I-Chart prepared, go over the columns and discuss the questions with the students. Help them grasp the ideas that they are reading to answer the questions, and to think about new questions they might want to ask about the reading. Show them how to record information in the boxes appropriately. This is a matrix and if your students may not have experience filling in a matrix, they may need a little help.

STEP 2. Work on the "What We Know" Information

In the first row of the I-Chart, students record what they already know about the topic and the questions. See the end of this lesson for an example of student-recorded information from multiple texts.

STEP 3. Notice What We Wonder About

Call students' attention to the "Other Interesting (but Maybe Trivial) Facts" and "New Questions" boxes. Ask your students what they might wonder about, talk to them about stopping when something in the reading grabs their attention, and show them how to record their observations and questions in these boxes while reading. If they want to record an interesting fact, or a question, before they start reading, they may also record it in the appropriate box of the I-Chart. Students will repeat this process with each text they read.

STEP 4. Work Through the I-Chart With Multiple Texts

Once students read a print article or online resource, discuss it with them, or have them reflect on the information in the text. Students may start to make connections between the questions on the I-Chart and the information in the text. Have them record their thoughts, ideas, and questions, as well as any facts and details they retrieve from the text, in the corresponding boxes on the chart. It is important for students to stay organized so they record their notes in the correct boxes. You may need to model this the first time students work with multiple texts. You may also notice the I-Chart is a matrix; to get a better grasp on developing a matrix, see the *Matrix Graphic Organizer* on page 122. Your students might not have experienced a matrix, and may need a little help filling it in.

Work through each question running across the top of the I-Chart and remind students to think about the answers to the questions and refer to the text to justify their answers. Let the students do this step on their own—don't provide the answers for them. Remember, doing the work on their own, with just the right amount of scaffolding, will help your students become strong and independent learners.

STEP 5. Write a Summary

Once students finish reading the texts they chose for their inquiry, have them look over their notes and write a summary on what they learned through the inquiry. Remind them of the steps in writing a summary (see *Four Rules for Summary Writing* on page 188).

I-Chart (Multiple Sources)

NAME: _____   DATE: _____

Topic: _____

ANSWERS TO QUESTIONS I ASKED ABOUT THE TEXT

	Source 1 Title _____	Source 2 Title _____
What I Know		
Facts and Details		
Other Interesting Facts (even if they are minor/trivial)		
New Questions I Have		

Available for download at **www.corwin.com/nonfictionnow**

Source: Adapted from Hoffman (1992).

I-Chart (Multiple Sources)

NAME: Sample Student   DATE:

Topic: Natural Disasters - Oil Spills

ANSWERS TO QUESTIONS I ASKED ABOUT THE TEXT

	Source 1 Title Oil Spill	Source 2 Title 10 Most Disatrous Accident
What I Know	• Oil Spills are hard to clean • Spills harm the environment and animals	• Long term Damages • tanker spills less than pipe leak
Facts and Details	• pipe bent and broke • safeguards failed • 35,000 barrels leaked each day	• Exxon Valdez tanker burst open • steering mistake • 50 million gallons of oil spilled
Other Interesting Facts (even if they are minor/trivial)	• pipe is 6.625 inches and 21 inches in diameter • leaked near bottom of well	• permanent damage to Alaskan wildlife and entire coast ecosystem
New Questions I Have	• why was the safeguard broken?	• did the oil company recieve punishment for the spill?

Source: Adapted from Hoffman (1992).

Four Rules for Summary Writing

1. **Collapse lists:** If you see a list of things, think of a word or phrase that can be a name for the whole list.

2. **Use topic sentences:** Look for a sentence that summarizes the whole paragraph. If you don't see one, make one up for yourself.

3. **Get rid of unnecessary detail:** Some information can be repeated, or the same thing is said in different ways. Other information may be trivial.

4. **Collapse paragraphs:** Some paragraphs explain others, and some expand a beginning paragraph. Keep the necessary paragraphs and join together information from paragraphs that connect.

Source: Brown, Day, & Jones (1983); Hare & Borchardt, 1984

Get the Gist to Get Good at Section-by-Section Summarizing

When to Use: During reading when you want students to practice checking their comprehension and learn how to speak and write about their thinking.

Students don't always have to take away deep comprehension from a reading; sometimes having a more surface-level understanding of the reading will suffice. A surface-level understanding will be sufficient for students as they work through reading, but not if they need to have a deep understanding of a new concept. We don't always read for complete and deep understanding, however; we often read to get the gist of a text. When students work on getting the gist of a text, they summarize small sections in their own words. Students can practice "getting the gist" using the *Summarizing With Notes Graphic Organizer* in Chapter 3. The *Scanning Text Features Graphic Organizer* also appears in Chapter 3 as a way to help students understand their textbooks while reading, but it also works well to help students get a surface-level understanding of other texts. Getting the gist is a summarizing activity that students do while reading (Akhavan, 2008).

Lesson Objective: During reading, make a short statement about what has been read.

Materials Needed: Copies of selected article; copies of *Get the Gist Graphic Organizer.*

Grouping: Whole class or small group.

Time: 15–20 minutes.

STEP 1. Review the *Get the Gist Graphic Organizer* to Set a Purpose for Reading

In Chapter 3, I introduced you to a graphic organizer called *Scanning Text Features Graphic Organizer Filled Out Based on a Section of a Textbook* to teach students how to get the gist of a reading by completing the organizer as a prereading activity. Here, I have modified the graphic organizer a bit to focus your students on summarizing sections of the text as they read. The *Get the Gist Graphic Organizer* walks students through grasping a simple, or superficial, understanding of a reading. While we don't always want our students to grasp only a superficial understanding of text, this is often the first level of understanding they take away from a first reading. You can help them go deeper into comprehending the text at a later time. To get ready for reading, walk students through the *Get the Gist Graphic Organizer*, pointing out how they will read, pause, and note (in their own words) what they "get" about the section of the article just read.

STEP 2. Read and Take Notes

Once you have shown students how to use the graphic organizer, let them read and take notes on what they "get" about the text. At this time, you can go around the classroom, coaching students to use fix-up strategies (see the sidebar in Chapter 6, page 66) when their comprehension breaks down (when they just aren't "getting" the text). You can also use this time as a formative assessment, noting students' reading behaviors, fluency, and comprehension. Take notes on what you notice about your students' abilities. These notes can provide you with valuable information about what trips up your students, and what you can teach in future lessons to help them either tackle, read through, or comprehend a text. I don't recommend that you relegate this reading activity to homework (at least not all of the time), as you will miss the opportunity to gather important information about your students' abilities.

STEP 3. Discuss Notes on the Gist of the Article

After all students have read the article and taken notes, gather them together to discuss what they understand about the text. You can do this in two ways. One way is to have a whole-class discussion. Another way is to organize the students in groups of four or five and have them share with one another. The good thing about having students share in small groups is that all students will get a chance to talk about their thinking—what they do or don't understand about a reading. This is a time for them to build upon one another's comments to have a rich discussion of what makes sense and what doesn't make sense. Remember, doing this step as a whole group is perfectly fine also; just use a randomizing technique (like popsicle sticks with students' names on them) to ensure students stay engaged in the discussion.

Key to this discussion is that students do three things:

1. Share their thinking.

2. Refer to their notes to accurately share.

3. Refer to the text to clarify, take further notes, or make annotations.

NAME: _____ **DATE:** _____

Title of Text: _____

Page	Notes From Text (use bullets)	What I Think This Means

Here's the Gist of the Text

Get the Gist

NAME: Sample Student   DATE:

Title of Text: Oil Spill Disaster in the Gulf

Page	Notes From Text (use bullets)	What I Think This Means
18	• 2,500 sq. miles of oil spilled	I think this means oil spills are huge problems.
1B	• spilled oil moves	
19	• wetlands are a priority zone	I think this means areas with sea-life and animals are most important
19	• coastal waters are priority zones	
20	• Booms are floating barriers used to move the oil	I think this means oil spills are hard to clean, and take special equiptment
20	• Skimmers vacuum oil from water	
21	• oil was burned to remove it	I think this means that only time will tell the extent of the damage
21	• extent of damage is unknown	

Here's the Gist of the Text

The Gist of the text is that oil spills are huge problems that are extremely hard to clean up. Also, the true extent of the damage will not be known until years to come.

Posing the Five Ws, One H to Promote Summarizing Reading

When to Use: When you want students to learn to interrogate a text in order to summarize it.

Proficient readers pose different types of questions as they work to understand a text. One group of questions that works well is the journalist's Five Ws, One H—who, what, when, where, why, and how. These questions help students not only understand the text, but summarize what they have read.

Lesson Objective: Ask questions of text to gather specific details (who, what, when, where, why, and how) in order to summarize the text.

Materials Needed: A copy of the article you have chosen for each student; chart paper or a projector to record questions and the group-written summary.

Grouping: Whole class or small group.

Time: 30–40 minutes.

STEP 1. Organize for Reading

Hand out the article. Say,

> "Class, today we are going to practice asking questions to help us summarize what we have read. Asking questions can help us figure out the main ideas in a text. I want you to think like journalists while we read this article. We are going to ask the type of questions we might ask if we were reporting on a story, or something that happened. We are going to practice together while reading this article *[explain the article a bit]*. I'm going to keep track of our questions here on the board *[or chart]*."

STEP 2. Start Reading and Ask a Question

Read the first couple of paragraphs in the text. Stop reading, ask students to review the text, and tell them that together you are journalists inquiring into happenings in the text for a report. Describe the Five W, One H (see *The Five W, One H Questions*) questions and ask students to think of one question they could ask. Have the students share their question with a partner, and then call on students to share with the class. Allowing students to share their thinking with a partner before sharing with the whole class is important because it gives students time to practice thinking of a Five Ws, One H question, and also gives them a chance to practice asking their question of another person before asking it of the whole class. This simple engagement strategy will get all of your students thinking and prepared with a question.

STEP 3. Practice Posing the Five W Questions

Read a few more paragraphs in the text and have the students working in groups think of a few Five W questions that relate to the part of the article just read. Elicit question ideas from the class and record them on the board. Questions might include:

- Who are the people in this article?
- What happened? or What seems to be really important?
- When did the main events take place?

- Where did the events occur?
- Why did the people in the text do what they did?
- How did the people make things happen?

Once students answer the five Ws, ask them to address the H. They can go back to the text and revisit for details. You can ask:

- How did the issue occur?

At the end of the question brainstorming, have students read a couple of paragraphs on their own, ask their own question, and then answer it. Students can record the questions they ask and the answers from the text in a notebook. Remember, your job is to coach the students through the process. Let the students do the thinking. Provide gentle thinking prompts, but don't come up with the questions or answers for them. Keep their thinking muscles active!

STEP 4. Continue Reading the Article, Asking and Answering Questions

Make sure that by the time the students finish reading the article, they have 3–4 questions with answers recorded in their notebooks.

STEP 5. Write a Summary

Have students work in groups to review their questions before writing a short summary. If they feel they have not answered the journalists' guiding *who, what, when, where, why,* and *how* questions, students may revisit the text and ask a few more questions to tease out all of the facts. Write these questions on the board. Elicit ideas from the class for the summary and write it out on the board or chart paper. Encouraging the students to paraphrase the answers to the five Why questions and the one How question in their own words is a good place to start.

The Five W, One H Questions

- Who is it about?
- What happened?
- When did it happen?
- Where did it happen?
- Why did it happen?
- How did it happen?

Using On-the-Fly Summaries to Check Student Understanding

When to Use: When you want to check for understanding by having students orally summarize.

On-the-fly summaries are oral summaries that act as comprehension checks so you can make sure your students comprehend what they read. Teaching students to give an oral summary is relatively quick, and they can use the skill often when reading nonfiction to make sure they understand the text.

Lesson Objective: Quickly identify main points of reading selection.

Materials Needed: A textbook section to demonstrate the technique; copies of an assortment of articles.

Grouping: Partners, two students paired together.

Time: 5–10 minutes.

STEP 1. Pair and Prepare

Pair students together to jointly choose an article. Allowing them to choose the article that most interests them helps to build their desire to read.

STEP 2. Demonstrate Through a Think-Aloud

Say,

> "I want you to work together to quickly summarize what you are reading. Watch me do this first. I am going to read a section of this textbook section. Then I am going to pause for a second or two and try to tell you the main points of what I just read."

Demonstrate using a section of the selected textbook. In this think-aloud, emphasize that you are trying to remember what you read—you are not checking the text to be exact. Say,

> "Now that you watched me do this, do you notice how I am summarizing the text? I am thinking about what I read and trying to remember what it said and then saying it out loud. Now it's your turn."

STEP 3. Have Students Practice Together

Have students read their selected articles to one another, stopping frequently and saying what they just read out loud by remembering the main point. The focus is on the students giving an oral summary of the text, not a retelling. If they can't remember what they read, tell them to try rereading and saying the main point out loud. Your job during this activity is to listen to what the students say to each other. Are they confused? Do they comprehend? Are they on track? Make notes as necessary to use the information as an assessment of fluency and comprehension.

Using Visual Summaries to Support Learning

When to Use: When you want to engage students who learn in different modalities.

    Some of our students learn visually. In fact, a study showed that 40% of all college students are visual learners (Felder & Solomon, 1999); if we extrapolate that down to the elementary grade levels, we can assume that a whole lot more of our students learn visually than we might have expected. So, we need to think more creatively about students summarizing what they have read in our classrooms. Visual learners remember best what they see (Felder & Solomon, 1999) and students can see pictures, diagrams, flow charts, timelines, and videos. We can capitalize upon this learning style by having students create visual summaries, or pictorial depictions of information (Clarke, Flaherty, & Yankey, 2006). We can engage students in creating picture montages using traditional software programs like PowerPoint, or using online applications like Pinterest, Flickr, Facebook, and student-created blogs. This lesson is limited only by your imagination!

Lesson Objective: Create a visual summary of information read in an article or a book.

Materials Needed: Copies of an assortment of articles; a computer with access to the Internet; document software such as Microsoft Word.

Grouping: Whole group for lesson, individual or partners for summary creation.

Time: 20 minutes for the reading, several sessions in the classroom or after class to create the visual summary.

STEP 1. Prepare

You may not be familiar with, or comfortable using, all of the ways to create a visual summary. See Step 3 for a list of suggestions, including diagrams, photo collages, and social media. You don't necessarily need to model the creation of a visual summary—especially if the students want to do a digital summary and you don't know how to use the software or the application—but it is important to set the stage for this work by helping students understand what a visual summary is. If you assign this as homework, I encourage you to allow the students to use the application with which they are most comfortable.

STEP 2. Assign Articles and Read the Text

I recommend allowing students to choose their own article or text from an assortment. When students choose their own reading, they tend to be more engaged with the reading. Have students read the text and take a few notes in the margins about the important ideas. I encourage you to do this step in class so you can coach the students in their reading and note taking. Encourage students to use fix-up strategies (see the sidebar in Chapter 6, page 66) if they do not understand what they have read. You can also pair students up to read with a buddy.

STEP 3. Create the Visual Summaries

Students can create a visual rendition of their reading in a variety of ways. Whatever the project, students need to include the title and the author of the article. I also suggest they include a short bulleted list of Big Ideas as a key to the thinking behind the images. Choose one of the following steps to follow based on the type of visual summary (diagram, photo collage, PowerPoint) you expect students to create for the assignment. The following list includes only suggestions:

- **Diagram:** A graphic to represent ideas in the text; can include words, figures, shapes, pictures, or drawings. See *Sample of Diagram Visual Summary* for an example based on the article "The First Teddy Bear" in the Appendix.
- **Collage:** A one-page montage of cut and pasted pictures from magazines, or a digital collage using images from the Internet or a software program.
- **PowerPoint presentation:** A presentation created with only a few slides, including pictures, photos, diagrams, shapes, or other visual digital images.
- **Social media summary:** A digital montage of pictures, photos, or words posted to social media sites like Facebook (on a student or teacher page), Pinterest, and Flickr.
- **Blog:** A short description of the article read and a visual montage of the Big Ideas from the article or text.

STEP 4. Share

Your students have just been involved in a creative and fun process. Don't miss the opportunity for them to share their reading and visual summaries with one another. Arrange for students to share in small groups or in front of the class. Sharing provides a great opportunity to bring in the Common Core State Standards for Speaking and Listening for your grade level (check this out at www.corestandards.org). Our students need abundant opportunities to express themselves and explain their work in front of others.

Sample of Diagram Visual Summary

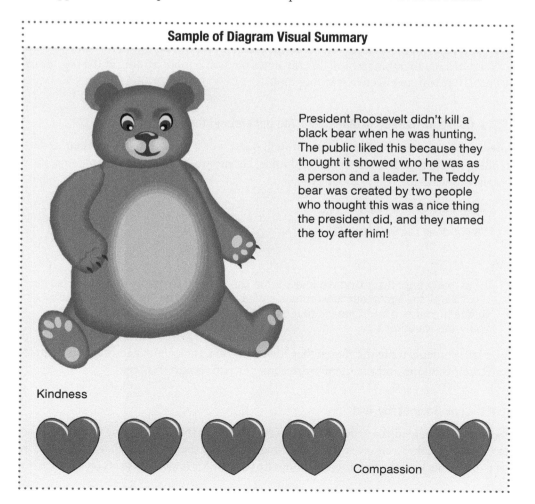

President Roosevelt didn't kill a black bear when he was hunting. The public liked this because they thought it showed who he was as a person and a leader. The Teddy bear was created by two people who thought this was a nice thing the president did, and they named the toy after him!

Kindness

Compassion

Teaching the Four Rules of Summary Writing

When to Use: When first introducing summary writing skills.

Direct instruction is very helpful to students when used in appropriate doses—that is, if we provide too much direct instruction, our teaching can become laborious and stifling. If we don't provide enough direct instruction, and hope students figure things out for themselves (deductive instruction), students may not learn the summarization skills necessary to succeed in content-area classes beyond elementary and middle school. So use your judgment, and look for when your students seem bored by the demonstrations and eager to give it a go on their own. This process for summary writing is based on the work by Hare and Borchardt (1984). See *Four Rules of Summary Writing* for a visual of the lesson flow.

Materials Needed: A copy of the article you have chosen for each student; a chart or projector to record notes, ideas, and the summary; sticky notes.

Grouping: Whole class broken down into small work groups for discussion.

Time: 40 minutes.

STEP 1. Read

Have the students read the text to themselves, or with a partner. If you choose instead to read the article out loud, make sure to do the reading yourself. Do not have students read out loud in a round-robin fashion (see my notes on round-robin reading at the beginning of Part III. It isn't an effective teaching tool!).

STEP 2. Question Yourself to Make Sure You Understand the Text

After reading the text, walk students through questioning themselves about their understanding of the text. It is important to do this, because to summarize, the students must understand what the text is about. Ask:

"What is this text about?"

"What does the writer say?"

Say,

"It is really important that we know what the general theme of the article is.
"Think for a moment to yourselves what you think the *theme* is. Say the theme to yourself and then write it on a sticky note so you don't forget what you were thinking."

Have students write the theme they identified on a sticky note and then tell them to share their thinking and the theme with someone sitting next to them.

STEP 3. Look Back at the Text

Have students reread the article to make sure what they think the theme is matches the text. If needed, they can revise their thinking about the theme. After they do this quick scan and recheck, encourage them to annotate the text for important parts (see the lesson

Annotating Text in the "Prereading and Think-Aloud Lessons for Main Idea and Details" section of Part III). Say,

> "Now that you have checked your thinking about the theme with a partner and with the text, I want you to look back at the text again and star [★] important parts of the text. Write a star next to the parts you think are important. Then we will check our thinking together."

Lead the students in a discussion about what they starred as important parts of the text. Model this process by starring the article you are projecting (use a document camera and an LCD projector if you can) based on what the class is suggesting and coming to a consensus on. Don't just show the class what you think needs to be starred! The idea is to get your students to do the thinking and also to articulate their thinking out loud, justifying their reasons for starring a portion of a text.

STEP 4. Rethink

Teach the students to rethink their thinking to check themselves. Say,

> "Now before we write a summary of this article, let's double check our thinking. We are going to read the first paragraph again *[you have already had the students read the article in Step 1]*. Then we are going to think one more time about what we wrote as the theme, and what we might have starred as important in this article. So, here are the steps I want you to take:
>
> - Read a paragraph, then look at the theme you wrote down.
> - Check for a match.
> - Look at the parts in the paragraph you starred as important.
> - Check for a match.
> - Revise if you need to."

Walk students through these steps with the first paragraph, modeling and doing a think-aloud to showcase your thinking during the process. Direct students to repeat this process with multiple sections of the article. Such a "thinking check" shouldn't take them too long. Next, before they move on to writing a summary of the article, have them underline or highlight the topic sentence of each paragraph. If a topic sentence is missing, model how to write one in the margin of the text.

STEP 5. Write

Now that you have prepped students and their thinking processes to hone in on the article, theme, details, and topic sentences, you can help them write a summary by teaching them the *Four Rules of Summary Writing*. Model each step of the process (see *Tips for Teaching Each Rule as a Process*) before expecting students to write a summary on their own. Allowing students to practice a few times with a partner or in a group also helps.

Try posting the rules in your room for ongoing reference. Here are the *Four Rules of Summary Writing* in shortened form. You can use these as a guide for making a poster:

- Rule 1: Collapse lists.
- Rule 2: Use topic sentences.
- Rule 3: Get rid of unnecessary detail.
- Rule 4: Collapse paragraphs.

THE 4 RULES OF SUMMARY WRITING

Rule 1: Collapse lists.

Rule 2: Use topic sentences.

Rule 3: Get rid of unnecessary detail.

Rule 4: Collapse paragraphs.

Tips for Teaching Each Rule as a Process

Before and after students have drafted their summaries, you can turn the following teaching points into mini-lessons or moments in conferring:

- **Collapse lists:** If a list of items appears in a nonfiction text, teach students to substitute a word or phrase.

- **Use topic sentences:** Teach students to use the topic sentences they find in the article; help them learn to rephrase and make the sentences their own.

- **Get rid of unnecessary detail:** Summaries are short. Teach students how to get rid of unimportant details. Let them know that even published authors of the articles they read can be repetitive, so it's their job to notice these flaws. The rule: Say it once, then move on to the next significant idea.

- **Collapse paragraphs:** Authors use a basic structure in their writing. Teach students to recognize it so they can glean the most important parts (see the "Lessons for Getting Main Idea by Understanding Text Structures" section of Part III). For example, some paragraphs explain; other, often subsequent, paragraphs elaborate with further detail about an initial paragraph; some paragraphs may seem more artful/writerly, designed to set a scene with description that engages but doesn't add a distinct critical new dose of information or idea. Teach students to use an "eagle eye" to determine which paragraphs are most important and have them write about those in the summary, leaving the others out.

STEP 6. Check and Double Check

Have students check their summaries one more time. Say,

> "I want you to read your summary to yourself *[or a partner]*. Ask yourself if the summary matches the article. Also check that you have a good, succinct summary. You may need to revise a bit. Think about if you repeated yourself, if you left anything out, and if the summary has only the important information in it."

STEP 7. Polish and Share!

Sometimes when students write a summary after moving through the steps, the result is a jilted text with unnatural-seeming sentences. Have them read their summaries out loud to a partner and see if they flow. The students may need to add some connecting words (*but, and*, etc.).

Creating Summaries

When to Use: When your students need explicit instruction and/or additional help with summary writing.

Lesson Objective: Write a short summary after reading an article.

Materials Needed: Copies of the article you have selected for the class; notebooks; chart paper or a document camera and projector.

Since this is an explicit lesson in writing summaries, have all the students use the same text, and use the same text in your modeling of the lesson as well. This way, using their own copy of the article, students can follow along with what you do and say.

Grouping: Whole class.

Time: 30 minutes.

STEP 1. Be Explicit

There are times for allowing students to work through reading and writing summaries on their own, discovering their own processes. However, researchers like Gerald Duffy (2002) and Tom Trabasso and Edward Bouchard (2002) have found that explicit instruction in summary writing helps students become better "comprehenders" of text and write better summaries, a skill they will need in middle school, high school, and college. So, this lesson is about being explicit—discussing, modeling, and doing together.

STEP 2. Teach the Steps

In this summary writing think-aloud lesson, you model the following steps with the students while thinking about the article you read together, and plan the class summary. Don't teach each step here—go over the steps with the class so the students know the order to follow as a group. Teach each step explicitly through a think-aloud after you read the article together.

- Read
- Select important information
- Delete unnecessary or trivial information
- Combine ideas
- Delete important, but repeated, information
- Select or write a topic sentence for paragraphs
- Substitute a word for phrase for a list of ideas or items
- Paraphrase into own words

STEP 3. Read the Text

Remind students that when they read in order to write a summary, they need to read actively. You can even model being an active reader. Say,

> "We are going to be active readers today because our purpose for reading is to summarize what we've read. It is easier to write a summary if you take some actions when you read. Let's read the first paragraph together, and then we are going to brainstorm some ways we can annotate the text."

(See the lesson *Annotating Text* in the "Prereading and Think-Aloud Lessons for Main Idea and Details" section of Part III). Brainstorm with the class some possible annotations and model writing at least once in the margin.

> "Now, let's reread the paragraph to see what notes we can take about it. A good note to write down would be the topic sentence of the paragraph."

Model finding the topic sentence and recording it in a notebook. Then continue reading the article out loud to the students, stopping at the end of each paragraph to annotate, and take notes on the topic sentences and other details. As you move through the article, remind students to read, annotate, take notes, and reread. Post these reminders on a wall, or project them on the board, so they can become a visual reminder of what to do while reading when they venture out on their own to read an article and write a summary.

STEP 4. Teach Each of the Steps and Take Notes

Now is when you are going to model the steps you went over with the students at the beginning of the lesson. Teach each step explicitly through a think-aloud. Remember, in a think-aloud (see the "Prereading and Think-Aloud Lessons for Main Idea and Details" section of Part II), you talk out loud about your thinking as you go through the steps. This allows students to "see" our thought processes and begin to own them for themselves. Once you state each step, think out loud about what you should do with the step and the article, elicit ideas from the class, and write the ideas down on a chart or projectable image. *Don't start the writing yet.* This is the note-taking phase (Daily Duo Step 4). As a reminder, the steps are as follows:

- Read
- Select important information
- Delete unnecessary or trivial information
- Combine ideas
- Delete important, but repeated, information
- Select or write a topic sentence for paragraphs
- Substitute a word for phrase for a list of ideas or items
- Paraphrase into own words

STEP 5. Write

Once you finish reading, taking notes, and rereading, launch into writing a summary together as a class. Brainstorm with the class each part of the summary and model the writing on a chart or on an image you project with the document camera. Remember to funnel your thinking (when you funnel thinking while writing, you start with a Big Idea, like the mouth of a funnel, and pop out a short statement about the big idea. Think of the shape of a funnel: The Big Idea goes in the top, and the short statement comes out of the small end of a funnel),

Oill Spill Diasters

There have been many oil spill diasters. One diaster occurred a long time ago very close to where we live. This spill happened in Kern County, only 1 ½ hours away from Fresno. It happened in 1910 and was the worst oil spill on U.S. Soil. 9 million barrels of oil were spilled and the well gushed for 18 months. This is interesting because we never heard about it before.

Catastrophic Records

Class-Written Summary

paraphrase information and ideas into your own words, and follow the summary writing steps above. *Class-Written Summary* is a short summary written with a class of fifth graders about a section of the book *Oil Spill Disaster in the Gulf* (Chiang, Crane, Hamalainen, & Jones, 2010).

STEP 6. Check for Accuracy Against the Text

Students can get so involved in writing a summary that they forget to compare their summary against the text to check for accuracy, and to see if they captured the Big Ideas. Remind them to reskim the article and then reread their summary to see if they match.

Using Backward Summaries to Develop Reasoning

When to Use: When students understand how to summarize well, and they are ready to extend their thinking by analyzing previously written summaries.

The Common Core State Standards expect students to be able to cold-read a text and recognize and evaluate the validity of its reasoning. Additionally, the College and Career Readiness Anchor Standards for Reading expect students to be able to summarize key supporting details and ideas (see R.1, R.2, and R.8). The CCSS assessments will probably include items for which the answers about a text are actually provided, and students will have to justify why the answers are correct. To practice justifying thinking about reading, this lesson has students work to prove why a summary is a good summary of a text, referencing the original text to justify their answers. It's a tall order, I know, but this lesson will help your students prepare for these higher-level comprehension tasks.

Lesson Objective: Evaluate a summary and justify the evaluation by referencing the original text.

Materials Needed: Copies for all students of one of the articles from the Appendix that is summarized at the end of this lesson ("The Consequences of Modern Agriculture" and "Cancer Is a Scary Word," page 205), or any original text that is available to you (or that you create) and that you can summarize; copies of the accompanying summary—or use a single copy and project it using a document camera and a projector.

Grouping: Whole class or small group.

Time: 45 minutes.

STEP 1. Read the Summary

Hand out or project the summary so that all students can see the text clearly. Have students read the summary and then predict what the article is about and what details will be in the article.

STEP 2. Read the Article

Have the students read the article. They can read individually or in groups, or you can read the article to the students (just remember, avoid round-robin reading).

STEP 3. Compare

Display the summary side by side with the article, or have students put the summary and article next to each other on their desks. Have students compare the summary to the article. This is a backward process (they should do this *after* they learn to write summaries), and the students can refer to the *Four Rules for Summary Writing* to see if the summary adequately represents the text. Have students check to see if the following things match:

- The big idea of the article is described as the big idea in the summary.
- Lists in the article appear in the summary as a description using a word or a phrase.
- Big ideas of the paragraphs and details appear in the summary.
- Details in the summary appear in the article.

STEP 4. Justify Answers

Once students scan the article and relate it to the summary, have them evaluate the statements in the summary, underlining the sentences in the article that back up the ideas in the summary.

STEP 5. Wrap Up

Once students develop confidence evaluating summaries, have them write their own summaries and switch with a partner—or if students work in pairs, have them switch with another pair—and take turns evaluating the logic of the summary, referencing the text to justify their answers.

Summary 1

"The Consequences of Modern Agriculture"

We may face shorter life spans than our ancestors based on what we eat. Today, our food is produced through industrialized techniques that endanger the quality of our food supply. These techniques can make us ill, and also are not healthy, quality choices for the animals raised for food. We raise animals in factory-style situations, and use chemicals like fertilizers and pesticides to ensure crop growth. Also, convenience foods, on the rise in our world based on industrialized farming, are not as healthy. As a result, many Americans are facing major health problems like hypertension and diabetes.

Summary 2

"Cancer Is a Scary Word"

Cancer occurs in a person's body when cells that are not normal grow very fast and form tumors. Also, cancer can spread when cells break apart and travel to other parts of the body. Cancer can be scary because people die from cancer. Cancer isn't contagious, and kids can't catch cancer from another person. Kids can't cause themselves to get cancer, but it does help to live a healthy lifestyle so you won't get cancer when you grow up. Most of the people who get cancer are adults.

College and Career Readiness Anchor Standards for Reading 1, 2, and 8

Key Ideas and Details

1. Read closely to determine what the text says explicitly and to make logical inferences from it; cite specific textual evidence when writing or speaking to support conclusions drawn from the text.

2. Determine central ideas or themes of a text and analyze their development; summarize the key supporting detail and ideas.

Integration of Knowledge and Ideas

8. Delineate and evaluate the argument and specific claims in a text, including the validity of the reasoning as well as the relevance and sufficiency of the evidence.

Four Rules for Summary Writing

1. **Collapse lists:** If you see a list of things, think of a word or phrase that can be a name for the whole list.

2. **Use topic sentences:** Look for a sentence that summarizes the whole paragraph. If you don't see one, make one up for yourself.

3. **Get rid of unnecessary detail:** Some information can be repeated, or the same thing is said in different ways. Other information may be trivial.

4. **Collapse paragraphs:** Some paragraphs explain others, and some expand a beginning paragraph. Keep the necessary paragraphs and join together information from paragraphs that connect.

Source: Brown, Day, & Jones (1983); Hare & Borchardt (1984).

Understanding Key Vocabulary

Traditionally, we have taught students to pay attention to lists of words that we hand out at the beginning of a new chapter in a textbook. And I confess I used to often say as I distributed the list, "These words are important!" as though saying that would somehow better ensure students would actually learn the words. Ah, magical thinking. Now I know better.

In this section, I share an approach to developing vocabulary that creates an opportunity for *our students* to think about important words. Yes, here again, it's all about putting responsibility on our students to spot the key language in a nonfiction text. And of course we stand by on the sidelines, demonstrating, thinking aloud, and coaching.

The other sea change these lessons represent is that in the last decade or so, researchers like Beck, McKeown, and Kucan (2002) and Stahl and Nagy (2006) have discovered that the concepts are what counts. That is, we have to look at the texts we teach to decide for ourselves which words support the concept, and then we have to plan how to help students spot these words, too, and wrestle their meanings to the ground on their own.

Think of switching your vocabulary instruction from passive lessons to active lessons. Active lessons get students to think about, and identify, vocabulary *they* think is important to focus on. Active lessons also get students working with words, creating definitions for themselves as they engage in lively thinking and conversation about word meanings. A jump start to effective and powerful vocabulary instruction, the lessons in this chapter are designed to help your students comprehend what they read, and learn new words in the process.

Three Pieces of Advice From Me to You

As you delve into the lessons, keep these points in mind:

1. **Make the lessons your own.** The lessons are thorough enough for you to pick up and teach as is, but by all means, feel free to change them and do what works best for your objectives and your students.

2. **Teach for independence.** As you put the lessons into play, focus on *students doing* and not *teacher doing.* Set an egg timer, your iPhone alarm—whatever it takes to make sure you wrap up a demonstration on the spot if it exceeds 15 minutes. Really! Students learn by doing.

3. **Experiment with different articles.** Use the articles in the Appendix to teach the lessons, but then roam! A lot of great articles are available online, in newspapers, and in magazines in bookstores—get in the habit of finding, filing, and using them. Remember, too, that you can do potent mini-lessons (under 5 minutes), for example reading aloud or projecting just a very small portion of the piece.

As you jump in and teach, remember to have fun!

Knowing Words Well Enough to Generate Them

When to Use: Before, during, and after a content unit, when you want students to develop a knowledge of words beyond familiarity.

We know words at various levels and to different degrees. We don't know all the words in our vocabularies to the same level or degree. There are three degree levels to knowing words:

- **Association:** When we first encounter a word, we might not understand the word's meaning, but we can make correct associations about the word based on the context (Marzano, 2004).
- **Comprehension:** The next level is comprehension. At this level, we may know the word's meaning in the context in which it is used, but we don't have the word in our repertoire—we don't use it, and we definitely cannot define it (Stahl, 1999).
- **Generation:** The third level of knowing words is generation, when we know a word really well, use it in our daily vocabulary, and completely understand all uses of the word (Marzano, 2004; Stahl, 1999). We can "generate" such words at will from our memories and use them correctly and effectively in writing and speaking.

Lesson Objective: Use a word multiple times to develop understanding of the word.

Materials Needed: A copy of the article you have chosen to share with the class, enlarged or projected on the board using a document camera. You can also use a section of a textbook or other media, like a website that has information about the topic you are exploring with the class.

Grouping: Whole class or small group.

Time: 15–20 minutes.

STEP 1. Prepare

To prep for this lesson, decide on a list of words to target based on a topic area and then assess students' knowledge of those words. Working with words that the preassessment shows the students have little to no knowledge of is optimal.

The reason for working with words your students don't know is that the goal of this lesson is to move your students from the association level to the comprehension level of new words presented in a topic area. Do keep your instruction targeted at this level, as it is important to first assess your students' knowledge of the words you have chosen. This preassessment is important because it doesn't do you, or your students, much good to teach words that they already know. For an example of a preassessment, see *Preassessment of Words for Content Areas*. This lesson is designed to jump-start the students' level of knowing a word. Fill in boxes with target words (or have students write words) in the column labeled "Word." Then have students consider their knowledge of the word. If they don't know it, they check the column labeled "Never Heard of It." If they think they know it, they check the column labeled "I Think I Know It." If they are confident they know the meaning of the word, and could teach it to someone else, they check the column labeled "I Can Teach the Definition to a Friend."

Identify words in a topic area by skimming a few texts related to the area. You can use the articles in the Appendix, or a single article from the Appendix and a website that provides additional information, or a textbook section. An example of a word list from a website on the Revolutionary War (www.ushistory.org/declaration/revwartimeline.htm) appears in *Word List for Revolutionary War*. This list is short, keeping to only a few key

WORD LIST FOR REVOLUTIONARY WAR

Independence
colonial
Militia
continental congress
Revolution
Dissent
Defend
constitution

words so as not to overwhelm students with vocabulary before they start reading.

STEP 2. Provide Context

Discuss the topic area with students. I recommend you complete a *What We Know Chart* for the topic area to tap prior knowledge from the class collective and help build background knowledge for students with limited understanding of the topic. The *What We Know Chart* is adapted from the I-Chart in the "Lessons That Support Students While Reading for Main Idea and Details" section of Part III (see the *Inquiry Charts* lesson on page 146). For an example, see *What We Know Chart*.

STEP 3. Engage in Meaningful Use

Word knowledge is developed through meaningful use of words. A few suggested activities for meaningful use include the following:

- **Sentence strip frames:** Have students write the words and accompanying concepts and definitions on sentence strips. Then have them use the sentence strips to teach each other the words and definitions, create a "word wall" or "word bank" in the classroom, and/or create a personal sentence strip using index cards.

- **Word of the day:** Choose one of the important words from the current unit of study, or content being studied, and highlight it as the *word of the day*. Post the word around the room, have students use the word in whole- and small-group discussion, play games with the word, create a PowerPoint slide to project the word, and have students teach one another the word's concept and meaning. One teacher even installed a small changeable message sign in his science classroom and ran the word of the day across the screen during his lessons.

- **Poster words:** A poster word is a word printed large on an 11 × 18–inch (or larger) sheet of paper and then illustrated or decorated to demonstrate the concept of the word. The poster can also include the definition. Poster words are created by students, for students, and can be shared by students in groups or as part of a presentation, and/or be posted in the classroom.

- **Dazzling descriptive words:** This technique comes from my book, *Accelerated Vocabulary Instruction: Strategies for Closing the Achievement Gap for All Students* (Akhavan, 2007). Use large pieces of butcher, or chart, paper and create a web. Put the target word in the middle of the web and have students elicit words and phrases that connect to the concept of the word. Write these phrases and words around the target word in the web.

- **Semantic maps:** Semantic maps can help you harness the power of imagery for students who are visual learners. You can use a web for this as well, but have students make the web individually in a notebook. Say the target word and have students notice the flood of images that pop into their minds upon hearing the target word—this works really well after an initial discussion about the word and the word concept. Then students fill in the word web based on the images that came to mind, using both pictures and words.

STEP 4. Provide Repetition

Don't just provide a single activity with a word on a given day and then drop the word. Repeat using the word with different activities and ensure you are using the word yourself when discussing the topic area. Encourage students to use the target words when talking with a partner or group about the topic. Post topic words in a specific area of the classroom so students can readily access them when talking and writing.

Preassessment of Words for Content Areas

NAME: _____   DATE: _____

DIRECTIONS: Think about how well you know the words in the left-hand column. Put a checkmark in the box that shows how well you know the word.

Word	Never Heard of It	I Think I Know It	I Can Teach the Definition to a Friend, and It Is

What We Know Chart

NAME: _____   DATE: _____

Topic:	What We Know	Facts and Details We Think We've Got a Handle On

Assessing Word Knowledge

When to Use: When modeling for students how to recognize key vocabulary on their own.

In this lesson, you teach students to identify important vocabulary in a text, which is a little different from having them merely identify the words you have already declared are important. So often teachers hand word lists to students to study because the words are important for understanding a text, but this doesn't build any skills in judgment about texts or develop any discrimination skills to determine what is most important in a text. We do this all the time when we make choices about what words students should learn in a topic area or in an article, so why not teach the students to do this thinking? Not only will it keep them more engaged as their own thinking is reinforced, but the action also shows that you believe in them as learners and makes the students active and responsible for their learning—they must avoid being passive about their learning by just letting us (or a publisher) figure out the words they need to know.

Lesson Objective: Students identify key vocabulary and self-assess knowledge of key vocabulary in an article.

Materials Needed: Copies of the article you have chosen for each student; a chart or projector to record notes and ideas; highlighters and pens; copies for each student of *Do I Know This Word? Assessment Sheet* (you can find the sheet at the end of this lesson and enlarge it and make copies for students) (Akhavan, 2007).

Grouping: Whole class.

Time: 10 minutes or longer depending on the length of the article.

STEP 1. Demonstrate the Thinking Behind Identifying Key Vocabulary

When your students read nonfiction, they need to be aware of important words they don't know. Self-awareness helps students develop a purpose for figuring out word meanings. Teaching students to identify words they don't know is much different from presenting them with a list of words that might be hard for them. It is the difference between passive and active learning.

The best way to teach this thinking is through a think-aloud (see the "Prereading and Think-Aloud Lessons for Main Idea and Details" section of Part III). Project a text on the board or pass out copies. Use a different article from the one you have chosen for the students to read. This is highly effective if you use an article at your reading level—perhaps a choice from *National Geographic* or *Scientific American*—because you are showing students how you think through the identification of words you may not know, and using an article written at the students' level may seem inauthentic. Also, the students won't have to read your article; they'll just have to watch you think through it. Think aloud to reveal your thoughts to students about words that you might find difficult. Highlight, circle, or underline these words so the students can see them, and reveal your thinking about why they might be the key words you need to pay attention to when reading for meaning. Clues for identifying these words include the following:

- Repeated words
- Words appearing throughout the text
- Content-area words that appear often
- Words that also appear in graphics or other text features
- Words that seem to have sentences that describe them

Once you think through the text, identifying key words, write the words on the *Do I Know this Word? Assessment Sheet* in the left-hand column. Walk through the self-assessment categories at the top of the page for each word. In the "Self-Assessment" column, I suggest you "pretend" to not know some of the words so that students can see that even you (the teacher!) need to pay attention to words and figure out word meaning when reading. To figure out the word meaning for the "What I Think It Means" column, model for students how to guess (infer) word meaning from the sentences around the unknown word. If you really cannot figure it out, leave that box blank until you look up the definition and then go back and fill it in. The last column, "Actual Definition," is a perfect opportunity to model looking up a word in the dictionary. When you do this, don't just grab the first definition that appears for the word; double-check the context of word use from the article, and then choose a definition. It is really important to model and think aloud while demonstrating this process because kids tend to just pick the first definition that appears in a list, and they don't consider context in choosing the correct definition.

STEP 2. Guide Students While They Identify and Assess Their Knowledge of the Vocabulary

Once you finish the think-aloud with the demonstration text, it is time for students to practice identifying words they think are key and assessing their knowledge of each. Let the students skim the text and highlight or circle words they think are important in the article. The students may then move on, writing these words on the assessment sheet independently. Encourage the students to fill in the self-assessment section on the graphic organizer. If students only choose words they already know, encourage them to stretch to words that may be less familiar.

STEP 3. Share

Work with students in small groups or as a whole class to share what words they identified and take a class poll on their self-assessment results of word meanings. Discuss word meaning with the students—accessing online word dictionaries or referring to text features like an index for support and clarification.

Do I Know This Word? Assessment Sheet

NAME: _____ DATE: _____

DIRECTIONS: Think about how well you know the words in the left-hand column. Put a checkmark in the box that shows how well you know the word.

Word	Self-Assessment ☐ I know it – I don't know it	What I Think It Means	Actual Definition

Source: Akhavan (2007).

Word Definition Cards

When to Use: Before beginning a content unit.

Beck, McKeown, and Kucan (2002) have identified three tiers, or categories, of vocabulary word types. The first tier comprises basic words that rarely need instruction in meaning. Students develop an understanding of these words in conversation and reading. Second-tier words are useful words that appear across genres and content areas. These words appear frequently in reading and are often conceptually difficult for students to understand (Beck et al., 2002). Third-tier words are content-area words, or words that appear in a specific domain of knowledge. In the articles appearing in this book, you will find both Tier 2 and Tier 3 words that students might need to work with to understand. This lesson can apply to either category of words.

Lesson Objective: Create reference cards to learn word definitions and word use.

Materials Needed: Copies of the reproducible *Word Card* (Akhavan, 2007) for each student, or several blank index cards sized 5 × 8 inches for each student.

Grouping: Whole class to launch, and then for individual use.

Time: 10 minutes.

STEP 1. Provide Background on Key Vocabulary

In this lesson, you provide the key vocabulary you want students to learn. The vocabulary can be from a topic area or an article and can include Tier 2 and Tier 3 words. First, post and/or pass out the key vocabulary list. Go over the list three times. The first time, just say the words. Then, during the second pass over the list, read the words and ask the students if they know what the words might mean. Allow students with correct knowledge about the words to share. Then have students share with a partner to discuss on their own the key points about the word's definition. Finally, read the list for a third time, marking the words that no one knows with a star [★]. Then provide background on these words that no one knows.

STEP 2. Have Students Create a Definition Card for Each Word

Instruct students to use the reproducible *Word Card* or teach them to set up the index cards for two-column notes. Demonstrate how to write the word on the left and the definition *in their own words* on the right. The students will use their knowledge of the class discussions to fill in the definition in their own words.

STEP 3. Have Students Store and Reference Words as Needed

Students complete the cards or the *Word Card* graphic organizer. Check the cards for accuracy of definitions, and have students keep them handy in their desks or another place close by. Store blank cards on a ring or in an index card box, or use a folder with brads or pockets to store copies of the reproducible *Word Card*.

NAME: _____   **DATE:** _____

Word	Definition in My Own Words

Source: Akhavan (2007).

Four-Square Word Map

When to Use: After launching a content unit, when students are ready to grapple with really understanding key vocabulary.

A concept map is a graphic organizer that helps students learn word concepts. This is based on the idea of schema theory, a theory of knowledge. A schema is a data structure for storing information in the brain (Rumelhart & Norman, 1981), and we have schemata representing all of the concepts that we know. Good vocabulary instruction attempts to hook into these schemata, connecting new concepts and associated words with existing knowledge. This isn't a traditional approach to vocabulary instruction, where the teacher tells the students what words mean or the students look up words in the dictionary (I share my thoughts about that type of instruction in the lesson *Inferring Word Meanings* later in this chapter), but it is an approach that can lead to longer retention of word meanings.

Lesson Objective: Develop conceptual understanding of a word including discriminating between examples and nonexamples of a word.

Materials Needed: A copy of the selected article for each student; 8½ × 11–inch paper for all students or a copy of the *Four-Square Word Map* (Akhavan, 2007) for each student.

Grouping: Whole class or small group.

Time: 15–20 minutes.

STEP 1. Present the Concept

Discuss the concept from the article that is the prevailing front-runner for importance. Other concepts may be presented in the article, but at first, go with the most obvious concept. Discuss this concept with the students, eliciting their ideas about what it means. Reading all or part of the article with the class may help to develop a rich conversation.

STEP 2. Present the Unknown Word

Once you have engaged the class in a great conversation about the concept—waking up the students' brains about prior knowledge they might have about the concept—it is time to present the word to the class. Write the target word in the Box 1 of the *Four-Square Word Map*.

STEP 3. Discuss the Word; Solicit Examples

Next, prompt the students to think of examples of the concept. In Box 2, write down the words or phrases that the students think exemplify the word. The idea is for students to remember a word concept by thinking of previous knowledge that represents, or can help them remember, the word concept.

STEP 4. Continue to Discuss the Word; Solicit Nonexamples

Next, in Box 3, write the ideas that students come up with for nonexamples of the word concept. Remember, we are not focused on antonyms because the objective is to teach the *concept*, not the word. So elicit suggestions from the students regarding nonexamples of the concept. The word learning comes with the connection to learning the concept.

STEP 5. Define the Word

In Box 4, record a definition of the word concept that you have been discussing. I find it helps students to remember the concept and associated words when they write the definition on their own. You can engage the class in a discussion about a good definition, or have students brainstorm on their own. After they brainstorm a definition, you can engage the class in purposeful use of a dictionary by looking up the word and comparing word meanings to the ideas, examples, and definition the students thought up.

STEP 6. Post the Four-Square Concept Map

Don't let these rich concept maps languish in students' notebooks or desks! Post them in the classroom to create word banks of concepts taught during the year.

Four-Square Word Map

NAME: _____   DATE: _____

1. Target Word	2. Examples
4. My Definition	**3. Nonexamples**

Available for download at **www.corwin.com/nonfictionnow**

Source: Akhavan (2007).

Inferring Word Meanings

When to Use: During reading in a content unit.

When inexperienced readers encounter an unfamiliar word, often they skip over the word and keep reading. The problem is that they usually don't try to figure out the word's meaning using the context of the text. They skip over it and never look back. For struggling readers, this practice can become debilitating when reading nonfiction because nonfiction often has numerous unknown words in any given text, and the students who "skip and move on" may severely limit their ability to comprehend. It is a good idea to teach students to skip words and read to the end of a sentence or section, in service of going back to think through the word, making inferences about what it might mean based on the sentences before and after the word in the text. This lesson reinforces students' thinking, and supports students in taking educated guesses about word meaning by carefully thinking about what the sentences are saying, and what text structures (see the "Lessons for Getting Main Idea by Understanding Text Structures" section of Part III) might be present to support the information in the text. These are clues to word meaning.

You might wonder why I do not recommend that students stop reading and look up the unknown word in a dictionary. First, good readers rarely do this. Even when technology makes it easy to look up a word, good readers usually just keep reading because they can infer the word meaning from the context of the text. Now, of course, if good readers' comprehension breaks down, they might stop and check the meaning of the word, but they do this rarely because it breaks the flow of the reading. Second, poor or struggling readers usually don't carefully consider the multiple definitions available for most words; they just choose the first definition, call it good, and move on, which does not help them understand the text, as the definition may be incorrect given the context.

Lesson Objective: Make an inference about word meaning based on context.

Materials Needed: A copy of the selected article for each student; a half-sheet of 8½ × 11–inch paper for all students.

Grouping: Small group.

Time: 15–20 minutes.

STEP 1. Pair and Prepare

Organize students in groups of 4, 5, or 6—large enough that students can help one another with brainstorming, but not too small to risk the students getting "stuck" in their thinking. Demonstrate use of the *Inferring Word Meaning* chart.

STEP 2. Students Read, ID, and Hypothesize

Working in groups, students help one another to make inferences about the words in the text that they have identified from their reading. To do this, group the students and familiarize them with the *Inferring Word Meaning* reproducible. Say,

> "Today I want you to trust your thinking. I want you to identify important
> words in the article you are reading, while you are reading. Then, as a group,
> I want you to decide what you think the words mean, go back to the text to
> see what sentences have helped you develop that thinking about the word,
> and then list what else you know about the word. To do this, you might notice
> the parts of the word or the use of the word in the sentence, or you might

221

share information you know about the word or related ideas. Don't be afraid to give this a go. There aren't any wrong answers; the answers come from your thinking about brainstorming as a group."

STEP 3. Write a Definition

After students brainstorm answers for the middle three columns of the *Inferring Word Meaning* chart—"What I think the word means," "What the sentences make me think it means," and "What else I know about the word"—have the students develop a definition together. One student can then write the definition on the page or the chart under the word. You can get the class started defining the word by saying,

> "I think you have developed a good understanding of the word's meaning *[say the word]* based on what the text says and what you already knew about the word. So, knowing these things, what is a good definition of the word? What could you write down?"

If students get stuck, give them a little nudge by discussing the word with them, and what the text says about the word.

STEP 4. Share

Once each group of students completes an *Inferring Word Meaning* chart with approximately five words and meanings, have them share with another small group in class to compare notes and thinking and the examined vocabulary words.

Inferring Word Meaning

NAME: _____   DATE: _____

Word	What I think the word means	What the sentences make me think it means	What else I know about the word	Definition of Word

Writing About Reading

Writing is an awfully good way of thinking. It's an unbeatable process for discovering and securing one's understandings. From making diary entries about the events in one's personal life to taking copious notes to try to understand a challenging topic, getting thoughts down on the page is a critical activity of an educated mind. In a book on teaching nonfiction, of course, we'll zero in on writing about reading as it pertains to learning in the content areas. The lessons and writing activities presented here will help you model and guide students to apply the information and ideas they have taken from texts—to think with it, bring their own stamp of understanding to it, and show on the page that they have read well enough to inform others about a topic. Try them with Daily Duo Step 6, *Writing About Reading*.

Technically, the genre we address is informational writing, because students are writing to inform others about content they have learned. Informational writing informs or describes. When students write an informational essay or report, they need to introduce a topic, provide an organized structure to the essay or report, and use the structure to discuss relevant supporting evidence. Most informational writing includes language and vocabulary specific to the topic of the piece. Additionally, students should be able to wrap up their informational pieces with a conclusion that makes sense given the information and details presented.

The ideas in this section will help you guide your students to write about their reading in brief informal ways (through exit tickets or logs) and formal ways (through essays and structured writing). Some ideas are presented as writing activities, and others as focus lessons, which are short, strategic, 5- to 15-minute lessons meant to launch writing activity in your classroom without devolving into lectures that eat into vital student writing time.

Whether or not you have writing workshop in your classroom, the lessons here assume a three-phase instructional design, which begins with a focus lesson, moves into sustained writing time (practice), and finally concludes with a share time (see

Chapter 6, especially the *Cheat Sheet* on page 59, for more information). Typically for a 30- to 40-minute writing session, the focus lesson lasts between 10 and 15 minutes (but can also be only 5 minutes if you are reteaching), and the share at the end lasts between 5 and 7 minutes. The time in between, between 25 and 30 minutes, is for students to practice writing. Dedicating a total of 40 minutes to writing a couple of times a week is preferable, and doable if you teach in a departmentalized setting and have approximately 50-minute periods. If you don't, you can cut the writing time or have students write for homework, but this is overall less effective as your presence is key for coaching these developing writers.

The Focus Lesson Structure

The lessons presented here follow a four-part lesson plan, much like the lesson plan introduced in the "The Focus Lesson: What to Do" section of Chapter 6 (page 60):

- **Connect:** You do a quick demonstration for students that gets across why the new content matters and how it may connect to what they already know.
- **Teach:** You model using think-aloud techniques and visuals to explicitly show how you interact with a text as a reader and a writer.
- **Give It a Go:** You engage students in active thinking about the objective of the lesson. Do this by inviting students to connect with one another, talking and sharing their processes as they try what you have just modeled for them.
- **Wrap Up:** You recap what you modeled and discussed with students and have them share their thinking and ideas about the information shared in the lesson. Then you send them off to write.

The Activities

The first three writing activities in this section do not need to be taught as focus lessons, but could be incorporated into your writing lessons or writing time.

The Focus Lessons

The five focus lessons following the activities provide you and your students with fuller demonstrations. These lessons are designed to help you guide students' learning and then release the responsibility to your students so that they will own the writing process for themselves.

Quick Writes

When to Use: When you want to get students thinking about new information or concepts presented, or when you want to do a formative assessment to see what your students understand from a lesson.

How to Use: Quick writes are exactly what they sound like: writing that is recorded quickly, and for a short amount of time. The quick write is an excellent tool to maintain student engagement using the 10-2 principle. Student attention when receiving new information lasts about 10 minutes; after 10 minutes, students need a 2-minute activity to engage their attention and help them consolidate new information (Saphier, Haley-Speca, & Gower, 2008). This movement between listening and engaging is called the 10-2 principle (Saphier et al., 2008), and you can use writing for the 2-minute engagement. Writing short bursts of text on new ideas and information can help your students begin to own the information for themselves. When using a quick write, direct students' thinking by connecting a prompt or question to the information you have shared, or to something they have read.

Lesson Objective: Write a short explanation or description of new information from a lesson.

Materials Needed: Writing materials; student notebooks to record writing.

Grouping: Whole class or small group.

Time: Depends on the length the lesson; quick writes can be incorporated 3–4 times during a 30- to 40-minute lesson.

ACTIVITY

Learning Logs

When to Use: Especially good for science and social studies; whenever you want students to keep track of their learning and thinking about a new topic or about their reading.

How to Use: Learning logs can provide a history of student thinking and reading comprehension over time. Fisher and Frey (2004) suggest using prompts to structure learning logs. Well-structured prompts focused on inquiry can guide students to think deeply about their reading and help them reflect on new topics, ideas, and what they have read. Questions that structure the learning logs might include the following:

- What have I learned from this reading?
- What don't I get?
- What do I think about what I read?
- What do I think is important about this topic?

Lesson Objective: Write answers to thoughtful questions to record thinking about a topic in a log.

Materials Needed: Booklets for learning logs or notebooks; marble composition books work well.

Grouping: Small group or individual.

Time: 5–15 minutes.

Admit and Exit Tickets

When to Use: Whenever you want to get a pulse on students' understanding.

How to Use: Admit and exit tickets are brief writing assignments that do two things—get and keep students on task, *and* help you assess comprehension of material or reading—that can take anywhere from 2 to 10 minutes. Your job is to collect them when students are done; collect admit tickets once students are organized and in the classroom at the start of the period, and collect exit tickets as they walk out the door. The emphasis is on students writing what they have learned.

Topics for admit tickets include the following:

- Elaborate on a question or inquiry from the homework assignment.
- Explain what you remember from the last time class was held.
- Think of and ask questions of previously covered material.

Topics for exit tickets include the following:

- Summarize key points from the lesson.
- Summarize key points or Big Ideas from the reading.
- Think of and ask questions of ideas discussed in class.
- Ponder the essential question for the lesson that was just taught.

Lesson Objective: Write a short statement based on the teacher prompt to show understanding of material discussed or learned.

Materials Needed: Sheets of paper large enough for students to write a response on them, or copies of one of the admit and exit ticket reproducibles.

Grouping: Whole class.

Time: 2–10 minutes.

Exit Ticket

NAME: _____

What did you really "get" from today's lesson?

Why is this important?

Exit Ticket

NAME: _____

If I were to give you a test on what we learned today, what should I put on the test?

What would your answer be if your question/idea was on the test?

NAME: _____

> What do you remember from yesterday's lesson?
>
>
>
> If you don't remember anything, why do you think you don't remember?

Admit Ticket

NAME: _____

> What big question do you have about last night's reading?
>
>
>
> What did you think about the text you read?

Available for download at **www.corwin.com/nonfictionnow**

Guided Writing

Guided writing is an activity to increase students' comprehension of content concepts by engaging in discussion, listening, reading, and writing. A research-based procedure that gets students thinking about prior knowledge and then extends their thinking with discussion and writing (Knipper & Duggan, 2006), guided writing has a few steps, including brainstorming, organizing and labeling ideas, and writing about the topic.

Lesson Objective: Using a guided process, students brainstorm, discuss, and then write about their ideas.

Materials: Writing materials; chart paper and markers; copies of articles that students have been reading.

Connect

Say,

> "Sometimes it is really hard to get started with your writing. When we get stuck in our writing, it really helps to first brainstorm ideas and then think about how we would write about our ideas. Today we are going to work together to brainstorm about what we could write."

Teach

Say,

> "Let's get out our articles and think about what we've been reading."

If students have annotated their articles (see the lesson *Annotating Text* in the "Prereading and Think-Aloud Lessons for Main Idea and Details" section of Part III), it is helpful in the brainstorming process, but not required.

> "Take a look at your articles and think about what we've been reading as a class. We are going to brainstorm some ideas together."

While students offer ideas and suggestions about what they have been reading, write down their ideas on the chart paper. After brainstorming with the students, model for them how to organize and categorize their ideas.

> "Now that we have brainstormed some ideas about what we've read, I'm going to show you a way to organize the thinking so we can write about our ideas. I'm going to use one color of marker to circle thoughts, ideas, and information that connect together. Watch me while I group a few ideas together. After I circle one group of thoughts together, I'm going to use a different color marker to circle and highlight another group of ideas that connect together."

Model how to organize the ideas together by color-coding.

Give It a Go

As a way of getting students active in the lesson, suggest that they think of labels for the categories you just created with the color-coding. Prompt students to talk through their ideas in groups of three or four.

Wrap Up

Have a few students share their ideas about the labels they brainstormed. Lead the students to talk about what they could write based on the ideas and the category labels. Together as a group, write a few sentences.

You can repeat this process often with your class to help the students think through their ideas and write out their thoughts about a reading.

At the end of this lesson, you will have produced a class-written short essay or summary on a shared reading. See *Class-Written Guided Writing Sample* for an example.

Summary of the Fall of the Persian Empire.

Following the death of Xerxes in 465 BC. no great leader stepped up. Murder in the royal family weakened the structure. Some stability came in 424 BC. with the ruling of Artaxerxes. But when he died, two brothers, Artaxerxes II and Cyrus III fought each other. Artaxerxes prevailed but unrest continued. The royal family kept killing each other for power. In 358 BC. King Philip of Macedonia plotted to take over the Persian Empire. He succeeded in defeating Darius III. Philip died and his son Alexander invaded Persia, succeeding in deeply penetrating the country. Persia fell to Alexander.

Class-Written Guided
Writing Sample

Microthemes

A microtheme is a technique for writing about reading where students draw together key ideas from their writing and capture that thinking on an index card. This technique, by Brozo and Simpson (2003), allows students to practice summarizing text and gives you a way to quickly assess their reading comprehension. You can work on microthemes in several ways: assign the class a topic to investigate, encourage students to analyze the articles they are reading, or have students respond to an open-ended question (Knipper & Dugan, 2006). Students often like writing microthemes because they can get into a topic, but are expected to write only an amount of text that fills an index card. They then can refer back to the cards when writing a longer piece or studying for a test.

Lesson Objective: Write a summary or analysis of a topic or article on an index card.

Materials: Index card; reading materials; chart paper and markers; one article of your choice for modeling.

Connect

Say,

> "We have been doing a lot of reading in class, and a lot of discussing of topics *[maybe a topic in social studies or science]*, and I want to show you a way of capturing your thinking about the topic, or about your reading."

Hold up a card with information filled in on it (see *Microtheme Card* for an example).

> "This is a microtheme card, and that is what I want to share with you."

Teach

Say,

> "A microtheme is a short piece of writing that you can do on your reading or on a topic you are investigating. A microtheme has two parts. One is the micro part, or the small amount of writing, and the second part is the theme, or the topic you have been reading about."

Write this on a large piece of chart paper; see *Microtheme Chart Example* for a sample teaching chart for this lesson.

> "If I were going to write a microtheme about something I am an expert in, something I know a lot about, I would have to choose *[pick a topic, like mowing the lawn or doing the dishes]*. I could write up a microtheme on *[your topic]* in just a few simple sentences."

Go ahead and model this writing on a card, or on the chart.

> "See how I did that? I recorded the most important parts about *[your topic]*. Now, you can do this with your reading as well. When you are reading, you can stop and take a few notes about what is most important with this topic and write those down as part of the microtheme. Or you can write your microtheme after reading an article."

Now you will model reading a short article, or part of a longer article, and writing the microtheme card after you finish the reading. Be sure to focus on the topic, or the theme, of the article.

Pass out an index card to each student.

"I want you to write up a quick microtheme right now. Think of something you know a lot about—maybe skateboarding or texting—and write up a short summary about what you know about that topic. I'm going to give you only three minutes to do this, so get started!"

Give It a Go

Have a few students share their microtheme on their expert topic. Ask the students to share what they understand about microthemes and how they can be used to record points from their reading. Send students off to continue reading or investigating their topics of interest. Provide index cards for their use.

Wrap Up

After this lesson, you'll have one or more index cards filled with information written in summary style about students' reading or investigations.

Invite students to share their microtheme cards with one another. Recap the objective of writing a microtheme and how these cards can help your students comprehend what they read.

Microtheme Card

TOPIC: US involvement in foreign affairs

Main Pts:
- US has history of involvement in other countries to protect national interests.
- US involves itself in other countries wars for humanitarian reasons, but also for political power.
- Recent developments in Syria are an example when the government used chemical weapons on the people. President Obama threatened to attack; but in the end the US didn't attack

Microtheme Card

Microtheme Chart Example

Microtheme

Topic Description:

Thought-Provoking Question: What do you think about . . . ?

Microtheme

Topic Description:

Main Points About the Topic:

Microtheme

Topic Description:

Think about the topic in depth. What significance does it have?

Microtheme

Topic Description:

Compare and contrast the main points of the topic.

Argumentative Writing

Argument is practiced in all places in our lives and society. One just has to turn on the television to a national news commentary show to see an argument in process. Argument is about putting an idea forth and supporting that idea, even through a dispute.

Teaching argumentative writing is a complex and demanding task because multiple genres can be considered argumentative writing—for example, letters, speeches, sermons, reports, and essays—and a specific type of genre doesn't exemplify the form (Newell et al., 2011). Additionally, teaching argumentative writing is difficult because most textbooks are written in descriptive and narrative forms. In argument, the writer makes claims and then provides evidence to back up the claims. This is fairly sophisticated thinking for developing readers and writers, as the writer needs to read a topic widely in order to make a claim, and then has to know how to reference multiple sources to back it up. Brooks and Jeong (2006) found that students who labeled their argument strategies as arguments, challenges, supporting evidence, and explanations were better able to create effective arguments in their writing. This leads us to this lesson, which helps students understand the structure of argument and label their own planning with strategies for writing a solid and sensible argument. Outlines that help students develop their arguments are very helpful to scaffold this learning, and I suggest one model—Claim, Reason, Evidence, Counterargument, Warrant—in this lesson.

I am suggesting here that you teach argument in relation to the grade level you are teaching—the Common Core State Standards provide an excellent spiral of expectation for argument writing as each grade level expectation builds upon the previous one. *CCSS College and Career Readiness Anchor Standards for Writing—Text Types and Purposes Standard 1* reviews the first Text Types and Purposes standard for Grades 6–12. Additions or changes to the standard are circled so you can see the development. I suggest you get familiar with your grade-level standard in this area so you know the extent to which you will need to teach argument in your class. This lesson outlines a beginning method for teaching argument—a discussion of the claim, evidence, and reasons. You can modify the lesson in any way that works for the grade-level expectation of the Common Core State Standards. Additionally, you can teach multiple mini-lessons during a unit on argumentative writing.

A strong argumentative essay has several parts, and even though you may not teach all of them, I am going to review them for your information. The parts include (usually in this order) the claim, the reason, the evidence, and the counterargument or rebuttal. Some sophisticated essays, particularly at the college level, also include a warrant. A warrant connects your reasons to your claims in a logical argument.

- **Claim:** Making a concise, clear statement about the main point
- **Reason:** Stating why you are making the claim
- **Evidence:** Backing up the claim with supporting ideas and information
- **Counterargument:** Presenting the opposite idea from what you have stated in your claim and providing a reason why your claim is correct and stronger
- **Warrant:** Connecting the claim and the evidence together in a statement of general belief

The order in an essay is usually claim, reason, evidence, counterargument, and warrant. Some essays, however, begin with the reason and then state the claim.

CCSS College and Career Readiness Anchor Standards for Writing—Text Types and Purposes Standard 1

Grade 6	Grade 7	Grade 8	Grades 9 and 10	Grades 11 and 12
Write arguments to support claims with clear reasons and relevant evidence.	1. Write arguments to support claims with clear reasons and relevant evidence.	1. Write arguments to support claims with clear reasons and relevant evidence.	Write arguments to support claims in an analysis of substantive topics or texts, using valid reasoning and relevant and sufficient evidence.	Write arguments to support claims in an analysis of substantive topics or texts, using valid reasoning and relevant and sufficient evidence.
a. Introduce claim(s) and organize the reasons and evidence clearly.	a. Introduce claim(s), acknowledge alternate or opposing claims, and organize the reasons and evidence logically.	a. Introduce claim(s), acknowledge and distinguish the claim(s) from alternate or opposing claims, and organize the reasons and evidence logically.	a. Introduce precise claim(s), distinguish the claim(s) from alternate or opposing claims, and create an organization that establishes clear relationships among claim(s), counterclaims, reasons, and evidence.	a. Introduce precise, knowledgeable claim(s), establish the significance of the claim(s), distinguish the claim(s) from alternate or opposing claims, and create an organization that logically sequences claim(s), counterclaims, reasons, and evidence.
b. Support claim(s) with clear reasons and relevant evidence, using credible sources and demonstrating an understanding of the topic or text.	b. Support claim(s) with logical reasoning and relevant evidence, using accurate, credible sources and demonstrating an understanding of the topic or text.	b. Support claim(s) with logical reasoning and relevant evidence, using accurate, credible sources and demonstrating an understanding of the topic or text.	b. Develop claim(s) and counterclaims fairly, supplying evidence for each while pointing out the strengths and limitations of both in a manner that anticipates the audience's knowledge level and concerns.	b. Develop claim(s) and counterclaims fairly and thoroughly, supplying the most relevant evidence for each while pointing out the strengths and limitations of both in a manner that anticipates the audience's knowledge level, concerns, values, and possible biases.
c. Use words, phrases, and clauses to clarify the relationships among claim(s) and reasons.	c. Use words, phrases, and clauses to create cohesion and clarify the relationships among claim(s), reasons, and evidence.	c. Use words, phrases, and clauses to create cohesion and clarify the relationships among claim(s), counterclaims, reasons, and evidence.	c. Use words, phrases, and clauses to link the major sections of the text, create cohesion, and clarify the relationships between claim(s) and reasons, between reasons and evidence, and between claim(s) and counterclaims.	c. Use words, phrases, and clauses as well as varied syntax to link the major sections of the text, create cohesion, and clarify the relationships between claim(s) and reasons, between reasons and evidence, and between claim(s) and counterclaims.
d. Establish and maintain a formal style.	d. Establish and maintain a formal style.	d. Establish and maintain a formal style.	d. Establish and maintain a formal style and objective tone while attending to the norms and conventions of the discipline in which they are writing.	d. Establish and maintain a formal style and objective tone while attending to the norms and conventions of the discipline in which they are writing.
e. Provide a concluding statement or section that follows from the argument presented.	e. Provide a concluding statement or section that follows from and supports the argument presented.	e. Provide a concluding statement or section that follows from and supports the argument presented.	e. Provide a concluding statement or section that follows from and supports the argument presented.	e. Provide a concluding statement or section that follows from and supports the argument presented.

Source: Copyright 2010. National Governors Association Center for Best Practices and Council of Chief State School Officers. All rights reserved.

Lesson Objective: Students create a short argumentative essay after reading a text, or several texts on the same topic.

Materials: Writing materials; chart paper and markers.

Connect

Say,

> "Last night I watched a news show where people were arguing with one another about an issue with great passion. In fact, at one point, it seemed like they were all yelling at one another. It made my blood pressure skyrocket! I hope that we can create some fabulous argument essays in class today. An argument makes a claim about something, and then you provide the evidence backing up the claim in hope of making your claim strong. This is your argument."

Teach

Say,

> "I think that writing arguments can be really fun. Argumentative writing has three parts: the claim, the reason, and the supporting information. Some essays also have a warrant. The warrant is the interpretation the author makes for the reader between the claim and the supporting information. You make this connection in your writing because you don't want your readers coming up with their own idea. You want them to agree with *your* idea! First, let's look at making a claim. *[You are going to model writing the claim on the chart paper using markers.]* A claim is something you are stating as a truth, something that is correct. It may not be correct, but you are stating it is, and then you are going to provide evidence that you are correct. Hmm . . . Let's think of something fun we could state as a claim."

Elicit simple ideas from the class. For the first example, use a simple idea so the students can see what a claim is without dealing with a new or difficult-to-understand topic. For example, try "The sun is helpful to our world because it is yellow" or "Our school is the best school because it is in *[your city's name]*." Or practice making a false claim that you will back up with evidence: "Our world would be better if our planet was closer to the sun." You can make any claim you want with the class—just remember that a claim is a conclusion based on evidence, or supporting material, that you must provide.

After you brainstorm a few claims, move on to writing the reasons for the claim. Brainstorm one strong reason about the claim with the class and write it on a large piece of chart paper. The reason is the "why" behind the claim. See *Example of Claim and Reason.*

Example of Claim and Reason

There are a lot of great basketball players in the NBA, but not all of them are validated for their success.   **Claim**

It takes more than one or two stars to make a great team, and some great players are on teams that just never win the championship game.   **Reason**

After you brainstorm a few claims, move on to providing the supporting material for one claim. Brainstorm this with the class as well and write it on the chart. The supporting material is the evidence the writer provides to convince the reader of the strength of the claim. See *Example of Claim and Supporting Evidence*.

Example of Claim and Supporting Evidence

There are a lot of great basketball players in the NBA, but not all of them are validated for their success. Claim

Some players are important whether they get attention by the media and the NBA or not. NBA players are validated for their greatness as a player when they win a championship. For example, Carmelo Anthony is known as a great scorer, but he hasn't won a championship. Now, he is getting older and has had injuries, so he might not have a chance to win a title. Evidence

Some players are great at their position, but they are overshadowed by players who have risen to stardom. Chris Paul is one of these players. He played for the Los Angeles Clippers in 2013, he is a six-time All-Star and possesses the sixth highest career player efficiency rating (PER) in NBA history, but his name is not known to the average person on the street.

Certain players are discussed often in media and become household names through advertising.

The next step in preparing to write an argument essay is to connect the claim and the supporting evidence together in a summary statement called the warrant. Depending on the age of your students, you may or may not teach them to write a warrant. If you want to teach writing a warrant, you might say,

> "We've done some good brainstorming about our claim, our reason, and the ideas we have that support the claim. Now, let's think of a warrant, a good sentence that sums up one evidence point and how it connects back to the claim. This sentence is the reason the evidence and the claim connect together. Crafting a good reason can be tricky, but remember, we don't want any readers to come up with their own conclusion. We are arguing that we are correct, or justified, so we need to guide the reader's thinking."

See *Example of Claim, Reasons, Supporting Evidence, and Warrant.*
Now say,

> "I want you to talk with a partner about an argument that you could make about something you know. Go ahead and talk for a couple of minutes, and then we are going to brainstorm some topics together."

Remember, the engagement is short—only a couple of minutes—this gives the students time to process new information by verbalizing their thinking with another student.

Example of Claim, Reasons, Supporting Evidence, and Warrant

There are a lot of great basketball players in the NBA, but not all of them are validated for their success.   **Claim**

It takes more than one or two stars to make a great team, and some great players are on teams that just never win the championship game.   **Reason**

Some players are important whether they get attention by the media and the NBA or not. NBA players are validated for their greatness as a player when they win a championship. For example, Carmelo Anthony is known as a great scorer, but he hasn't won a championship. Now, he is getting older and has had injuries, so he might not have a chance to win a title.

Some players are great at their position, but they are overshadowed by players who have risen to stardom. Chris Paul is one of these players. He played for the Los Angeles Clippers in 2013, he is a six-time All-Star and possesses the sixth highest career player efficiency rating (PER) in NBA history, but his name is not known to the average person on the street.   **Evidence**

Certain players are discussed often in media and become household names through advertising.

Perhaps the problem with sports today is that the media spotlights some players and not others despite consistent and excellent skills on the court over several seasons. Fans notice the amount of time some players get in the media, and that tends to make them support these players more, and others less, pushing some players to stardom over the less discussed, or highlighted, players.   **Warrant**

Give It a Go

Elicit a few ideas from the students about what they just discussed with their partners. Have the students explain their argument and perhaps share the claim and some evidence. Then send them off to write.

> "We have thought up some great ideas for arguments. Now I want you to go ahead and write an argument on your own."

Wrap Up

Students write a short argumentative essay on a topic of choice—something easy to practice, something from life experience, or, if your students are ready to apply creating an argument to their reading, something they have read.

Invite students to share their argument and the supporting details they have outlined to support their argument.

Extended Writing

In the past, students were writing in our content-area classrooms, but often they were writing short responses to questions after reading. The Common Core State Standards guide our work with students away from teaching one standard at a time, breaking the learning down into small pieces, which encourages us to have students read and answer questions, and then create extended writing pieces about their reading. Extended writing pieces can look many different ways. A student may write an essay after reading an interesting topic, create a piece of writing to solve a problem or outline a concept, write about his or her point of view, write a descriptive essay, or even express an individual interpretation about something read. Overall, extended writing focuses on the creative aspect of writing to learn, where students write to know and to understand, often using evidence from the texts that they have read to support their point.

Lesson Objective: Students create a short descriptive essay after reading a text.

You can choose to have students write a different type of essay (see *Types of Essays*)—just adjust the objective and the mini-lesson accordingly.

Connect

Say,

> "I want you to think about what you have been reading in a deeper way than what we've been focused on. I want you to write everything you know regarding the topic that you have been focused on in your articles (or in your inquiry project). We are going to write everything we know in a piece of writing called a descriptive essay."

Teach

Say,

> "An essay is a short piece of writing on a specific topic—we are going to discuss descriptive essays today, which are short pieces of writing that describe a topic. A descriptive essay has a few essential parts. It has an introduction, a body, and a conclusion [*all essays have these three parts, so if you choose to teach a different type of essay, as noted in* Types of Essays, *you can stick with this essay structure*].
>
> "In the introduction, you state your main idea and give some pointers as to what the rest of the essay is going to be about. Here is where you would state your thesis statement, if you have one."

Model writing a short introduction to an essay on "Life in Room X" (insert the name or number of your room). In this introduction, orient the reader to the main idea about life in your classroom and then brainstorm, with the students, two or three points that might appear in the essay. Then write these points down in the introduction as the preview of the essay (see *Life in My Classroom* for an example of a modeled descriptive essay).

Model writing the next paragraph(s).

> "Now, let's think about what we want to include in the essay. We decided we wanted to talk about how we work together, and what happens when we don't get along."

Go on to model writing a paragraph or two describing life in your classroom. Check to see if the class agrees with what you have written as an accurate description of the classroom life. Revise if necessary.

Then, model writing a conclusion to the essay. In the conclusion, you will recap the main idea and the supporting details. In essence, this is a summary of the essay. See *Life in My Classroom* for an example.

Say,

> "We've just created a descriptive essay together about life in our classroom. Remember in a descriptive essay you focus on informing the reader about your topic through describing. Now I want you to plan your own descriptive essay based on your reading. Take a look at your reading and write down a couple of jots *[jots are short bullet points, as described in the "Weeklong Daily Duo Layout" section of Chapter 6]* about information you could share in a descriptive essay. When we are informing readers about a topic, we are going to have to be correct in our facts and thoughts, so make sure to double-check your reading. I'm going to come around and see what you've jotted down."

Students can jot in a notebook, on index cards, or on sticky notes. As you move around the classroom, coach students on their thinking about the important things to share with a reader about their reading.

Give It a Go

Say,

> "Now, let's try writing a descriptive essay on our own. Remember, a descriptive essay has three parts: an introduction, a body, and a conclusion. Who would like to share what they are thinking of writing about?"

Lead a discussion with the class with students sharing their thinking and getting ready to write.

Wrap Up

Students write a short descriptive essay (or another type, as described in *Types of Essays*) on a topic of choice and based on their reading.

Invite students to share what they have written or planned out to write.

Life in My Classroom

Every day, as the late summer heat rises with the morning sun, we enter Room 16 ready to spend six hours together. I usually get there first, pushing open the heavy door and smelling the air—a mixture of dry erase markers and adolescent sweat—which wafts toward me. I flip on the lights and the room is illuminated, but it seems dull and dead as the chairs, brown and gray, sit empty waiting for my students to fill them up and give them purpose.

The early morning time is a sharp contrast to the boisterousness of the daily activity. Me and my students, we are a team, and we talk and laugh and discuss together. We work, and wipe our brows, and reflect on mistakes and "aha" moments together. We are not a quiet group.

While the morning is filled with the sounds of reading and writing, pages turning and pens scratching across the paper, the midday, just after lunch, is different. It is a time students work math problems, and solve problems on big pieces of blue butcher paper that sit awkwardly across desks that have been pushed together. Life in this classroom is collaborative, and we all own it. It's true that you might hear my voice about the din, once in a while, to bring some order, but more often, you will hear the voices of students self-organizing or pushing one another to learn.

Types of Essays

Four Major Types of Essays

Narrative

- Tells a true story
- Uses narrative devices like character, plot, and description

Basic Structure Example

- Intro, plot, characters, setting, climax, conclusion
- Follows story structure, and can be told from the point of view of the character, the event, or an idea

Descriptive

- Paints a visual picture of a person, a place, an experience, a situation, or another topic
- Creative nonfiction using descriptive detail

Basic Structure Example

- Intro, description (in list or narrative form), conclusion

Expository

- Gives facts
- Includes an explanation of a short idea or issue

Basic Structure Example

- Intro including thesis, supporting points, conclusion and/or claim

Argument

- Makes a point, or proves an opinion, theory, or hypothesis
- Writer investigates a topic; collects, generates, and evaluates evidence; and establishes a position
- Different from expository as expository writing is less involved, requires less research, and is shorter than argumentative writing
- Different from persuasive writing as the writer is not persuading readers to adopt his or her point of view

Basic Structure Example

- Intro, claim, reason, supporting material, warrant or conclusion
- Can also follow structures like pro and con, compare and contrast, or cause and effect, but still include the claim, reason, and supporting material

Additional Types of Essays

Persuasive

- Aggressively works to convince the reader to take the writer's side about a topic or issue
- Differs from argument as in argument the writer is trying not to win the opinion of the reader, but rather to give the reader perspective on a topic

Basic Structure Example

- Hook, intro, thesis (point of the paper), supporting points (1-2-3), restatement of thesis, conclusion ending with a bang or emotional point

Analytical

- Analyzes, examines, or interprets a book, poem, play, or work of art

Basic Structure Example

- Intro, analysis of text or art, personal response, conclusion

A Few Writing Structures for the Essay

Basic Structure

- Includes the thesis and supporting details, and is wrapped up with a conclusion

Basic Structure Example

- Intro including thesis, supporting points, conclusion

Compare/Contrast

- Explores similarities and differences. Can be written in two different structures—point by point (similarities and differences are featured throughout the essay) or block (similarities and differences are presented together for each point before moving on to the next point)

Basic Structure Example

- **Point by Point:** Intro, Point 1 similarities and differences, Point 2 similarities and differences, Point 3 similarities and differences, conclusion
- **Block:** Intro, features of Point 1, features of Point 2, features of Point 3, differences grouped together, conclusion

(Continued)

(Continued)

Cause/Effect

- Explores root causes of situation or issue
- Answers questions including "Why?" and "What were the results?"

Basic Structure Example

- Intro, analysis of text or art, personal response, conclusion

---

Pro/Con

- Explores positives and negatives of a topic, issue, theory, or hypothesis by presenting advantages and disadvantages and going from one side of the issue to the other

---

Basic Structure Example

- Intro, Pro Idea 1, Pro Idea 2, Pro Idea 3, Con Idea 1, Con Idea 2, Con Idea 3, conclusion and refuting of negatively presented ideas

or

- Intro, Con Idea 1 and refutation, Con Idea 2 and refutation, Con Idea 3 and refutation, conclusion

or

- Intro, Pro but Con Idea 1, Pro but Con Idea 2, Pro but Con Idea 3, conclusion

---

Discovery

- Builds toward a generalization or thesis

Basic Structure Example

- Intro, Point 1, Point 2, Point 3 (etc.), conclusion, thesis

Writing and Text Structure

In Chapter 4, we examined how to teach students to recognize text structure in the articles they are reading. In this lesson, you teach your students to write by employing a text structure to convey information. This mini-lesson is especially helpful after students finish researching a topic of interest, and have notes on their topic.

Lesson Objective: Students write about a content-area inquiry using a specific text structure to organize their writing.

Materials: Charts or other images of text structure diagrams from past lessons (for examples, see *Recognize Many Text Structures* in the "Lessons for Getting Main Idea by Understanding Text Structures" section of Part III); student notes from their inquiry, or topic of research.

Connect

Say,

> "We have worked a lot to understand text structures to help us as readers, and now we are going to use text structures to help us as writers. Today, we are going to look at ways to use text structure to help us write. We've been working on an inquiry about a topic we are interested in, and now we have lots of notes about our topic. What we need to figure out before we start writing is *how* we want to tell our readers what we have learned.
>
> "Let's look at the text structures we are familiar with. We're going to choose a text structure that might work for conveying our message to our readers."

Review the different text structures you have taught the class, such as those in *Recognize Many Text Structures* in the "Lessons for Getting Main Idea by Understanding Text Structures" section of Part III. It is important to use a visual or chart to list the type and definition of the text structures. When the lesson incorporates visuals, you support students who are visual or tactile learners, and those who need scaffolding to understand.

Teach

Say,

> "I have been thinking about my writing *[show your notebook, or pages with notes on them with information about an inquiry you are working on—if you don't have one, fake it a bit to help you with modeling]* and thinking about which text structure is going to help me convey the information clearly in my writing. I have been reading about the ancient civilizations Mesopotamia and Egypt *[these two ancient civilizations are taught according to California's sixth-grade social studies standards]* and thinking that one way I could write about what I have learned is by comparing and contrasting the two ancient civilizations. I could compare and contrast geographic regions, agricultural technologies, death rituals, and education. I'm going to pick one area and write a bit for you about how it would read if I were to use Compare and Contrast as a text structure."

Once you explain to the students what you are going to do, refer to the *Compare and Contrast Graphic Organizer* on page 123 (or any other text structure you prefer to use), and then model your writing in front of the students. Remember to write in a format that

Notes for Compare/Contrast Lesson

2 areas today only:
Geography & Daily Life

	Egypt	Ancient Mesopotamia Persia
Geography	• Nile cut through the desert land • natural barriers protected the land - cliffs & desert & marshland • rich dirt was for planting • the Nile flooded & covered farmland • life was centered around the Nile a few explored land around Egypt	• Early Persia was life between rivers between Tigris + Euphrates Rivers - floods lead to rich fertile ground - nomads lived in a dry and region w/ rocky soil
Daily Life	• clothing was simple • people wore jewelry that protected people from dangers • people wore scented body oils & makeup • there were no marriage ceremonies • music was important • a calender was used to mark lucky & unlucky days • wealthy were mummified	• They had markets • slaves were part of society • a justice system organized daily life • everyone worked the affluent were educated • funerals were solemn events • all men served in the military

Example of Teacher Notes

There are similarities and differences between early Egypt and Ancient Mesopotamia, with a focus on Persia.

Some parts of the geography were the same, and others different. Both had rivers that flooded, leaving behind rice, fertile land for farming. However, in Ancient Mesopotamia, early Persians were nomads living in a dry, arid region.

Daily life had a few similarities. Both wore simple clothing, and spent most days working or farming. In Egypt though, the rich wore makeup and jewelry to protect them from dangers. Both cultures focused on burial rituals, but Egyptians had no marriage ceremony.

Example of the Writing Sample

all students can see (for example, using a document camera), and while you are writing, be sure to talk out loud about your writing decisions. Refer to *Example of Teacher Notes* for an example of the teacher's notes for modeling this lesson. You can also use *Example of the Writing Sample* when you model your writing during the lesson.

Say,

"You've been watching me work on my writing using text structure; now it's your turn to think about this. Look at your notebooks for a little while and think about what your inquiry has been about. What text structure would support you to convey the information in your piece really well? Think about this, and then turn and talk with your partner about what you are thinking of doing with text structure and your writing."

Give It a Go

Say,

"It's almost time for us to go out and write. Before we go, can anyone share their thoughts about what they are going to do today with their writing? Tell us how you are going to use text structure to help your reader understand your writing, and if you know which text structure you want to use, talk about that too."

Wrap Up

By the end of this lesson, students will have writing pieces that use a text structure to convey information. Students choose the text structure that best fits what they have been reading about and the information they want to convey.

Invite students to share the progress on their work at the end of the writing time. Guide students to focus on what text structure they chose and how they used it to organize their writing and share information with their readers.

Appendix

THE READY-TO-USE TEXTS

A Day at School in Kyrgyzstan

by Kathryn Hulick

It's 7:30 a.m. and I'm on my way to school. I'm wrapped in a gigantic coat, hat, and scarf to keep out the winter chills as I walk. It's still dark out, but I pass vendors setting up shops, families driving donkey carts, and men standing outside their cars. I also pass groups of students, who wave to me and say, "Hello, Miss Kathryn!"

I am their teacher, a Peace Corps volunteer in Kyrgyzstan, a small country in the mountains of Central Asia. When I arrive at school, I climb the stairs to the third floor and unlock my classroom. It's a large room, with a row of windows and posters and maps all over the walls. The white board I bought leans against an ancient, unusable blackboard across the room from the windows. I flick the lights. Nothing happens. *"Svet Jok,"* I think to myself, the Kyrgyz words for "No electricity." Although the sun is rising, it's still dark in the building. My first class, 11th grade, piles into the room, speaking among themselves in a mix of Russian and Kyrgyz. My job is to teach them English. It's going to be hard to follow my lesson plans when the students can't even see the white board, and it's so cold in the room that we're all still wearing our bulky coats and hats! Luckily, the lights blink on near the end of my first lesson. I ask my students to finish writing letters to their pen pals in America for homework.

A Kyrgyz high school goes up to the 11th grade. After graduation, many students will get married. The brightest students will go to university for five years, however most of them will end up back in this village, raising families, taking care of livestock and farming beans and potatoes. A select few will work their way to a job in the capital city of Bishkek. The common dream, however, is to travel to America or Europe, which is only possible if they first learn English.

For now, they are still students and teenagers. They giggle and whisper to each other in my class. They write to their pen pals about Britney Spears and 50 Cent, who they like as much as popular Russian, Turkish, and Kyrgyz pop stars. They watch American action movies, dubbed in Russian, on TV. A few kids have cell phones and collect clips of music to play for their friends. They do homework, take tests, play sports, and organize talent shows. But being students is just one aspect of their lives. When they go home after school, the girls make soup and bread from scratch, haul water in buckets and basins, and take care of younger siblings. The boys tend cows and sheep, learn to repair cars, and work in the fields.

Even in school, students are responsible for more than their homework. Students stay together in the same group of about 20 kids from first grade until graduation, meaning that classmates are like brothers and sisters. Each class has its own homeroom, and the students are responsible for the upkeep of this room. That's right, the students spend at least one afternoon every week with buckets, mops and dusting cloths cleaning their own classroom! When the weather is warm in the spring and fall, the director of the school may call a *subotnik*, which means that instead of classes, the whole school works outside cleaning up trash, gardening, and raking.

But today it's the middle of December. I wait ten minutes for my next class and finally one girl peeks in, "Sorry, Miss Kathryn! We have no lesson today. We are in the *Actovnly Zal.*" That's Russian for "auditorium." I follow her downstairs and discover my students lined up on the stage, singing a song about winter to a group of teachers. If there's a performance going on, there probably won't be any lessons for the rest of the day. As I settle in to watch the show, I am full of hope for the futures of these students of mine, who juggle being teenagers, housekeepers, farmers, custodians, and entertainers all at once.

Big Drinks Are Back

A State Judge in New York Strikes Down a Ban on Large-Sized Sugary Beverages

by Alice Park for *TIME* with AP reporting

March 13, 2013

On Monday, State Supreme Court Justice Milton Tingling struck down New York City's ban on big sugary drinks just hours before it was supposed to take effect. The law would have banned the sale of sugared beverages larger than 16 oz. at New York restaurants, mobile food carts, sports arenas and movie theaters.

Tingling said the ban would have left people with many other ways to consume sugary drinks. "The loopholes in this rule effectively defeat the stated purpose of this rule," he wrote.

Although the ban was widely supported by health professionals, it was not popular with food retailers or many city residents. They asked, why single out sugared sodas, when there are many reasons why people are overweight? And if sugared beverages are being targeted, why not take stronger measures against other sources of sugar, such as candy and other sweets?

The American Beverage Association (ABA) and other opponents of the rule supported the judge's decision. "The court ruling provides a sigh of relief to New Yorkers and thousands of small businesses in New York City that would have been harmed by this unpopular ban," an ABA spokesperson said.

Health in the Big Apple

New York City Mayor Michael Bloomberg led the ban on large drinks. He aimed to cut obesity rates in the U.S., where at least two-thirds of American adults are considered overweight. Bloomberg says the city will appeal the judge's decision. "We believe the judge is totally in error in how he interpreted the law, and we are confident we will win on appeal," Bloomberg said.

More than half of New York City adults and nearly 40 percent of the city's public elementary and middle school students are considered overweight.

New York City's Board of Health members believe that banning mega-sized drinks is an important step toward helping consumers not only to drink fewer calories, but may also encourage people to make other healthy changes to their diet. The board reviewed data showing that sugared drinks make up 43 percent of the added sugar in the average American diet. Now, with big drinks back on store shelves, New Yorkers will make their own choices about how to stay healthy.

What do you think? Should the government ban large sugary drinks to help consumers make healthier choices? Or should people be allowed make their own choices about beverage size?

Cancer Is a Scary Word

Cancer is a scary word. Almost everyone knows someone who got very sick or died from cancer. Most of the time, cancer affects older people. Not many kids get cancer, but when they do, very often it can be treated and cured.

Good News

The number of kids who beat cancer goes up every year because of new treatments. Hurray for the researchers who discover new medicines and other ways of putting cancer cells in their place.

What Is Cancer?

Cancer is actually a group of many related diseases that all have to do with cells. Cells are the very small units that make up all living things, including the human body. There are billions of cells in each person's body.

Cancer happens when cells that are not normal grow and spread very fast. Normal body cells grow and divide and know to stop growing. Over time, they also die. Unlike these normal cells, cancer cells just continue to grow and divide out of control and don't die when they're supposed to.

Cancer cells usually group or clump together to form tumors (say: TOO-mers). A growing tumor becomes a lump of cancer cells that can destroy the normal cells around the tumor and damage the body's healthy tissues. This can make someone very sick.

Sometimes cancer cells break away from the original tumor and travel to other areas of the body, where they keep growing and can go on to form new tumors. This is how cancer spreads. The spread of a tumor to a new place in the body is called metastasis (say: meh-TASS-tuh-sis).

Causes of Cancer

You probably know a kid who had chickenpox—maybe even you. But you probably don't know any kids who've had cancer. If you packed a large football stadium with kids, probably only one child in that stadium would have cancer.

Doctors aren't sure why some people get cancer and others don't. They do know that cancer is not contagious. You can't catch it from someone else who has it—cancer isn't caused by germs, like colds or the flu are. So don't be afraid of other kids—or anyone else—with cancer. You can talk to, play with, and hug someone with cancer.

Kids can't get cancer from anything they do either. Some kids think that a bump on the head causes brain cancer or that bad people get cancer. This isn't true! Kids don't do anything wrong to get cancer. But some unhealthy habits, especially cigarette smoking or drinking too much alcohol every day, can make you a lot more likely to get cancer when you become an adult.

Source: http://kidshealth.org/kid/cancer_center/cancer_basics/cancer.html. Used with permission of the Nemours Foundation.

The Child, the Tablet, and the Developing Mind

by Nick Bilton

I recently watched my sister perform an act of magic.

We were sitting in a restaurant, trying to have a conversation, but her children, 4-year-old Willow and 7-year-old Luca, would not stop fighting. The arguments—over a fork, or who had more water in a glass—were unrelenting.

Like a magician quieting a group of children by pulling a rabbit out of a hat, my sister reached into her purse and produced two shiny Apple iPads, handing one to each child. Suddenly, the two were quiet. Eerily so. They sat playing games and watching videos, and we continued with our conversation.

After our meal, as we stuffed the iPads back into their magic storage bag, my sister felt slightly guilty.

"I don't want to give them the iPads at the dinner table, but if it keeps them occupied for an hour so we can eat in peace, and more importantly not disturb other people in the restaurant, I often just hand it over," she told me. Then she asked: "Do you think it's bad for them? I do worry that it is setting them up to think it's O.K. to use electronics at the dinner table in the future."

I did not have an answer, and although some people might have opinions, no one has a true scientific understanding of what the future might hold for a generation raised on portable screens.

"We really don't know the full neurological effects of these technologies yet," said Dr. Gary Small, director of the Longevity Center at the University of California, Los Angeles, and author of "iBrain: Surviving the Technological Alteration of the Modern Mind." "Children, like adults, vary quite a lot, and some are more sensitive than others to an abundance of screen time."

But Dr. Small says we do know that the brain is highly sensitive to stimuli, like iPads and smartphone screens, and if people spend too much time with one technology, and less time interacting with people like parents at the dinner table, that could hinder the development of certain communications skills.

So will a child who plays with crayons at dinner rather than a coloring application on an iPad be a more socialized person?

Ozlem Ayduk, an associate professor in the Relationships and Social Cognition Lab at the University of California, Berkeley, said children sitting at the dinner table with a print book or crayons were not as engaged with the people around them, either. "There are value-based lessons for children to talk to the people during a meal," she said. "It's not so much about the iPad versus nonelectronics."

Parents who have little choice but to hand over their iPad can at least control what a child does on those devices.

A report published last week by the Millennium Cohort Study, a long-term study group in Britain that has been following 19,000 children born in 2000 and 2001, found that those who watched more than three hours of television, videos or DVDs a day had a higher chance of conduct problems, emotional symptoms and relationship problems by the time they were 7 than children who did not. The

251

study, of a sample of 11,000 children, found that children who played video games—often age-appropriate games—for the same amount of time did not show any signs of negative behavioral changes by the same age.

Which brings us back to the dinner table with my niece and nephew. While they sat happily staring into those shiny screens, they were not engaged in any type of conversation, or staring off into space thinking, as my sister and I did as children when our parents were talking. And that is where the risks are apparent.

"Conversations with each other are the way children learn to have conversations with themselves, and learn how to be alone," said Sherry Turkle, a professor of science, technology and society at the Massachusetts Institute of Technology, and author of the book "Alone Together: Why We Expect More From Technology and Less From Each Other." "Learning about solitude and being alone is the bedrock of early development, and you don't want your kids to miss out on that because you're pacifying them with a device."

Ms. Turkle has interviewed parents, teenagers and children about the use of gadgets during early development, and says she fears that children who do not learn real interactions, which often have flaws and imperfections, will come to know a world where perfect, shiny screens give them a false sense of intimacy without risk.

And they need to be able to think independently of a device. "They need to be able to explore their imagination. To be able to gather themselves and know who they are. So someday they can form a relationship with another person without a panic of being alone," she said. "If you don't teach your children to be alone, they'll only know how to be lonely."

The Consequences of Modern Agriculture

Our ancestors raised their own food—fish, meat, vegetables, and grains. In the pursuit of a stable food supply, practices changed. Now, the production of our food has been industrialized, meaning that we have turned raising food into a business and that the product (food) is produced in large quantities, cheaply. This process, the industrialization of food production, at first was seen as positive but now has consequences that could not have been anticipated.

These practices have led to spectacular increases in food productivity, but there are downfalls. We raise and eat more animals than we physically need, leading countries with access to this abundance of food to face national health problems like obesity, hypertension, and diabetes. Additionally, in the pursuit of economy and efficiency, we raise animals under especially cruel conditions, and farming methods depend on synthetic fertilizers and pesticides and factory-style practices for raising animals.

Industrialized agriculture does make the food we eat less nutritious than its wild or more naturally raised counterparts. It also adds to environmental issues as the production and transport of the food relies on burning large amounts of fossil fuels. Industrialized farms depend on large quantities of water, and water is consumed at unsustainable rates.

The 20th-century American diet—high in meat, refined carbohydrates, and junk food—is driven by this industrialized food production. One could say our modern agricultural techniques are a destructive form of food production. The actions we take to bring balance back and create sustainable food production will destroy or preserve our environment and determine the individual life expectancy and quality of life for people living in industrialized societies.

Disney Channel Stars Speak Out Against Cyberbullying

by Jill Serjeant, Reuters

April 05, 2012

LOS ANGELES (Reuters)—Even some young Disney Channel stars, as popular as they seem to be, have suffered at the hands of bullies, and now dozens of them are urging kids to stand up against bullying—not by lashing out, but by speaking up.

In a campaign launching on Thursday on Disney Channel, Disney XD and Disney.com, actors like Billy Unger, Bridgit Mendler and Bella Thorne are urging 6 to 14-year-olds to treat each other better, both in the playground and online.

The campaign also encourages parents to teach their children how to use cell phones, social networking sites and gaming websites responsibly, and gives advice on what to do when cyberbullies strike.

Unger, 16, who plays a bionic teen in the hit Disney XD series "Lab Rats," recalls in one public service announcement for the campaign how he was taunted with nicknames like "small fry" and "shortie" when he was in elementary school.

Unger told a teacher who met with his parents. But what also helped, he said, was a casting agent telling the budding young actor that being short was a good thing for a kid entering the entertainment industry.

"So from that point on, when people called me small fry or shortie I was like, 'yeah, you're right and I am proud of it,'" Unger says in his message.

China Anne McClain of "A.N.T. Farm," Zendaya of "Shake It Up" and Debby Ryan of "Jessie" are also taking part in the Disney campaign, run jointly with the non-profit group Common Sense Media.

Kids Inspired by Other Kids

"When kids see other kids who have had experiences they can relate to, that is so much more profound and inspiring than hearing from an adult," said Caroline Knorr, parenting editor of Common Sense Media.

"These Disney Channel characters are real people, and kids really look up to them ...So for them to come out and say 'this happened to me' or to advocate for good digital citizenship, it will make a huge impact," Knorr said.

Disney Channel SVP of original programming Adam Bonnett said the family friendly network felt it had a duty to speak out against cyber-bullying.

"As the media platforms and viewing patterns of our audience become more interactive, it's become more important for us to reinforce the significance of positive social communication," Bonnett said.

The campaign, which is expected to run for several months, directs kids and parents to a dedicated website http://www.Disney.com/commonsense for information and advice.

"We don't advocate responding or retaliation because we feel cyberbullies are looking to get a reaction and it is best to just ignore it," said Knorr, who advises kids to turn off their phones, or block access to online "friends" who turn nasty.

Although confiding to a teacher or trusted adult is important, Knorr said 'tweens and older kids often prefer to turn to friends first, rather than parents.

"Kids are reporting that it is way more important to have peers support them in a bullying situation than parents. The instinct for parents is to rush in and try to fix everything."

But parents also have a huge role to play.

"Parents really need to have a conversation with their kids, when they give them a cell phone or allow them do social networking, about what responsible behavior is.

"These are not toys. You can't just hand your kid a cellphone and assume they will use it responsibly," Knorr said.

(Reporting by Jill Serjeant; Editing by Bob Tourtellotte)

The Dynamic Duo

Ten-Year-Old Ashley Amdor and Her Diving Dog, Napoleon, Are Making a Splash

by Kyla Oliver

JULY 09, 2012

Napoleon climbs up the ladder, takes a running start and leaps into the pool. He splashes down, and the crowd cheers. As Napoleon swims to the edge of the pool, he looks excited. It might sound a lot like a diving event at the Olympics, but this sport is for a different type of competitor—the furry, tail-wagging type. It is called dog diving.

Napoleon, a black Labrador retriever, has been participating in the sport for two years. That is not the only thing that makes Napoleon special. The person who trains him and handles him at dog-diving events is Ashley Amdor, a 10-year-old kid!

Get in the Game!

Ashley became interested in the sport of dog diving while at a state fair near her home in Albuquerque, New Mexico. She saw the dog divers competing to leap the farthest into a pool, and thought Napoleon would be good at the sport because he loves the water.

When her parents tried working with Napoleon he didn't do well, so Ashley decided to try it herself. With Ashley as his trainer, Napoleon caught right on, leaping as far as 24 feet at a time! Working together, Ashley and Napoleon have forged a special bond. "Napoleon is my best friend," Ashley told TFK. "He loves me for who I am and has taught me to treat others that way."

"Ruf" Competition

On June 30, Ashley and Napoleon participated in a competition in Denver, Colorado. Dogs showed off their skills in several fur-raising events, from jumping over hurdles to catching flying disks. As usual, Napoleon focused on the diving portion of the competition.

To warm up, Ashley took Napoleon on a walk, had him practice fetching and stretched him out. "Napoleon was scared when he first arrived at the competition," said Ashley. "But when he focused, he did a good job." Leaping into the water to grab his favorite toy, Napoleon took sixth place out of nine.

It was not enough to qualify for the upcoming "Dog Olympics," officially known as the Purina Pro Plan Incredible Dog Challenge. But that won't stop Napoleon and Ashley from pressing on. In August, the duo will participate in the Dock Dogs competition. Sounds like a great way to spend the dog days of summer!

The First Teddy Bear

by the National Park Service, U.S. Department of the Interior

Did you know that the Teddy Bear was invented in honor of President Theodore Roosevelt? It all began when Theodore Roosevelt was on a bear hunting trip near Onward, Mississippi on November 14, 1902. He had been invited by Mississippi Governor Andrew H. Longino, and unlike other hunters in the group, had not located a single bear.

Roosevelt's assistants, led by Holt Collier, a born slave and former Confederate cavalryman, cornered and tied a black bear to a willow tree. They summoned Roosevelt and suggested that he shoot it. Viewing this as extremely unsportsmanlike, Roosevelt refused to shoot the bear. The news of this event spread quickly through newspaper articles across the country. The articles recounted the story of the president who refused to shoot a bear. However, it was not just any president, it was Theodore Roosevelt the big game hunter!

A political cartoonist by the name of Clifford Berryman read the article and decided to lightheartedly lampoon the president's refusal to shoot the bear. Berryman's cartoon appeared in the Washington Post on November 16, 1902. A Brooklyn candy shop owner by the name of Morris Michtom saw the cartoon and had an idea. He and his wife Rose were also makers of stuffed animals, and

Clifford Berryman's 1902 cartoon that lampooned T.R.'s bear hunt.

Michtom decided to create a stuffed toy bear and dedicate it to the president who refused to shoot a bear. He called it "Teddy's Bear."

After receiving Roosevelt's permission to use his name, Michtom mass produced the toy bears which were so popular that he soon founded the Ideal Toy Company. To this day the Teddy Bear has worldwide popularity and its origin can be traced back to Theodore's fateful hunting trip in 1902.

Source: http://www.nps.gov/thrb/historyculture/storyofteddybear.htm. Used with permission of the National Park Service, U.S. Department of the Interior.

The New Colossus

by Emma Lazarus

Not like the brazen giant of Greek fame,

With conquering limbs astride from land to land;

Here at our sea-washed, sunset gates shall stand

A mighty woman with a torch, whose flame

Is the imprisoned lightning, and her name

Mother of Exiles. From her beacon-hand

Glows world-wide welcome; her mild eyes command

The air-bridged harbor that twin cities frame.

"Keep, ancient lands, your storied pomp!" cries she

With silent lips. "Give me your tired, your poor,

Your huddled masses yearning to breathe free,

The wretched refuse of your teeming shore.

Send these, the homeless, tempest-tost to me,

I lift my lamp beside the golden door!"

Source: Lazarus, Emma, "The New Colossus," *A Century of Immigration, 1820–1924* (handwritten) (sonnet), Library of Congress.

Note: See more at http://www.poets.org/viewmedia.php/prmMID/16111#sthash.G6Epj5ce.dpuf

Ozone and the Greenhouse Effect: Environmental Issues That Affect Our Lives

Humans have had an impact on Earth's environment. It is important to be aware of these impacts so that we can make changes to preserve the Earth. Two important environmental issues are the greenhouse effect and ozone reduction. There are differences between the greenhouse effect and ozone reduction. These differences can be very confusing. However, there are a couple of similarities: The greenhouse effect and ozone reduction are affected by molecules that are released into the atmosphere by activities people engage in every day.

The greenhouse effect is the process of the trapping of the sun's warmth in the planet's atmosphere. What are these gases? These gases include water vapor, carbon dioxide, methane, and nitrous oxide. These gases make life on Earth possible. The problems with the gases occur when greenhouse gases increase, and affect the atmosphere and climate. This results in the elevation of the average temperature of the Earth's surface. The Earth naturally produces some of the gases, but the burning of fossil fuels and clearing of vegetation in forests has intensified the effect.

Another issue is ozone reduction. Ozone reduction makes the earth vulnerable to solar radiation. There is a protective layer around the Earth called the ozone layer. This layer is deep within the stratosphere that encircles the Earth. It is a special form of oxygen. Manmade chemicals, called chlorofluorocarbons, enter the stratosphere, and they destroy some of the ozone. When the protective ozone layer is destroyed, harmful UV radiation from the sun enters the atmosphere and reaches Earth's surface. Exposure to this radiation causes skin cancer, eye damage, and other health problems.

Ozone reduction and the greenhouse effect are two environmental issues that scientists study in order to discover ways to reduce the harmful effects of these phenomena.

Pin the Tail on the Dolphin

by Emily Anthes

Winter's life began with a phenomenal stroke of bad luck.

In December 2005, when the Atlantic bottlenose dolphin was just a few months old, she was swimming with her mother in Mosquito Lagoon, along central Florida's Atlantic coast. Somehow, she got herself tangled in a crab trap. An eagle-eyed fisherman spotted her struggling and called in a wildlife rescue team. They found the calf gasping for air, her heart racing. The volunteers gently positioned the dolphin on a stretcher, carried her out of the water, and drove her across the state to the Clearwater Marine Aquarium.

She was in bad shape when she arrived—exhausted, dehydrated, and sporting numerous cuts and abrasions. She could barely swim, and trainers stood in the tank with her, holding her little body up in the water. No one knew whether she'd make it through the night. But she was a survivor, lasting through those initial hours and the following days, too.

Slowly, with bottle-feeding and round-the-clock care, the team nursed the calf back to health. As Winter began to stabilize, though, other problems emerged. A line from the crab trap had been wrapped so tightly around her tail that it had cut off the circulation. The tissue was necrotic: The dolphin's skin started peeling off, and the tail itself began to decay. One day, Winter's caretaker found two of her vertebrae at the bottom of the pool. Winter was getting her strength back, but her tail was clearly a goner. And what kind of future could there possibly be for a dolphin without a tail?

Though she didn't know it, in one way, Winter was lucky—she was born in the twenty-first century, and there has never been a better time for an animal to lose a body part. Materials ranging from carbon-fiber composites to flexible, shape-shifting plastics are making it possible for us to design artificial appendages for patients that fly, trot or swim; prosthetists have succeeded in creating a new beak for an eagle, a replacement shell for a turtle and a false foot for a kangaroo. Surgical techniques are enabling vets to give cats and dogs bionic legs that are permanently implanted in their bodies, and advances in neuroscience hold out the promise of creating prostheses that can be directly controlled by the brain.

Whereas affixing sensors and tags to animal bodies could help save entire species, artificial tails and paws represent the other end of the spectrum, a way to provide a (sometimes literal) leg up to unlucky individuals. Prosthetic devices aren't appropriate for every animal—indeed, one of the challenges prosthetists face is determining what's in the best interest of bodies that look nothing like our own—but when we get it right, our custom-designed and individually engineered devices are helping us aid animals one life and limb at a time.

Polymer Balls Raise Alarm

by Consumer Reports

A recent recall of toys made of a material that can expand significantly when ingested has revealed a potential health risk that the Consumer Product Safety Commission considers serious enough to warrant a broader investigation.

In December 2012, Cleveland-based Dunecraft recalled about 95,000 packages of marble-sized toys that expand in water. That recall came three months after doctors at Texas Children's Hospital reported in the journal Pediatrics that an 8-month-old girl swallowed one of the brightly colored balls from a set of Dunecraft's Water Balz. It had to be surgically removed after it expanded inside her, blocking her small intestine.

The doctors warned that such cases might become more common because superabsorbent polymers such as those used to make the Dunecraft toys are increasingly prevalent not only in other toys but also in widely available household products, such as water-retaining pellets used for gardening or in flower arrangements. Some day-care providers actually use those versions as playthings for babies and preschoolers. In the dry state, the polymer beads are tiny but could pose life-threatening risks.

"If one of these is in the airway and doubles within 2 to 4 hours, a child can go from not breathing well to not breathing at all," says Paul Krakowitz, M.D., a pediatric ear, nose, and throat surgeon and vice chairman of surgical operations at the Cleveland Clinic.

"We view the recall with Dunecraft and the incident involving the 8-month-old girl to be very serious and as a result, CPSC staff are taking a broader look at this product class," said CPSC spokesman Scott Wolfson.

Two cases were recently reported among children in Pakistan, one of whom died as a result. Malaysia banned the sale of such products in August 2011 after hospital reports of seven children needing surgery after ingesting them. Italy has imposed a ban, and New Zealand says they should not be promoted as children's toys or craft products.

"These are colorful and look cute when you watch them expand, but they could have disastrous effects if they are ingested, so any of these superabsorbent polymer products should be kept out of the reach of children or pets," says Oluyinka O. Olutoye, M.D., a pediatric surgeon at Texas Children's Hospital who operated on the baby whose case was reported in Pediatrics.

Robots 101

What Is a Robot?

At its most basic a robot is a machine that senses the world, processes the sensor information with a computer and then does something in response to that information (such as moving or turning).

A robot isn't just a computer. A desktop computer can "sense" that you are typing or moving the mouse, but the computer itself doesn't move or act in the physical world.

Where Can I Find a Robot?

Many everyday objects around you are a lot like robots. A car with cruise control senses how fast the car is moving and then changes the car's acceleration so that the car's speed stays constant. A thermostat in a room senses what temperature the room is and then it turns on a heater or air conditioner to bring the room to the right temperature.

Many people assume all robots are characters in science-fiction movies like the *Terminator* or R2D2 in *Star Wars*. In fact, robots are used all over the world, right now! Robots build cars, clean houses, help soldiers and doctors, are played with by kids and explore other planets. They may not look like the robots we see in the movies but they are still doing important jobs. Robots can also be very powerful tools for learning. Kids all over the United States are using robots in their classrooms and out-of-school to help them learn science, technology, engineering, and math (STEM) topics in new and innovative ways.

How Do Robots Learn About the World Around Them?

Robots are often equipped with a variety of sensors that allow them to collect information about their environment. Depending on its task, a robot might have a wide variety of sensors. Some of the most common sensors that robots use include:

- Cameras to find objects, people, or other robots
- Global Positioning System (GPS) receivers to determine the robot's location
- Laser rangefinders to determine the distance between the robot and other objects
- Light sensors to detect how bright the robot's environment is
- Temperature sensors to detect how hot or cold the robot's environment is
- Touch sensors to tell the robot if it has bumped into something

Who Makes Robots?

Robotics is a multi-disciplinary field; it takes a lot of different expertise to design, build and program a robot. Often mechanical engineers, electrical engineers, computer scientists, industrial engineers and industrial designers are all involved.

Mechanical engineers design all of the physical parts of the robot—parts like the chassis, motors, arms and hands, wheels, tracks or legs. Electrical engineers design all of the circuits and wiring that the internal computer will use to control the robot. Computer scientists program the robot; they write the software that takes the information from the robot's sensors, processes it and then tells the robot how to act. For robots that are mass-produced, industrial engineers are needed to figure out how a factory can make all of the robot's parts and in what order they should be put together. Industrial designers look at all the different parts of the robot and figure out how it will look on the outside—what color will its chassis be? Where should the company logo go?

What Does the Future Hold for Robotics?

In the future robots may be used to help doctors examine patients who are far away, to help carry injured people out of disaster areas, to assist senior citizens or people with disabilities or even to inspect bridges for signs of wear. Scientists and engineers all *over* the world are developing robots that can help people in homes or outside, on land, in the water and in the air. Keep your eyes open and watch for these amazing robots!

Robots 101 is brought to you by iRobot SPARK in celebration of National Robotics Week.

For more cool robot activities, visit spark.irobot .com and www.nationalroboticsweek.org!

Source: Used with permission of iRobot SPARK and National Robotics Week.

Text-Message Bullying Becoming More Common

by Reuters

December 01, 2011

A growing number of American children say they have been picked on via text messaging, including having rumors spread about them or being threatened, a study says.

Of more than 1,000 middle school and high school students surveyed in 2008, 24 percent said they had been "harassed" by texting—up from 14 percent in a survey of the same students the year before, according to findings published last week in Pediatrics.

In the study, "harassment" meant that peers had spread rumors about them, made "rude or mean comments" or threatened them.

Outright bullying, which was defined as being repeatedly picked on, rose to 8 percent of students surveyed from just over 6 percent the year before.

The researchers, led by Michele Ybarra of Internet Solutions for Kids Inc. in San Clemente, Calif., said the findings suggest children's texting needs attention but not that parents should be alarmed.

"This is not a reason to become distressed or take kids' cellphones away. The majority of kids seem to be navigating these new technologies pretty healthfully," Ybarra said.

The study included 1,588 10- to 15-year-olds who were surveyed online in 2006. The survey was repeated in 2007 and 2008, with about three-quarters of the original group taking part in all three.

When it came down to Internet-based harassment, as opposed to texting, there was little change over time. By 2008, 39 percent of students said they had been harassed online, with most saying it had happened "a few times." Fewer than 15 percent said they had ever been cyberbullied.

Even when students were picked on, most seemed to take it in stride, which researchers said was a good sign.

Of those who said they had been harassed online, 20 percent reported being "very or extremely upset" by the most serious incident, down from 25 percent in 2006.

Ybarra and other experts said the main message for parents was to try to help their children manage their relationships in a healthy way, because the issue was fundamentally a relationship problem.

Cyberbullying remained a smaller problem than the old-fashioned kind, they said.

"Meanness and bullying are still much more likely to occur face to face," according to David Finkelhor, who directs the Crimes Against Children Research Center at the University of New Hampshire in Durham.

The Trash Dump at Sea

On January 10, 1992, an accident happened at sea. The Evergreen Ever Laurel, a cargo ship much like a floating warehouse, encountered rough waters at sea. The waves were 36 feet high and the winds hurricane force. The great Evergreen Ever Laurel mostly floated through the storm, but at some point, an accident happened. Two columns of containers broke loose from their steel strappings and fell into the ocean. One of those cargo containers was filled with 28,800 plastic turtles, ducks, beavers, and frogs. They splashed into the mid-Pacific, close to the International Date Line (44.7°N, 178.1°E). These Floatees took a trip, and between August and September 1992, after 2,200 miles adrift, hundreds of them beached near Sitka, Alaska.

The floating toys became a mystery. How did they come to beach in Alaska? Where did they come from? One beachcomber-turned-investigator began to research the origin of the floating toys. Donovan Hohn began studying the voyage of the small Floatee toys and published what he learned in his book, *Moby-Duck: The True Story of 28,800 Bath Toys Lost at Sea* (2011). Hohn's book, and the stories he told about the toys, raised awareness about trash at sea.

Not all of the Floatees were found by beachcombers. In fact, there is a large amount of debris at sea. One patch of debris covers as much area as the state of Texas, and another, considered the largest, is in the North Pacific and is called the Great Pacific Garbage Patch. This floating garbage dump is about 1,000 miles off the coast of California and extends from Hawaii to San Francisco. The garbage patch is now covering an area twice the size of the continental United States. It has about 3.5 million tons of garbage, and 80% of the garbage is plastic. The garbage is extremely harmful to animals. Sharks, turtles, whales, seals, and sea birds get caught in the trash heap in the ocean.

Many scientists believe the Great Pacific Garbage Patch is a relic of our modern, throwaway living. Cleaning it up isn't a task that any one country can afford to undertake. In addition, the patch grows every day from the debris thrown from cargo ships or oil platforms. Eventually, plastic breaks down into very small bits and enters the food chain because animals eat the tiny plastic pieces. Just think about it—what goes in the ocean eventually ends up on your dinner plate.

References

Friendly Floatees. Retrieved from http://en.wikipedia.org/wiki/Friendly_Floatees

Hohn, D. (2012). *The great escape: Bath toys that swam the Pacific*. Retrieved from http://www.theguardian.com/environment/2012/feb/12/great-escape-bath-toys-pacific

Hohn, D. (2011). *Moby-Duck: The true story of 28,000 bath toys lost at sea and all of the beachcombers, oceanographers, environmentalists, fools, including the author, who went in search of them*. New York: Viking.

Silverman, J. (n.d.). *Why is the world's biggest landfill in the Pacific Ocean?* Retrieved from http://science.howstuffworks.com/environmental/earth/oceanography/great-pacific-garbage-patch.htm

What Are Hurricanes?

by Dan Stillman, Institute for Global Environmental Strategies

Hurricanes are large, swirling storms with winds of 119 kilometers per hour (74 mph) or higher. That's faster than a cheetah, the fastest animal on land.

The storms form over warm ocean waters and sometimes strike land. When a hurricane reaches land, it pushes a wall of ocean water ashore. This wall of water is called a storm surge, which along with heavy rain can cause flooding, especially near the coast.

NASA studies hurricanes to learn how they form and to better predict where they will go.

Once a hurricane forms, weather forecasters predict its path and how strong it will get. This information helps people prepare for the storm before it arrives.

How Are Hurricanes Categorized?

A hurricane is categorized by its wind speed using the Saffir-Simpson Hurricane Scale.

Category 1: Winds 119–153 km/hr (74–95 mph)—faster than a cheetah

Category 2: Winds 154–177 km/hr (96–110 mph)—as fast [as] or faster than a baseball pitcher's fastball

Category 3: Winds 178–209 km/hr (111–130 mph)—similar to the serving speed of many professional tennis players

Category 4: Winds 210–249 km/hr (131–155 mph)—faster than the world's fastest rollercoaster

Category 5: Winds more than 259 km/hr (155 mph)—similar to the speed of some high-speed trains

What Are the Parts of a Hurricane?

Eye: The eye is the "hole" at the center of the storm. Winds are light and skies are only partly cloudy, sometimes even clear, in this area.

Eye wall: The eye wall is a ring of thunderstorms swirling around the eye. The wall is where winds are strongest and rain is heaviest.

Rain bands: Spiral bands of clouds, rain and thunderstorms extend out from a hurricane's eye wall. These bands stretch for hundreds of miles and sometimes contain tornadoes.

How Does a Storm Become a Hurricane?

A hurricane starts out as a tropical disturbance, an area over warm ocean waters where rain clouds are building. A tropical disturbance sometimes grows into a tropical

S118E07919

The eye of Hurricane Dean is shown as it moved through the Caribbean.

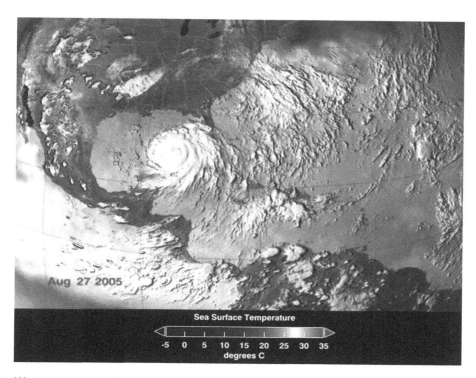

Aug 27 2005

Sea Surface Temperature

-5 0 5 10 15 20 25 30 35
degrees C

Warm water in the Gulf of Mexico and the Caribbean during the late summer months helps to fuel hurricanes.

depression, an area of rotating thunderstorms with winds of 62 km/hr (38 mph) or less. A tropical depression becomes a tropical storm if its winds reach 63 km/hr (39 mph). A tropical storm becomes a hurricane if its winds reach 119 km/hr (74 mph).

What Makes Hurricanes Form?

Scientists don't know exactly why or how a hurricane forms. But they do know that two main ingredients are necessary: warm water and winds that don't change much in speed or direction as they go higher in the atmosphere.

Warm ocean waters provide the energy needed for a storm to become a hurricane. Usually, the surface water temperature must be 26 degrees Celsius (79 degrees Fahrenheit) or higher for a hurricane to form.

The rate at which wind speed or direction changes with height is called vertical wind shear. Low vertical wind shear—winds that change very little going up through the atmosphere—is needed for hurricane development. High vertical wind shear—winds that are changing significantly with height—tends to rip storms apart.

How Are Hurricanes Named?

One reason hurricanes are named is because more than one may exist at the same time. Names make it easier to keep track of and talk about storms.

A storm is given a name if it reaches tropical storm strength. That name stays with the storm if it goes on to become a hurricane.

Each year, tropical storms are named in alphabetical order as they occur. The names come from lists of names that are maintained and updated by the World Meteorological Organization.

There are six lists of names. Each year starts with the next list. The same lists are reused every six years. Names of storms that are very deadly or costly are removed from the lists and replaced with new names.

How Does NASA Study Hurricanes?

NASA satellites take pictures of hurricanes from space. NASA scientists use data from satellites and other sources to learn more about hurricanes. The data helps them understand how hurricanes form and get stronger. The data also helps to improve the models that weather forecasters use to predict the path and strength of hurricanes.

NASA's Aqua satellite measures clouds, rainfall and sea-surface temperatures. NASA's CloudSat satellite also collects information on clouds. NASA's Tropical Rainfall Measuring Mission satellite observes the three-dimensional pattern of rainfall in hurricanes. TRMM also helps forecasters locate a hurricane's eye, especially when it is hidden under clouds. These measurements help show how strong a storm might be.

The SeaWinds instrument on NASA's QuikSCAT satellite measures wind speed and direction. These measurements enable earlier detection of developing hurricanes.

Did you know that dust storms from Africa might affect hurricanes? NASA's Terra and Aqua satellites have a tool that tracks dust coming off of Africa. The tool MODIS helps scientists study the impact of dust on hurricane formation and strength.

NASA research aircraft fly into and above hurricanes to gather detailed storm data. NASA has also flown an unmanned aircraft into areas of a hurricane that are too dangerous for manned aircraft.

The Convection and Moisture Experiment is one of several NASA field research missions that have studied hurricanes. These missions use a combination of instruments on satellites, on aircraft and on the ground. The missions study the development, track, strength and rainfall of hurricanes.

NASA has also created computer animations of hurricanes using rain, wind and temperature data from multiple satellites. These animations could help forecasters more accurately predict storm damage.

How Will NASA Study Hurricanes in the Future?

NASA is developing several instruments that will help scientists better understand hurricanes. They will also help scientists improve models used to forecast the storms.

The Hurricane Imaging Radiometer is designed to work from an airplane or satellite. From above, HIRAD will see through a hurricane's heaviest rains and thickest clouds to measure strong winds at the ocean surface. These measurements will help improve models used to forecast hurricanes.

Another instrument in development is the High-Altitude Imaging Wind and Rain Airborne Radar. HIWRAP is a Doppler radar that will fly on high-altitude aircraft and provide a three-dimensional view of hurricane winds and precipitation.

Also, an instrument named TWiLiTE will measure wind profiles in clear air near storms. TWiLiTE stands for the Tropospheric Wind Lidar Technology Experiment.

NASA is forming a hurricane science team that will use NASA satellite and field data to research hurricanes. Research topics will include hurricane formation, intensification and precipitation. The team will also research the role of Saharan air in limiting hurricane formation.

Source: http://www.nasa.gov/audience/forstudents/5-8/features/what-are-hurricanes-58.html. Used with permission of NASA.

The Wonder of Diamonds

Have you ever noticed a flash of fire when a woman's diamond ring caught a ray of sunshine? Diamonds are the sparkly stones that adorn women's engagement rings. Even though diamond jewelry is highly prized, we don't often think about why!

A diamond isn't just a pretty rock. It is a rare and beautiful mineral that formed deep in the Earth in localized places around the world. Diamond is the hardest known substance in the world. Diamonds are used for industry, and diamond gems are used in jewelry and other art. Of the diamonds in the world, only 20% are of gem quality. The remaining diamonds have industrial uses (Fleet, Hart, & Wall, 2006). Let's explore the types of diamonds, how diamonds are formed, and the history of diamonds.

What Is a Diamond?

Diamonds have a simple and elegant crystal structure. Diamonds are made entirely of carbon. This was discovered by the English chemist Simon Tennant. Carbon has two polymorphs, graphite and diamond. In diamond, each carbon atom is bonded to four other atoms in a tetrahedral formation. The carbon atoms are densely packed in an array with strong bonds. This combination of the array and the bonds creates a very strong framework. This formation leads to the three main properties of diamond: hardness, incompressibility (density), and thermal conductivity. Diamonds have extreme values for these properties.

Hardness of Diamond

The Mohs scale of hardness is on a continuum from 1 to 10. The hardest substance on the scale is diamond at 10. To understand the hardness this represents, it is important to know that the Mohs scale of hardness does not have even intervals. Corundum is a mineral considered to be level 9 on the hardness scale, and diamond is 5 times harder than corundum. This is unlike graphite, the other polymorph of carbon, which is soft and has a Mohs scale of hardness score of 1 or 2. The hardness of diamond makes it useful in industry. It is often used as a cutting tool, as in diamond-studded drill bits and saws, because diamond is the hardest substance in the world.

Incompressibility

Diamond has the lowest molar entropy at room temperature of any mineral. This indicates a high degree of internal order. Diamond is not easily compressed, as it is formed, and withstands the incredible force of the pressure in the mantle of Earth. The standard molar entropy of diamond is 2.377, which is less than graphite. This makes the internal energy of diamond lower as it has a more compact structure and the volume is smaller, and therefore diamond doesn't compress at high pressures.

Thermal Conductivity

Diamond has excellent thermal conductivity, with 5 to 25 watts per centimeter. This thermal conductivity level is 4 times greater than that of copper and 6 times greater than that of silver. This makes diamond very useful in industry. For example, in sawing, there is a lot of friction between the saw and the materials being cut, and diamond in diamond saws quickly carries the heat away. While diamond has excellent thermal conductivity, it is a poor conductor of electricity. This is unusual as most solids that conduct heat aren't poor conductors of electricity. This is unlike graphite, the other polymorph of carbon, which is a good conductor of electricity. Diamond has a high melting point, which is 3,550 degrees Celsius.

Types of Diamonds

There are natural and synthetic diamonds. Natural diamonds are formed deep within the Earth's mantle, whereas synthetic diamonds are created in a lab. The process that forms natural diamonds is extensively studied, but is mostly unknown.

Natural diamonds are old and formed in the ancient lithosphere. Diamonds we find today were formed about 3 billion years ago at a depth of 140–200 km beneath the Earth's crust. The areas where they formed were underneath ancient continents in locations called keels. Keels are the oldest parts of the continents; this is the base, or the cartons, of the continents. Diamonds form from high pressure and high temperatures. The pressure that forms diamonds is considered to be about 45 thousand times that of the Earth's atmosphere. The temperature that formed diamonds is estimated to be above 950 degrees.

There are several types of natural diamonds. In addition to the diamond minerals found on continents and formed in the interior of the Earth, there are natural polycrystalline diamonds called carbonado and framesite. Polycrystalline diamonds are formed on the Earth's crust from ultrahigh-pressure conditions. *Carbonado* is the term for the multigranular diamond aggregates from the Central African Republic and Brazil. *Framesite* is a broader term to describe the microcrystalline diamonds found all over the world. These ultrarare diamonds form where continents collide and plate tectonics occur.

The rarest of all diamonds is the nanodiamond. Nanodiamonds are found in meteorites. The finding of meteorite diamonds is not new, as these were discovered in the Canyon Diablo meteorite in 1891. At that time, it was assumed that these miniscule diamonds formed by shock metamorphism when the meteorite hit the Earth. New theories of the formation of nanodiamonds have been formulated. In 1987, the first presolar grains were recognized in meteoritic components. The term *nanodiamond* was coined to describe the meteorite diamonds because of the few nanometers in diameter of the diamonds. Huss and Lewis (2005) write that the diamonds were formed in space, not upon impact with the Earth. Ten different minerals from meteorites have been identified as presolar, and one of these minerals is diamond. The nanodiamonds are considered presolar because of the type of noble gases that they contain. The meteorites were formed from the ejecta of dying stars that existed before the solar system formed. The source of carbon in space comes from stars that grew and disintegrated before the solar system existed. Astrophysicists have found evidence of diamonds in stars. Recently a white dwarf, a collapsed star in the Centaurus galaxy, was found to consist completely of diamond (Fleet, Hart, & Wall, 2006). These diamonds form from a very different process than the diamonds formed in the high-pressure conditions of the mantle of Earth, because these diamonds form in the low pressure of space.

Color of Diamonds

Diamonds are usually colorless but rarely do come in a variety of colors. One in 500 to one in 1,000 gem-quality diamonds are colored. Color occurs from variances in pressure when the diamond was formed, or the presence of other elements, in addition to carbon. The presence of nitrogen makes diamonds yellow, and the presence of boron makes diamonds blue. The colors of pink and red are caused by atomic scale defects in the diamonds' structure. Green is caused by radiation damage of the diamond structure. Black diamonds are caused by the presence of mineral inclusions or by irradiation.

Diamond Location and Transport to the Earth's Surface

While the process of how diamonds were formed over 3 billion years ago remains highly debated and researched, how the diamonds are transported to the Earth's surface and where they are located is clearly known.

Diamonds are located around the globe, but mostly found in South Africa, Russia, Australia, East South America, Canada, and South India. Diamonds were brought to the Earth's surface through a rare volcanic eruption called kimberlites and lamproites. These eruptions picked up the diamonds from deep inside the Earth and moved them upward. The diamonds ascended fast enough to preserve their form and structure. This is important because as the diamonds moved up through the Earth's layers, they would have experienced temperature and pressure changes, which would have changed the diamonds into graphite.

The magmas that brought diamonds to Earth's surface arise differently than other magmas. They begin rising at the speed of a slow-moving car and then finish by traveling 100 times faster. This type of acceleration is important in transporting diamonds because the diamonds don't alter to graphite at the pressure and the temperature decrease on the ascent. Also, at this speed, the diamonds are not oxidized to carbon. The eruptions cause pipes, called diatreme pipes, that are shaped like carrots. These pipes are like express elevators to raise the diamonds. Only 6,000 pipes formed by these types of eruptions are known, and one in 200 pipes contain diamonds in quantities that are economically useful to mine. The diamond-filled pipes were discovered in 1871 in South Africa. These pipes no longer form as the last eruption of this type occurred about 47 million years ago.

Humans have used diamonds for thousands of years. Evidence suggests that diamonds were used to polish stone axes in China in 2500 BC. A few diamonds have been found in the archeological digs in Greece and Rome, but these were unworked stones found in rings. Diamonds were used for adorning the rich and the powerful beginning in medieval times. The 1980s started a new industry for the uses of diamonds. Once such use is a surgical scalpel with a blade of optical-grade synthetic diamond though which laser light can be directed to cauterize as the scalpel cuts.

References

Fleet, A., Hart, A., & Wall, F. (2006). Diamonds: Geology, gemmology, technology. *Geology Today, 22*(1), 23–28. doi:10.1111/j.1365-2451.2006.00545.x

Huss, G. R., & Lewis, R. S. (1994). Noble gases in presolar diamonds I: Three distinct components and their implications for diamond origins. *Meteoritics and Planetary Science, 29*(6), 791–810. doi:10.1111/j.1945-5100.1994.tb01094.x

Reproducible Forms

ABC Brainstorming

NAME: _____   DATE: _____

A		**N**	
B		**O**	
C		**P**	
D		**Q**	
E		**R**	
F		**S**	
G		**T**	
H		**U**	
I		**V**	
J		**W**	
K		**X**	
L		**Y**	
M		**Z**	

Available for download at **www.corwin.com/nonfictionnow**

Source: Adapted from Jones (1998).

NAME: _____ DATE: _____

A	N
B	O
C	P
D	Q
E	R
F	S
G	T
H	U
I	V
J	W
K	X
L	Y
M	Z

OUR SUMMARY

Thesis Statement From Our Summary

Available for download at **www.corwin.com/nonfictionnow**

Source: Adapted from Massey & Heafner (2004).

Admit Ticket

NAME: _____

What do you remember from yesterday's lesson?

If you don't remember anything, why do you think you don't remember?

Admit Ticket

NAME: _____

What big question do you have about last night's reading?

What did you think about the text you read?

Available for download at **www.corwin.com/nonfictionnow**

Daily Duo Focus Lesson Plan

Lesson:

Unit:

Objective:

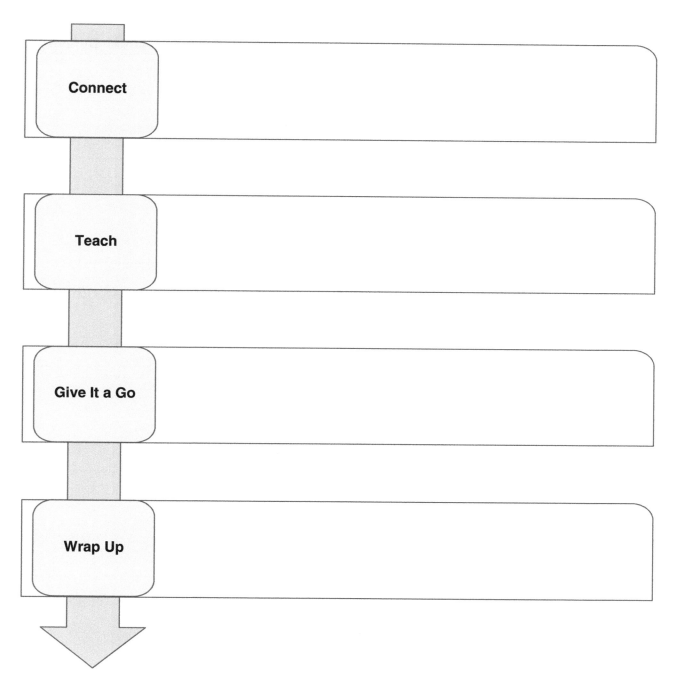

Connect

Teach

Give It a Go

Wrap Up

Available for download at **www.corwin.com/nonfictionnow**

Do I Know This Word? Assessment Sheet

NAME: _____   DATE: _____

DIRECTIONS: Think about how well you know the words in the left-hand column. Put a checkmark in the box that shows how well you know the word.

Word	Self-Assessment ☐ I know it – I don't know it	What I Think It Means	Actual Definition

Source: Akhavan (2007).

Exit Ticket

NAME: _____

What did you really "get" from today's lesson?

Why is this important?

Exit Ticket

NAME: _____

If I were to give you a test on what we learned today, what should I put on the test?

What would your answer be if your question/idea was on the test?

Available for download at **www.corwin.com/nonfictionnow**

Four-Square Word Map

NAME: _____ DATE: _____

1. Target Word	2. Examples
4. My Definition	**3. Nonexamples**

Get the Gist

NAME: _____   DATE: _____

Title of Text: _____

Page	Notes From Text (use bullets)	What I Think This Means

Here's the Gist of the Text

I-Chart

NAME: _____ DATE: _____

QUESTIONS TO ASK ABOUT THE TEXT: What is most important about what I read? What are the big ideas? What are the details supporting the big ideas? What else do I need to know?

Topic/Source: _____

ANSWERS TO QUESTIONS I ASKED ABOUT THE TEXT

What I Know	
Facts and Details	
Other Interesting Facts (even if they are minor/ trivial)	
New Questions I Have	

Available for download at **www.corwin.com/nonfictionnow**

Source: Adapted from Hoffman (1992).

282

I-Chart (Multiple Sources)

NAME: _____   DATE: _____

Topic: _____

ANSWERS TO QUESTIONS I ASKED ABOUT THE TEXT

	Source 1 Title _____	Source 2 Title _____
What I Know		
Facts and Details		
Other Interesting Facts (even if they are minor/trivial)		
New Questions I Have		

Available for download at **www.corwin.com/nonfictionnow**

Source: Adapted from Hoffman (1992).

283

Inferring Word Meaning

NAME: _____   DATE: _____

Word	What I think the word means	What the sentences make me think it means	What else I know about the word	Definition of Word

Available for download at **www.corwin.com/nonfictionnow**

List, Group, Label Graphic Organizer

NAME: _____   DATE: _____

List words in
this column.

Group similar words
together.

Label each group of
words. The label should
describe the grouping.

_____

_____

_____

_____

Student Response Log

NAME: _____   DATE: _____

Paragraph	What Was Interesting From the Text	My Thoughts

Available for download at **www.corwin.com/nonfictionnow**

Analyzing Sections • TEXTBOOK TAMER

NAME: _____ DATE: _____

Section heading/page number: _____

IMPORTANT FACT 1	IMPORTANT FACT 2	IMPORTANT FACT 3
Summary of Information About Fact 1	Summary of Information About Fact 2	Summary of Information About Fact 3
Summary Sentence About Fact 1	Summary Sentence About Fact 2	Summary Sentence About Fact 3

Available for download at **www.corwin.com/nonfictionnow**

NAME: _____   DATE: _____

Three Important Ideas
(Outline your ideas)

1.

2.

3.

Summarize the Text

Interpret the Text
(Jot why the text's meaning is important or why it is not)

Make a Judgment
(State your opinion about the text)

Available for download at **www.corwin.com/nonfictionnow**

NAME: _____ DATE: _____

Important Ideas
(Look at the text features)

Get the Gist
(Summarize key points)

Important Vocabulary
(Bold words, important terms)

NAME: _____   DATE: _____

Cut tabs apart on middle line. Line up the top of the Skimming Tab with the first sentence on your page, on the right-hand side of the book. Write margin notes by writing on the Skimming Tab.

Page number: _____

Skim over the page to gather information and ideas. Write margin notes below.

Page number: _____

Skim over the page to gather information and ideas. Write margin notes below.

NAME: _____ DATE: _____

BEFORE READING: ASK, THINK, JOT

STEP 1: Ask yourself:

"Do I understand why I am reading this section?"

If you answered YES: Write the purpose below.

If you answered NO: Skim the section again, check your notes, and give it a try.

STEP 2: Skim the headings, bold words, and graphics.

Ask yourself: *"What is the section or page about?"* and *"What details support the main idea?"*

(Write your jots here)

STEP 3: Summarize what you read.

(Write your summary here)

Word Card

NAME: _____   DATE: _____

Word	Definition in My Own Words

Available for download at **www.corwin.com/nonfictionnow**

Source: Akhavan (2007).

References

Achieve. (2013). *The Next Generation Science Standards.* Retrieved from http://www.nextgen science.org/msls1-molecules-organisms-structures-processes

Achieve the Core. (2013). *The Common Core shifts at a glance.* Retrieved from http://www.achie vethecore.org/page/277/the-common-core-shifts-at-a-glance

Afflerbach, P., Pearson, P. D., and Paris, S. G. (2008). Clarifying differences between reading skills and reading strategies. *The Reading Teacher, 61*(5), pp. 364–373. doi:10.1598/RT.61.5.1

Ainsworth, L. (2011). *Rigorous curriculum design: How to create curricular units of study that align standards, instruction, and assessment.* Lanham, MD: Advanced Learning Press.

Akhavan, N. (2004). *How to align literacy instruction, assessment and standards and achieve results you never dreamed possible.* Portsmouth, NH: Heinemann.

Akhavan, N. (2007). *Accelerated vocabulary instruction: Strategies for closing the achievement gap for all students.* New York: Scholastic.

Akhavan, N. (2008). *The content-rich reading & writing workshop: A time-saving approach for making the most of your literacy block.* New York: Scholastic.

Alvermann, D. E., & Eakle, A. J. (2003). Comprehension instruction: Adolescents and multiple literacies. In A. P. Sweet & C. E. Snow (Eds.), *Rethinking reading comprehension* (pp. 12–29). New York: Guilford.

Anderson, L. W., & Krathwohl, D. R. (Eds.). (2001). *A taxonomy for learning, teaching, and assessing: A revision of Bloom's Taxonomy of educational objectives.* Boston: Allyn & Bacon.

Anderson, V., & Hidi, S. (1989). Teaching students to summarize. *Educational Leadership, 46*(4), 26–28.

Andreassen, R., & Braten, I. (2011). Implementation and effects of explicit reading comprehension instruction in fifth-grade classrooms. *Learning and Instruction, 21,* 520–537.

Applebee, A. N. (1985). Writing and reasoning. *Review of Educational Research, 54*(4), 577–596.

Armbruster, B. B., Anderson, T. H., & Meyer, J. L. (1991). Improving content-area reading using instructional graphics. *Reading Research Quarterly,* 26(4) (Autumn, 1991), 393–416

Armbruster, B. B., Anderson, T. H., & Ostertag, J. (1987). Does text structure/summarization instruction facilitate learning from expository text? *Reading Research Quarterly, 22,* 331–346.

Baker, L. (2002). Metacognition in comprehension instruction. In C. C. Block & M. Pressley (Eds.). *Comprehension Instruction: Researched-Based Best Practices* (pp. 77-95). New York: Guilford Press.

Barone, D. (2010). Comprehension in the primary grades. In K. Ganske & D. Fisher (Eds.), *Comprehension across the curriculum: Perspectives and practices, K–12* (pp. 75–95). New York: Guilford Press.

Beck, I. L., McKeown, M. G., & Kucan, L. (2002). *Bringing words to life.* New York: Guilford Press.

Beers, K., & Probst, R. E. (2013). *Notice and note: Strategies for close reading.* Portsmouth, NH: Heinemann.

Birr Moje, E. (2010). Comprehending in the subject areas: The challenges of comprehension, grades 7–12. In K. Ganske & D. Fisher (Eds.), *Comprehension across the curriculum: Perspectives and practices, K–12* (pp. 46–72). New York: Guilford Press.

Blachowicz, C. L. Z., & Fisher, P. (2002). *Teaching vocabulary in all classrooms.* Columbus, OH: Merrill/Prentice Hall.

Block, C. C., & Israel, S. E. (2004). The ABCs of performing highly effective think-alouds. *The Reading Teacher, 58*(2), 154–167.

Bromley, K. (2003). Building a sound writing program. In L. M. Morrow, L. B. Gambrell, & M. Pressley (Eds.), *Best practices in literacy instruction* (pp. 143–165). New York: Guilford.

Brooks, D., & Jeong, A. (2006). The effects of pre-structuring discussion threads on group interaction and group performance in computer-supported collaborative argumentation. *Distance Education, 27*(3), 371–390. Retrieved from http://myweb.fsu.edu/ajeong/pubs/ Brooks2006PrestructThreads.pdf

Brown, A. L., Day, J. D., & Jones, R. S. (1983). *The development of plans for summarizing texts* (Technical Report 268). Center for the Study of Reading, University of Illinois at Urbana-Champaign. Retrieved from https://www.ideals.illinois.edu/bitstream/handle/2142/18024/ ctrstreadtechrepv01983i00268_opt.pdf?sequence=1

Brown, C., & Broemmel, A. (2011). Deep scaffolding: Enhancing the reading experiences of English language learners. *New England Reading Association Journal, 46*(2), 34–40.

Brozo, W. G., & Simpson, M. L. (2003). *In readers, teachers, learners: Expanding literacy across the content areas* (4th ed). Upper Saddle River, NJ: Merrill Prentice Hall.

Brummett, B. (2010). *Techniques for close reading.* Thousand Oaks, CA: Sage.

Buehl, D. (2007). A professional development framework for embedding comprehension instruction into content classrooms. In J. Lewis & G. Moorman (Eds.), *Adolescent literacy instruction: Policies and promising practices* (pp. 192–211). Newark, DE: International Reading Association.

Chiang, M., Crane, C., Hamalainen, K., & Jones, L. (2010). *Oil spill disaster in the Gulf.* New York: Scholastic.

Chou, M. (2012). Implementing keyword and question generation approaches in teaching EFL summary writing. *English Language Teaching, 5*(12), 36–41.

Clarke, I., II, Flaherty, T. B., & Yankey, M. (2006). Teaching the visual learner: The use of visual summaries in marketing education. *Journal of Marketing Education, 28*(3), 218–226. Retrieved from http://search.proquest.com/docview/204409218?accountid=10349

Coiro, J. (2003). Reading comprehension on the Internet: Expanding our understanding of reading comprehension to encompass new literacies. *The Reading Teacher, 56,* 458–464.

Coiro, J., & Dobler, E. (2007). Exploring the online reading comprehension strategies used by sixth-grade skilled readers to search for and locate information on the Internet. *Reading Research Quarterly, 42*(2), 214–257.

Dreher, M. J. (2002). Children searching and using information text: A critical part of comprehension. In C. C. Block & M. Pressley (Eds.), *Comprehension instruction: Research based practices* (pp. 289–304). New York: Guilford.

Duffy, G. G. (2002). The case for direct explanation of strategies. In C. C. Block & M. Pressley (Eds.), *Comprehension instruction: Research-based best practices* (pp. 28–41). New York: Guilford Press.

Duke, N. K., & Pearson, P. D. (2002). Effective practices for developing reading comprehension. In A. E. Farstrup & S. J. Samuels (Eds.), *What research has to say about reading instruction* (3rd ed., pp. 205–242). Newark, DE: International Reading Association.

Dymock, S. (2005). Teaching expository text structure awareness. *The Reading Teacher 59*(2). doi:10.1598/RT.59.2.7

Dymock, S. J., & Nicholson, T. (1999). *Reading comprehension: What is it? How do you teach it?* Wellington: New Zealand Council for Educational Research.

Felder, R. M., & Brent, R. (2005). Understanding student differences. *Journal of Engineering Education, 94*(1), 57–72. Retrieved from http://www4.ncsu.edu/unity/lockers/users/f/felder/public/Papers/Understanding_Differences.pdf

Felder, R. M., & Solomon, B. A. (1999). *Index of learning styles.* Retrieved from http://www4.ncsu.edu/unity/lockers/users/f/felder/public/ILSdir/styles.htm

Fisher, D. (2008). *Effective use of the Gradual Release of Responsibility Model* [Author monograph]. Boston: Glencoe.

Fisher, D., & Frey, N. (2004). *Improving adolescent literacy: Strategies at work.* Upper Saddle River, NJ: Merrill Prentice Hall.

Fisher, D., & Frey, N. (2008). *Better learning through structured teaching: A framework for the gradual release of responsibility.* Alexandria, VA: ASCD.

Fisher, D., Frey, N., & Lapp, D. (2012). *Text complexity: Raising rigor in reading.* Newark, DE: International Reading Association.

Fountas, I. C., & Pinnell, G. S. (2001). *Guiding readers and writers (Grades 3–6): Teaching comprehension, genre, and content literacy.* Portsmouth, NH: Heinemann.

Fuchs, D., Fuchs, L. S., Mathes, P. G., & Martinez, E. A. (2002). Preliminary evidence on the social standing of students with learning disabilities in PALS and No-PALS classrooms. *Learning Disabilities Research & Practice, 17*(4), 205–215. doi:10.1111/1540-5826.00046

Ganske, K. (2010). Active thinking and engagement: Comprehension in the intermediate grades. In K. Ganske & D. Fisher (Eds.), *Comprehension across the curriculum: Perspectives and practices, K–12* (pp. 96–118). New York: Guilford Press.

Graves, M. F. (2006). Teaching word-learning strategies. In *The Vocabulary Book* (pp. 91–118). New York; Newark, DE; and Urbana, IL: Teachers College Press.

Gutherie, J. T., Hoa, A. L. W., Wigfiled, A., Tonks, S. M., Humenick, N. M., & Littles, E. (2007). Reading motivation and reading comprehension growth in later elementary years. *Contemporary Educational Psychology, 32,* 282–313.

Hare, V. C., & Borchardt, K. M. (1984). Direct instruction of summarization skills. *Reading Research Quarterly, 20*(1), 62–78.

Harste, J., & Short, K. (with C. Burke). (1995). *Creating classrooms for authors: The reading-writing connection* (2nd ed.). Portsmouth, NH: Heinemann.

Hebert, M., Gillespie, A., & Graham, S. (2012). Comparing effects of different writing activities on reading comprehension: A meta-analysis. *Read Writ, 26,* 111–138. doi:10.1007/s11145-012-9386-3

Herrington, A. J. (1981). Writing across the disciplines. *College English, 43*(4), 379–387. Retrieved from http://www.jstor.org/stable/377126

Hess, K., & Biggam, S. (2004). A discussion of "increasing text complexity." *Appendices for the New England Common Assessment Program Reading GLEs: Grades K–8.* Retrieved from http://www.nciea.org/publications/TextComplexity_KH05.pdf

Hoffman, J. (1992). Critical reading/thinking across the curriculum: Using I-charts to support learning. *Language Arts, 69*(2), 121–127.

Hulick, K. (2007). A day at school in Kyrgyzstan. *Faces, 24*(3).

Jacobs, G. E. (2011). *Writing instruction for Generation 2.0.* Lanham, MD: Rowman & Littlefield.

Jenkins, J. R., Matlock, B., & Slocum, T. A. (1989). Two approaches to vocabulary instruction: The teaching of individual word meanings and practice in deriving word meaning from context. *Reading Research Quarterly, 24*(2), 215–235. Retrieved from http://www.jstor.org/stable/747865

Jones, R. (1998). *ABC brainstorm.* Retrieved from http://www.readingquest.org/strat/abc.html

Keene, E. (2010). To understand: The small changes that make a big difference. In K. Ganske & D. Fisher (Eds.), *Comprehension across the curriculum: Perspectives and practices, K–12* (pp. 7–22). New York: Guilford Press.

Kern, D. (2012). Real-world reading and the common core state standards. *The NERA Journal, 47*(2), 71–73.

Kiefer, K. (1990). An alternative to curricular reform: Writing in the natural science/engineering curriculum. In *Proceedings of the Core Across the Curriculum Conference* (Keystone, Colorado, October 6–8). American Association for the Advancement of Core Curriculum.

King, A. (2007). Beyond literal comprehension: A strategy to promote deep understanding of text. In D. S. McNamora (Ed.), *Reading comprehension strategies: Theories, interventions and techniques* (pp. 267–290). Mahwah, NJ: Lawrence Erlbaum.

Klinger, J. K., & Vaughn, S. (1998). Using collaborative strategic reading. *Teaching Exceptional Children, 30*(6), 32–37.

Knipper, K. J., & Duggan, T. J. (2006). Writing to learn across the curriculum: Tools for comprehension in content area classes. *The Reading Teacher, 59*(5), 462–470. doi:10.1598/RT.59.5.5

Knoell, D. L. (2010). Selecting and using nonfiction in grades K–12 social studies and science. In K. Ganske & D. Fisher (Eds.), *Comprehension across the curriculum: Perspectives and practices K–12* (pp. 246–275). New York: Guilford.

Krathwohl, D. (2002). A revision of Bloom's taxonomy: An overview. *Theory Into Practice, 41*(4), 212–218.

Krathwohl, D., & Anderson, L. (2010). Merlin C. Wittrock and the revision of Bloom's taxonomy. *Educational Psychology, 45*(1), 64–65.

Kurland, D. (2000). *What is critical reading?* Retrieved from http://www.criticalreading.com/critical_reading.htm

Lazarus, E. (n.d.). The New Colossus. *PoemHunter.com.* Retrieved from http://www.poemhunter.com/poem/the-new-colossus/

Lemov, D. (2010). *Teach like a champion: 49 techniques that put students on the path to college* (K–12). San Francisco: Jossey-Bass.

Lesaux, N. K., Kieffer, M., Faller, S. E., & Kelley, J. G. (2010). The effectiveness and ease of implementation of an academic vocabulary intervention for linguistically diverse students in urban middle schools. *Reading Research Quarterly, 45*(2), 196–228.

"Making generalizations: Description of the strategy." (n.d.). University of California at Santa Barbara. Retrieved from http://education.ucsb.edu/webdata/instruction/hss/Generalizations/Description_of_Strategy.pdf

Martin, V. L., & Pressley, M. (1991). Elaborative-interrogation effects depend on the nature of question. *Journal of Educational Psychology, 83,* 113–119.

Marzano, R. J. (2004). *Building background knowledge for academic achievement: Research on what works in schools.* Alexandria, VA: ASCD.

Massey, D. D., & Heafner, T. L. (2004). Promoting reading comprehension in social studies. *Journal of Adolescent & Adult Literacy, 48*(1), 26–40.

McConachie, S. M., & Petrosky, A. R. (2010). Engaging content teachers in literacy development. In S. M. McConachie & A. R. Petrosky (Eds.), *Content matters: A disciplinary literacy approach to improving student learning* (pp. 1–14). San Francisco, CA: Jossey-Bass.

McKeown, M. G. (1985). The acquisition of word meaning from context by children of high and low ability. *Reading Research Quarterly, 20*(4), 482–496.

Means, B., & Knapp, M. S. (1991). Cognitive approaches to teaching advanced skills to educationally disadvantaged students. *Phi Delta Kappan, 73*(4), 282–289.

Meyer, B. J. F., & Ray, M. N. (2011). Structure strategy interventions: Increasing reading comprehension of expository text. *International Electronic Journal of Elementary Education, 4*(1), 127–152.

Myers, M. P., & Savage, T. (2005). Enhancing student comprehension of social studies material. *The Social Studies, 96*(1), 18–23.

Nagy, W., & Anderson, R. (1984). The number of words in printed school English. *Reading Research Quarterly, 19,* 304–330.

National Governors Association Center for Best Practices & Council of Chief State School Officers. (2010). *Common Core State Standards for English Language Arts.* Washington, DC: Authors.

Neufeld, P. (2005). Comprehension instruction in content area classes. *The Reading Teacher, 59*(4), 302–312.

New York City Department of Education. (n.d.). *Inquire.* Retrieved from http://schools.nyc.gov/inquire

Newell, G. E., Beach, R., Smith, J., & VanDerHeide, J. (2011). Teaching and learning argumentative reading and writing: A review of research. *Reading Research Quarterly, 46*(3), 273–304.

Ogle, D., & Blachowicz, C. L. Z. (2002). Beyond literature circles: Helping students comprehend informational texts. In C. C. Block & M. Pressley (Eds.), *Comprehension instruction: Research based practices* (pp. 259–274). New York: Guilford.

Otto, W., White S., Richgels, D., Hansen, R., & Morrison, B. (1981). *A technique for improving the understanding of expository text: Gloss and examples* (Theoretical Paper No. 96). Madison: Wisconsin Center for Education Research.

Pacific Policy Research Center. (2010). *21st century skills for students and teachers.* Honolulu, HI: Kamehameha Schools, Research & Evaluation Division.

Palfrey, J., & Gasser, U. (2008). *Born digital: Understanding the first generation of digital natives.* New York: Basic Books.

Partnership for 21st Century Skills. (2009). *P21 framework definitions.* Retrieved from http://www.p21.org/storage/documents/P21_Framework_Definitions.pdf

Paul, R., & Elder, L. (2008). *How to read a paragraph: The art of close reading.* Tomales, CA: Foundation for Critical Thinking.

Pearson, P. D., & Gallagher, M. C. (1983). The instruction of reading comprehension. *Contemporary Educational Psychology, 8,* 317–344.

Pearson, P. D., Roehler, L. R., Dole, J. A., & Duffy, G. G. (1992). Developing expertise in reading comprehension. In S. J. Samuels & A. E. Farstrup (Eds.), *What research has to say about reading instruction* (2nd ed., pp. 145–199). Newark, DE: International Reading Association.

Popham, J. W. (2007). The lowdown on learning progressions. *Educational Leadership,* April, pp. 83–84.

Pressley, M. (2002). Metacognition and self-regulated comprehension. In A. E. Farstrup & S. J. Samuels (Eds.), *What research has to say about reading instruction* (3rd ed., pp. 291–309). Newark, DE: International Reading Association.

Pressley, M., & Wharton-McDonald, R. (1997). Skilled comprehension instruction and its development through instruction. *School Psychology Review, 26,* 448–466.

Pressley, M., & Wharton-McDonald, R. (2002). The need for increased comprehension instruction. In M. Pressley (Ed.), *Reading instruction that works best: The case for balanced teaching* (2nd ed., pp. 236–288). New York: Guilford Press.

Pressley, M., Wood, E., Woloshyn, V. E., Martin, V., King, A., & Menke, D. (1992). Encouraging mindful use of prior knowledge: Attempting to construct explanatory answers facilitates learning. *Educational Psychologist, 27,* 91–110.

Richgels, D. J., & Hansen, R. (1984). Gloss: Helping students apply both skills and strategies in reading content texts. *Journal of Reading, 27*(4), 312–317.

Riley, J. R. (1992). Using the proficient reader protocol to evaluate middle school reading behaviors. *The Clearing House, 66*(1), 41–43.

Rumelhart, D., & Norman, D. (1981). Analogical processes in learning. In J. R. Anderson (Ed.), *Cognitive skills and their acquisition.* Hillsdale, NJ: Erlbaum.

Sanders, J., & Moudy, J. (2008). Literature apprentices: Understanding nonfiction text structures with mentor texts. *Journal of Children's Literature, 34*(2), 31–40.

Saphier, J., Haley-Speca, M. A., & Gower, R. (2008). *The skillful teacher: Building your teaching skills.* Acton, MA: Research for Better Teaching.

Schmar-Dobler, E. (2003). Reading on the Internet: The link between literacy and technology. *Journal of Adolescent & Adult Literacy, 47*(1). Retrieved from http://www.readingonline.org/newliteracies/lit_index.asp?HREF=/newliteracies/jaal/9-03_column/index.htm

Schoenbach, R., & Greenleaf, C. (2009). Fostering adolescents' engaged academic literacy. In L. Christenbury, R. Bomer, & P. Smagorinsky (Eds.), *Handbook of adolescent literacy research.* New York: Guilford Press.

Serravallo, J. (2013). *Independent reading assessment: Nonfiction.* New York: Scholastic.

Sinatra, R. C. (2000). Teaching learners to think, read and write more effectively in content subjects. *The Clearinghouse, 73*(5), 266–273.

Singer, H., & Donlan, D. (1980). *Reading and learning from text.* Boston: Little, Brown.

Singer, H., & Donlan, D. (1982). Active comprehension: Problem-solving schema with question generation for comprehension of complex short stories. *Reading Research Quarterly, 17*(2), 166–186.

Sporer, N., & Brunstein, J. C. (2009). Fostering the reading comprehension of secondary school students through peer-assisted learning: Effects on strategy knowledge, strategy use, and task performance. *Contemporary Educational Psychology, 34,* 289–297.

Stahl, S. A. (1999). *Vocabulary Development.* Cambridge, MA: Brookline.

Stahl, S. A. (2006). Understanding shifts in reading and its instruction. In K. A. Dougherty Stahl & M. C. McKenna (Eds.), *Reading research at work* (pp. 45–75). New York: Guilford.

Stahl, S. A., & Nagy, W. E. (2006). *Teaching word meanings.* Mahwah, NJ: Erlbaum.

Stanovich, K. E. (1986). Matthew effects in reading: Some consequences of individual differences in the acquisition of literacy. *Reading Research Quarterly, 21*(4), 360–407. doi:10.1598/RRQ.21.4.1

Sternberg, R. J. (1987). Most vocabulary is learned from context. In M. G. McKeown & M. E. Curtis (Eds.), *The nature of vocabulary acquisition* (pp. 89–105). Hillsdale, NJ: Erlbaum.

Sutherland-Smith, W. (2002). Weaving the literacy Web: Changes in reading from page to screen. *The Reading Teacher, 55,* 662–669.

Taba, H. (1967). *Teacher handbook for elementary social studies.* Palo Alto, CA: Addison-Wesley.

Tovani, C. (2000). *I read it, but I don't get it: Comprehension strategies for adolescent readers.* Portland, ME: Stenhouse.

Trabasso, T., & Bouchard, E. (2002). Teaching readers how to comprehend text strategically. In C. C. Block & M. Pressley (Eds.), *Comprehension instruction: Research based practices* (pp. 176–200). New York: Guilford Press.

Tuchman Glass, K. (2012). *Mapping comprehensive units to the ELA Common Core Standards, K–5.* Thousand Oaks, CA: Corwin.

Weaver, C. A., III, & Kintsch, W. (1991). Expository text. In R. Barr, M. L. Kamil, P. Mosenthal, & P. D. Pearson (Eds.), *Handbook of reading research* (Vol. 2, pp. 230–244). White Plains, NY: Longman.

Whitman, A., & Goldberg, J. (2008). *Brain development in a hyper-tech world.* Briefing Paper, The Dana Foundation.

Williams, J. P. (2007). Literacy in the curriculum: Integrating text structure and content area instruction. In D. S. McNamora (Ed.), *Reading comprehension strategies: Theories, interventions and techniques* (pp. 199–218). Mahwah, NJ: Lawrence Erlbaum.

Williams, L. (2005). *Environmental science demystified: A self-teaching guide.* New York: McGraw-Hill.

Wormeli, R. (2005). *Summarization in any subject: 50 techniques to improve student learning.* Alexandria, VA: ASCD.

Photo Credits

Page 13: © Winzworks

Page 14: www.CartoonStock.com

Page 257: Clifford Berryman © 1902

Page 266: NASA

Page 267: NASA

Page 267: NASA

Index

BECAUSE ALL TEACHERS ARE LEADERS

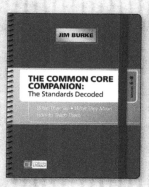
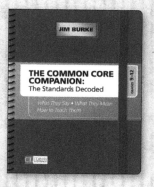

CORWIN
A SAGE Company

The Corwin logo—a raven striding across an open book—represents the union of courage and learning. Corwin is committed to improving education for all learners by publishing books and other professional development resources for those serving the field of PreK–12 education. By providing practical, hands-on materials, Corwin continues to carry out the promise of its motto: **"Helping Educators Do Their Work Better."**